Contents

Foreword

Until the middle of this century the two main components of gamebird management were predator (including poacher) control and hunting methods. In the late 1940s when the swords of the Second World War were beaten into the proverbial ploughshares there came to the hands of farmers powerful new tools: machines such as bulldozers and combine harvesters and broad-spectrum herbicides and insecticides. Of course our countryside has for centuries been changed by man's activities, but these new 'ploughshares' increased our power to modify it by orders of magnitude.

Working at the Rothamsted Experimental Station, I was horrified at the new-found ease with which the farm manager could remove old headlands or spray wild flowers (or weeds – according to one's viewpoint) on the verges. Thus it was with some eagerness that I participated in a study on the possible impact on partridges of the widespread use of DNOC in cereals. Already there were those who linked these changes in agricultural practice with a reduction in the crop of gamebirds, but this brief *ad hoc* study merely emphasised how little was known of the ecological links in agricultural systems.

Ecologists were traditionally concerned with 'natural systems': there was an unspoken assumption that man damaged such systems so that their study would be as invalid as a means of unravelling the functioning of ecosystems as would be observations of caged lions as a basis for the understanding of hunting behaviour. In fact agroecosystems often provide the ecologist with field experiments on a scale that the traditional research budget would never support, and so it proved for me, when in the early 1960s I commenced a programme of work on the decline of the partridge. It was funded by the late Lord Rank and undertaken on his farmland. There were a multitude of uncertainties: Was chick death the key factor? Were insects essential for chicks? How many did they need? Did nutrition and weather interact in causing death? How far would a partridge chick need to travel to catch enough insects? And then, because so little was known about crop insects as a whole, rather than a particular pest species, what is the density of insects in crops of different types and with different herbicide treatments? There were a whole host of other questions deriving from work centred on the behaviour of the adult bird; for instance, was there an inherent difference in the viability of eggs and chicks, depending on the 'condition' of their parents?

This book shows how far we have come in the last two decades in both knowledge and attitudes. It addresses itself to the management of wildlife in the countryside. It does not provide a detailed recipe for each particular species, rather it distills the fundamental management techniques from current ecological knowledge. It shows that ecology is now in a position to make practical contributions to wildlife management and the conservation of nature – two activities that are, fortunately on increasingly convergent paths.

A study of the authoritative chapters in this book shows also how, contrary to earlier prejudices, 'game animals' have provided excellent material for the investigation of many fundamental ecological questions. Records have been accumulated over many years; varying degrees of predator-control and artificial culling practised and recorded, whilst experimental tests have been possible of the various hypotheses concerning the dynamics of natural populations. Thus this book will, I am sure, prove of great interest to ecologists, as well as to conservationists, farmers and all interested in wildlife.

The publication of this book is timely: our countryside is under pressure as never before. It is not only a matter of man's increased technological power, to which I have already referred, but also of pressures generated by current financial and social attitudes. High interest rates have led to demands for high and immediate returns on capital; 'land must earn its keep' is the accountants' cry! On the other hand, in our growing population of town dwellers there is a widespread and increasing appreciation of the countryside coupled with the ownership of a motorcar in which to visit it. It is only by applying sound ecological principles to countryside management that these conflicting demands can be met without the destruction of what everyone values.

This book shows how science can be applied so that we can simultaneously use and conserve wildlife in our own countryside.

Sir Richard Southwood FRS
Merton College
Oxford
April 1987

Preface

This book is about the application of science to the conservation and management of animal populations in the wild. We have chosen examples largely from the world of British gamebirds, partly because this is the subject on which we have both worked for a number of years, and partly because we believe they exemplify how an understanding of empirical theories can be applied to improve the abundance of species.

Environmental issues have become increasingly important in the world of politics and amongst the population at large. More and more frequently a 'scientist', 'ecologist' or 'conservationist' appears in the media giving their solution to yet another ecological crisis or passing emotive comment on some environmental issue. Sadly, few such scientists have had exposure to the practical problems of dealing with species extinction, habitat destruction or whatever problem may be under debate. Similarly, those faced with protecting natural resources on a day-to-day basis rarely think of, or turn to science for a solution. This is not true, however, in the world of gamebird ecology and management where, as we hope this volume demonstrates, an application of the principles of ecology has been of practical use in the conservation of wild populations. We hope that these examples will rekindle the enthusiasm of those scientists and conservationists in other disciplines.

Each chapter of this book reviews the theoretical background to a particular field of ecology, be it predation, harvesting strategies, or whatever, and then provides empirical evidence to support that theory from studies of gamebirds. The contributors then go on to discuss the implications of both the theory itself and the evidence presented for the management of gamebirds and their habitat, whenever possible citing specific examples of where a knowledge of ecology has directly led to the enhancement of gamebird numbers.

The chapters themselves have been arranged in order first to introduce the reader to gamebirds and their ecology and, second, to deal with specific ecological processes affecting populations. This leads to the final analyses which show how, by bringing together these various processes in various forms of mathematical model, wise management and harvesting strategies can be optimized. Thus Chapter 1 is an introduction to what is meant by the terms gamebird, ecology and conservation. This is followed by a description of the habitats in which British gamebirds live and some of the environmental changes taking place within these areas. The following two chapters provide analytical descriptions and reviews of general population changes in gamebirds and gamebird life history strategies (factors affecting survival, recruitment and productivity). A knowledge of each of these subjects is necessary as a prelude to examining the relationships between ecological processes and management. Chapters 4, 5 and 6 each deal with predation, parasites and habitat quality respectively, all of which can be closely and directly related to management but within the constraints set by the birds' mating systems (Chapter 7). Chapter 8 assesses the value of harvesting theories in determining maximum sustainable yields and the final chapter examines the value of population simulation models and other types of mathematical modelling tools for determining good gamebird management strategies.

Many people read, commented and helped us with the job of editing. We particularly wish to thank Dick Potts, Des Thompson, Sir Richard Southwood and David Newborn for their generous and rapid response to our multitude of requests. Many of the authors helped referee the contributions by the others but we should also like to thank Kate Lessels, Adam Watson, Rhys Green, Robert Moss and Trevor Lewis. Most people in the Game Conservancy helped in one way or another and we would like to offer our sincere thanks to Richard Van Oss, Mike Swan, Caroline Hunt, Patsy Hitchings and Corinne Duggins. Our wives, Mary Hudson and Gillian Rands deserve special thanks and we are also very grateful to Richard Miles and Julian Grover of BSP Professional Books for their tolerance and efficiency.

Our intention with this volume is to present an integrated review of the relationship between the ecology of a group of species and their management. It is aimed at all those interested in the application of ecology to conservation be they students of ecology or agriculture or conservationists, farmers or land managers with an interest in the scientific management of wildlife populations. We hope you enjoy reading it as much as we have enjoyed our roles as editors.

Peter J. Hudson
Michael R. W. Rands.

April 1988

1 Gamebirds, Ecology, Conservation and Agriculture

Michael R. W. Rands, Peter J. Hudson and Nicolas W. Sotherton

1.1 Introduction

Gamebirds display a fascinating array of ecological characteristics that have attracted the wide-ranging interests of naturalists, sportsmen and scientists. The natural history of game has been described elsewhere (Vesey Fitzgerald, 1946; Marchington, 1984; McKelvie, 1985) and we have no desire to summarise this information once more, nor is this volume concerned with gamebird ecology *per se*. Instead, our objective is to describe and examine the principles of ecology and the application of such principles to the management and conservation of wildlife. We have chosen gamebirds simply to exemplify the approach since this is a group that has been both managed and studied in detail. The management of many natural populations is still based on intuition and could, in our opinion, be greatly improved by the ecological approach developed in this volume.

The term 'gamebirds' is somewhat vague; it can include all birds that are legitimately hunted or just the bird species that fall within the taxonomic order known as the Galliformes. Although this book refers to a wide range of animal species, emphasis is placed on the Galliformes, a group of some 245 species which inhabit a wide range of terrains. In Western Europe, where few natural habitats remain, gamebirds have become closely associated with man and his use of the land: an association which arises largely because gamebirds provide both food and recreation, and one that has resulted in a number of scientific studies of British game.

The choice of gamebirds to demonstrate the application of ecological principles to wildlife management stems from three unusual features of this group. First, man has tried to manage gamebird populations for several hundred years to ensure that they may be harvested in a sustainable manner. Second, regular shooting of game has yielded statistics of the numbers shot over relatively long time periods; these may be used to indicate long-term trends in population size and significant ecological changes in the countryside (an approach used by Potts, 1986). Such long strings of data contrast markedly with the information available on farmland passerines and other wildlife species for which few population data existed prior to 1962 (O'Connor and Shrubb, 1986). Thirdly, gamebirds are somewhat unusual amongst the animal kingdom in that their ecology has been specifically studied by scientists with the final objective of determining and developing management recommendations.

1.2 Gamebirds

The order Galliformes contains six families:

(1) Grouse (*Tetraonidae*); includes the ptarmigan and capercaillie.
(2) Pheasants and quails (*Phasianidae*); as well as the pheasant and quail this group also includes the partridge, snowcock, peafowl and tragopan.
(3) Guineafowl (*Numididae*); African birds with loud cackling calls.
(4) Megapodes (*Megapodiidae*); birds that lay their eggs communally in sand or mounds of rotting vegetation: mainly from south-east Asia and Australia.
(5) Curassows and guans (*Cracidae*); frugivorous tropical birds from Central and South America.
(6) Turkeys (*Meleagrididae*); two species from North and Central America.

The group is represented in every continent of the world with the exception of Antarctica, although only ten occur in wild free-living populations in Britain (Cramp and Simmons, 1980). Their status, habitat and estimated total breeding population are summarised in Table 1.1. Of these, only the quail, golden pheasant and Lady Amherst's pheasant have not been the subject of ecological field studies while the red grouse and grey partridge have been intensively studied since 1905 and 1930 respectively.

Gamebird management techniques have inevitably focused on methods of increasing the number of birds available for shooting. Early management was designed to remove or minimise sources of mortality other than shooting, especially the more conspicuous threats such as predation. A wide variety of techniques were developed to destroy all potential predators and in some cases possible competitors as well. Although the temporary suppression of predator populations almost certainly increased the numbers of game available to be shot, little thought was given to the cost-effectiveness of this destruction or to the consequences of disturbing the ecological balance. Today the large-scale destruction of predators is often unacceptable, illegal or impractical. Moreover, a scientifically based prescription for the effective control of selected predators is still only in its infancy.

Table 1.1   The status, habitat and estimated population sizes of Britain's gamebirds (*sources*: Parslow, 1969; Cramp and Simmons, 1980; Lack, 1986; Game Conservancy, unpublished data).

Species	Status	Major Habitat	Estimated British Population
Red Grouse	N	Heather moorland	1 000 000
Ptarmigan	N	Montane plateau	10 000–15 000
Black Grouse	N	Moorland, forest edge	20 000–200 000
Capercaillie	RI	Coniferous woodland	2 000–20 000
Red-legged Partridges,*	I	Farmland and heath	200 000–400 000
Grey Partridge	N	Open arable farmland	1 000 000
Quail	N	Farmland	200–20 000
Pheasant	I	Woodland edge	20–30 million
Golden Pheasant	I	Conifer plantations	1000–2000
Lady Amherst's Pheasant	I	Woodland with dense undergrowth	200–400

Status:
    N = Native
    I = Introduced
    RI = Reintroduced

* Includes chukar partridge (*Alectoris chukar*) and hybrids.

The management of wild gamebirds has always included elements of habitat manipulation. The first inquiry into population fluctuations in red grouse concluded that burning heather vegetation in strips on a rotational basis was beneficial to grouse stocks (Lovat, 1911) and this has since become an established part of grouse moor management. On lowland farmland, where the habitat for gamebirds has been radically altered by the rapid turnover in types of arable rotations, special crops (typically kale, maize, artichokes, millet or root crops) are often planted to provide food and shelter. In addition, supplementary feed in the form of grain is regularly provided to hand-reared birds to prevent birds dispersing in search of natural foods (McCall, 1986). It is not our intention to review the diverse, practical management options currently used to improve a habitat for gamebirds, those aspects of habitat quality that have been shown to limit gamebird numbers are discussed in some detail later.

Another method for increasing the number of gamebirds available for harvesting is the release of captive-bred birds; a technique that is both cost-effective in the short term and can produce a substantial harvest. Comparisons of the survival of wild and hand-reared birds show the reared birds suffer from a greater mortality and lower productivity (Hill and Robertson, 1986). These findings seriously undermine the traditional belief that reared birds can make a significant contribution to future wild populations. The rearing and subsequent release of gamebirds has not, at least until very recently, come under the scrutiny of ecologists (see Potts, 1986, and Section 8.4.3).

1.3 Ecology and conservation

Ecology is the study of the interrelationships between living organisms and their environment; a study that aims to explain both the distribution and abundance of organisms. Ecologists study the ways in which variation in environmental factors, be they abiotic (such as the weather) or biotic (such as predation, competition or parasitism) affect the reproduction, density, longevity and a whole range of other features of a population or community of animals and plants. Since the environment of one organism is frequently composed of other organisms the interrelationships become very complex and it is rarely possible for the ecologist to examine the influence of one environmental factor on an organism in isolation, especially under natural conditions. Ecology is a relatively young science that has grown out of the more traditional disciplines of zoology and botany but has already advanced our understanding of the mechanisms limiting animal and plant populations, the selective forces influencing the evolution of species and the structure and functioning of biological communities.

While ecology has an important function in pure science, it also has many practical uses and the subject of applied ecology may be considered as the use of science to manage the environment and its inhabitants. This involves changing the environment in a manner that results in a desired alteration in the population of a particular organism. In reality populations are managed only if they are important to man (Wood, 1983). Thus, man may attempt to:

(1) Reduce the number of animals in a population because it is a pest species.

(2) Maintain a population of animals at a level which produces an optimal sustainable yield of an important resource such as meat, leather or sport.

(3) Increase the size of an animal population because he is concerned about its welfare; species that are selectively conserved in this way usually provide cultural benefits such as aesthetic enjoyment or interest.

Wildlife conservation is primarily concerned with managing the environment for either (2) or more often (3), and may be considered as a special case of applied ecology. Game conservation also involves (2) and (3), although in both instances it may be necessary to control pest species (1) to achieve this.

Conservation – in the biological sense – is still equated by some with preservation, as demonstrated by the belief of Margalef (1968) that 'genuine conservation forbids interference'. Others, accepting that man's influence on the environment is already so great, believe that conservation is essentially concerned with the interaction between man and the environment (Usher, 1983). This comes close to the definition of applied ecology and perhaps a useful working definition of biological conservation is the management of the interrelationships between man, other living organisms and the environment. Thus, for the successful conservation and management of a species it is necessary to understand the functioning of the ecosystems in which it lives and hence we can say that successful conservation depends on ecology.

The relationship between game conservation and wildlife conservation in general has an interesting history and one that suggests they have much more in common than many conservationists now suppose or will accept. Much of the initial driving force behind the conservation of species stemmed from a sporting interest; the game reserve long preceded the wildlife sanctuary (Fitter, 1986). In Britain the founders of one of the first voluntary wildlife conservation bodies (what is now the Fauna and Flora Preservation Society) were keen game conservationists and while early game management sometimes led to the wholesale destruction of certain non-game species, these early conservationists always viewed sustainable exploitation as an important element of species conservation. In this way, game conservation has demonstrated the importance of resource management rather than simple preservation and provides an instructive approach for wildlife conservation. Much of Britain's landscape has been moulded by game management and, to preserve certain ecological aspects of this, wildlife conservationists will need to use some of the techniques of game management. For example, much of Britain's 1.2 million hectares of moorland is maintained principally to sustain red grouse shooting, while at the same time the management procedures are of benefit to a wide range of other upland birds (Reed, 1985) including raptors. To maintain such conditions requires continued management inputs and on a number of upland nature reserves it has become necessary that some of the traditional aspects of grouse management continue to maintain the value of the reserve.

Here we require both an understanding of animal ecology and some control over the environment in which they live. Traditionally, wildlife conservationists have tended to concentrate on protecting sites which either contain a rare species or are relatively small, species-rich areas. Indeed, this was the focus of Britain's first conservation legislation which installed the Nature Conservancy and the National Parks Commission in 1949. Both these government bodies concentrated on site protection and to some extent their modern counterparts, the Nature Conservancy Council (NCC) and the Countryside Commission (CC), still do. However, it has become apparent that the long-term survival of wildlife requires an environmental policy for the entire countryside and not a selection of isolated sites. Such a policy will require not preservation but active management and will hinge on our knowledge of game conservation since this has played a major part in developing the ecological principles of management. This is the basis of this book.

Much of the countryside is farmed and agricultural developments cannot be viewed in isolation from game and wildlife conservation. Agriculture is responsible for the shape of the habitats in which most animals must live – in particular the gamebirds. A description of changes in agriculture in relation to gamebirds would therefore be judicious before an examination of the ecological principles of management.

1.4 Agriculture and gamebirds in Britain

In most countries of the world, agriculture dominates as the major land use; some 75% of Britain's land surface is farmed, with pasture and arable land predominating. The history and origins of the British landscape have been well documented (see, for example, Hoskins, 1970; Tittensor, 1981). However, in order to familiarise the reader with the changing environment in which our gamebirds live and amongst which game management must be carried out, we have chosen briefly

Plate 1.1 Modern agriculture has moulded over 80% of today's landscape in Britain. In the lowlands (a), arable crops and their associated pesticides have had a major impact while in the uplands (b) grazing pressure from livestock has played a significant role.

to review some of the more important changes in agriculture.

The term 'agricultural land' is a description of use that ranges from land which is subject to the frequent and far-reaching disturbances of arable rotation to land which is often described as semi-natural, such as heather moorland or downland (Cobham and Rowe, 1986). While agricultural disturbance of the land is nothing new in Britain (O'Connor and Shrubb, 1986), the last forty years have seen an ever-increasing intensity of agricultural methods aimed at maximising yields. This applies to some extent in the uplands but is particularly true of lowland farmland.

1.4.1 Lowland farmland

Britain is one of the most densely populated countries in the world and consequently supports a very intensive farming system. It is inevitable that major changes in farming will produce major ecological changes

in the countryside. While such changes have occurred continuously throughout the evolution of the British landscape, Moore (1965) suggests that three major developments are likely to have had most influence on farmland birds, including the lowland gamebirds. First, the clearance of forests to be replaced by agriculture; second, the change from the medieval open-field system to enclosed farms; and third, the introduction of less labour-intensive methods of production involving the increased use of chemicals and mechanised farm machinery. Of these, the first two were probably of overall benefit to partridges, quail and pheasants since the first provided extensive areas of traditional farmland and the second increased the length of permanent field boundaries available as nesting cover. On the other hand, since this also resulted in the loss of heathlands and forests, black grouse numbers declined in the lowlands and it can be argued that such agricultural developments have simply altered the structure of the gamebird community. The increase in field size, farming intensity and the use of agrochemicals that accompanied the third major change, have almost certainly been detrimental to many species of farmland wildlife and are at least partially responsible for the recent widespread and dramatic decline of lowland gamebirds (Potts, 1986).

Some 65% of farmland in Britain is arable, a proportion that has remained relatively stable since the 1960s (Munton, 1974) but from which the level of output has continued to rise. For example, wheat yields have increased from 2.9 tonnes/ha in 1952 to 7.7 tonnes/ha in 1984 (Royal Commission, 1979; MAFF, 1986). A major factor allowing this increase in yield has been the increased use of pesticides, both in the quantity distributed on the fields and the range of compounds used. In 1957, eleven active ingredients were approved for use in cereal fields in Britain but by 1985, cereal growers were using eighty different compounds on cereals, with substantial increases in the numbers of herbicides, insecticides and foliar applied fungicides (Table 1.2). The estimated annual usage of pesticides on British crops has also increased and by the mid-1980s, 99.8% of Britain's cereals were treated with a pesticide with the average cereal field being treated 5.3 times per year (Sly, 1986). From the 1970s to the present day, the area of farmland treated with herbicides and insecticides has doubled, while the use of fungicides has more than trebled (Table 1.3). Data from wheat crops between 1974 to 1982 show these trends to be similar throughout all types of arable land used by lowland gamebirds (Table 1.4).

Table 1.2 The number of pesticide active ingredients approved for use in UK cereal fields 1957–1985. (From MAFF, 1957, 1966, 1974, 1985.)

	1957	*1967*	*1975*	*1985*
Herbicides	5	16	27	37
Insecticides	4	7	12	19
Molluscicides	1	1	2	2
Fungicides				
seed dressings	1	1	2	3
foliar sprays	0	0	5	15
Plant growth regulators	0	0	2	4
Total	11	25	50	80

Nationally, annual insecticide use data can be difficult to interpret because the amounts used will often depend on the outbreak of cereal aphids during the summer. The inability to forecast the sporadic outbreaks has created a tendency among farmers to apply insecticides to wheat crops prophylactically (Sly, 1981). There has also been a tendency to move away from the use of more selective compounds towards those with a broader spectrum of activity against insects, including those known to be important to partridge and pheasant chicks (Green, 1984; Hill, 1985). Selective farmer surveys carried out between 1975 and 1977 showed that 59% of crops sprayed with insecticides were treated with pirimicarb (a relatively selective compound against non-target insects) whilst 9% were treated with dimethoate (a relatively non-selective compound) (Watt, Vickerman

Table 1.3 Estimated annual usage of pesticides on crops in agriculture and horticulture in England and Wales between 1971 and 1983 (treated '000 ha). (From Sly, 1986.)

Pesticide	*1971–74*	*1975–79*	*1980–83*
Insecticides, acaricides, molluscicides	1086	1718	2111
Seed treatments	3718	3753	3883
Fungicides	1895	2253	6715
Herbicides, defoliants	6003	7868	12402
Other pesticides	81	203	801
Total	127 83	15795	26012
Areas of crop and grass	5631*	9322	10511

* permanent grass not included

Table 1.4   The use of pesticides on winter wheat in England and Wales 1974–1982. (From Sly, 1977, 1984, Steed *et al.*, 1979.)

	1974	1977	1982
Total area grown ('000 ha)	1139	1025	1620
Area of crop treated ('000 ha)			
Insecticides	44	491	345
Fungicides	94	367	3274
Herbicides	1793	1647	4161
MCPA	253	124	195
2,4-D	87	56	38
bromoxynil/ioxynil mixtures	31	42	525
dicamba mixtures	209	166	91
2,3,6-TBA mixtures	127*	138	7
chlortoluron	–	52	430
isoproturon	–	127	454

* = 2,3,6-TBA only
– = data unavailable

and Wratten, 1984). In 1984, similar surveys showed that only 30% of crops sprayed were treated with pirimicarb whereas 43% were treated with dimethoate (Sotherton, unpubl. data).

Fungicide use has also increased on wheat crops over the last decade (Table 1.4). These official figures are supported by Potts (1986) who found that on a 62 km² study farm in West Sussex, none of the cereal fields had been sprayed with a foliar fungicide in the early 1970s. By the early 1980s, almost every field of cereals received at least one application of fungicide per year.

The spectrum of weed species killed by herbicides has also widened over this period. Weed species which are both the host plants of insects important to wild gamebird chicks and important plant food for adult partridges (Potts, 1970; Sotherton, 1982) are highly susceptible to the herbicides currently being used. Initially, some of these weeds, such as the *Polygonaceae* (the dock family), were relatively tolerant to the herbicides introduced for use on cereals in 1946 but broad-spectrum herbicides that kill such weeds have since been introduced. The most recent trend in herbicide technology has been the use of broad-spectrum, residual herbicides usually applied in the autumn which kill both grass and broad-leaved weeds and can reduce subsequent spring-germinating species such as the weeds known to be important to gamebirds.

The area of agricultural land in cereal production, and hence the area potentially available as habitat for lowland gamebirds, has increased over the last twenty years. In 1962, 2.6 million hectares of England and Wales were in cereal production (MAFF, 1973); by 1982, the area had increased to 3.44 million hectares (Sly, 1986). Over the same period the proportion of autumn-sown cereals had increased. As a consequence of this switch towards autumn drilling, stubbles are now more likely to be sprayed off with a defoliant herbicide or burnt after harvest to prepare the seed bed for the next crop. There is little information concerning the effects of the use of defoliant herbicides on non-target fauna. However, data suggest that the uses of these chemicals (e.g. paraquat, the most commonly used on stubbles) have increased: 43 500 ha of winter wheat sprayed in 1974 compared to 131 000 ha in 1982 (Sly, 1977, 1986). Disposal of straw by burning also removes insects that are important food items of gamebird chicks both in the short term (Vickerman, 1974) and in the longer term; in spring, areas burnt in the previous autumn have lower densities of insects than areas not burnt (Sotherton, 1980). It is difficult to assess the effects of straw burning in isolation but Potts (1974) found that large areas of burning and prolonged cultivation were generally followed by low numbers of preferred food items of gamebird chicks. This must be a significant factor when one considers that in 1976, MAFF estimated that over 2 million tonnes of straw were burnt (Royal Commission, 1979).

Early establishment of cereals and the shift towards cereal monocultures has also led to an increase in the practice of direct-drilling. The area of cereals established by direct-drilling increased from about 8000 ha in 1967 to 137 000 ha in 1974 (Cussans, 1975) but has declined since. Direct-drilled fields have a different weed flora than conventionally cultivated fields because fewer cultivations results in a reduction in the numbers of annual broad-leaved weeds, such as the *Polygonaceae*, with a corresponding increase in perennial broad-leaved weeds and grass weeds.

The practice of establishing grass leys by undersowing them into cereal fields is also a practice of cereal management favourable to the important chick food insects of wild gamebird chicks (Potts, 1970; Vickerman, 1978). However, because of the yield penalties involved in this technique and the decreased need for grassland on arable farms, especially in the Eastern Counties, the practice has greatly declined (Potts, 1970).

Since the 1960s, there has been a tendency towards growing cereals continually rather than in rotation. This would appear to be potentially advantageous to gamebirds although it does prevent undersowing. However, as we have seen, the production system has been accompanied by intensification and the use of farming practices which are, in fact, detrimental to gamebird populations. Increased pesticide use, a switch away from spring-drilling (and the associated differences in pesticide use between crop types), changes in stubble clearance and crop establishment have all created an agricultural regime that is not sympathetic to game.

Without a clearly defined agricultural policy towards cereals, it is difficult to predict the future for game in Britain. In the mid-1980s, Britain and Europe are over-producing cereals. Increasing the standards of cereal grain before some of the excess can be purchased, into intervention, may appear to be one method of decreasing surpluses. It may however encourage growers to improve grain quality by increasing their pesticide inputs and thus merely exacerbating the problem. Other proposed methods to reduce surpluses, such as a set aside policy (fallow land) or Payment in Kind (PIK) whereby cereals are ploughed into the soil before harvest, have also proved to be unsympathetic to gamebirds (Potts, 1986).

1.4.2 Upland agriculture

The uplands are an extensive part of Britain's land mass that predominate in the north and west of the country (Fig. 1.1). Most of this agricultural land is now included in the Less Favoured Areas Directive of the EEC and receives a number of subsidies and grants designed to stem depopulation, conserve the area and encourage tourism. Despite this relatively large area of land and the massive fiscal support, hill and upland farming account for only 7.5% of the total gross output from British agriculture (Eadie, 1985). In the lowlands, technological developments and intensification have led to substantial increases in the output per hectare since 1945 whereas outputs from the hills have remained relatively stable. Cooper and Thomas (1975) captured the essence of this when they said 'An agrarian Rip Van Winkle who had slept these last thirty years would be at a complete loss as a husbandman if he returned to a tillage farm, but if he were an upland farmer, his main problem would be one of getting to grips with subsidies'.

Some 5000 years ago most of Britain's hill land was still covered in woodland. A change to a cool, wet climate had already led to a reduction in this woodland although the rate of disappearance increased dramatically following the slash and burn agricultural practice used by early man. Demand for wood and the expansion of agriculture in the 18th century led to an almost complete destruction of natural woodland and its replacement by heather moorland. This set the scene for the red grouse populations to expand but at the same time the loss of the Caledonian forest was probably a major factor in the extinction of the capercaillie.

Early agriculture based on smallholdings and the crofting system was extensive in Scotland. Following the clearances, sheep farming intensified and the sheep population reached its highest level at the end of the 18th century. The interest in gamebirds in the uplands increased dramatically during Victorian times, in particular when Queen Victoria bought Balmoral estate and it became fashionable to own and be seen on an upland sporting estate. The capercaillie was successfully reintroduced and the current population are descendants of birds originally released by Lord Breadalbane in Tayside. The natural corollary of this increased interest in gamebirds was an increase in management inputs; keepers took over responsibilities for heather burning and predator control practices reduced the numbers of any

Fig. 1.1   The distribution of moorland in Britain.

predator that was considered a threat. Gamebird populations probably reached their greatest size at this time and bag records indicate that they remained so until the Second World War.

Agriculture in the uplands is naturally limited by the harsh climate, poor soils and difficult topography, although economic and social conditions have also played a part. Generally, these factors have limited most hill farms to livestock production and principally sheep production; out of some 5.43 million hectares of hill land in Britain 92% is rough grazing and grass. As with the lowlands, the major changes that have occurred have been since 1945. The number of sheep in the north and west of the country has doubled although the total sheep population has remained relatively stable as lowland farmers have moved from sheep into cereal production and some sheep-producing areas have been lost to other land uses.

With increased economic pressure on the hill farmer and an increase in the minimum viable size of farm there has been farm amalgamation and a reduction in the labour force. The traditional hill shepherds have all but gone in most areas so sheep tend to concentrate in small areas where they over-utilise the heather. This has been exacerbated further by providing supplementary feed and also by farmers keeping sheep on the hill for longer periods during the winter (Hudson, 1985, 1986a). It has been argued (Sinclair, 1983; Peel, 1983) that these practices have been encouraged by the system of headage payments given to farmers under the Hill Livestock Compensatory Allowance which in effect encourage over-stocking as opposed to supporting a system of quality production and a farming industry that could be intensified to some degree (Hudson, 1985).

Red grouse depend primarily on heather moorland and a reduction in the extent of heather has had serious repercussions on red grouse and upland land use. As the heather and grouse go, sporting values fall. Yet, even with reduced numbers, management inputs must be maintained to produce a sustainable grouse density. Put simply, while the area of productive ground has been reduced, the keepering levels have had to be maintained. Inevitably, the fall in land values and the low returns result in once productive ground being sold to alternative land uses such as commercial afforestation. In southern Scotland and areas of Wales, moorlands and grouse populations have been seriously reduced as a consequence of these events. In the Highlands of Scotland, over-utilisation of heather by red deer can have a similar effect. Counts of red deer by the Red Deer Commission show an increase in deer density, probably as a result of the hind cull being too low and increased afforestation excluding deer from traditional wintering areas. The problem for agriculture in the uplands is the downward spiral of reduced returns followed by reduced investments.

Although governments provide incentives for afforestation there is great concern about the rate at which this is currently taking place in the uplands. More than 70% of afforestation has occurred since 1950 and the current rate is not far short of the officially intended rate of 30 000 hectares per annum. As Eadie (1985) points out, this is a high rate of land-use transfer when one considers that only 4500 hectares of semi-natural vegetation are re-seeded per annum. The direct replacement of moorland with mass afforestation is of great concern to conservationists (NCC, 1986) and those using land adjacent to afforested areas. Plantations alter the ecology of the uplands: decomposition rates are reduced, water yield is reduced and acidity increases. Low levels of calcium, nitrates and phosphorus reduce tree growth and influence the growth of salmonoid fish in streams receiving water run-off.

Forestry plantations fragment upland bird populations and replace many of these valued species with lowland counterparts. An increase in the abundance of voles and other lowland species in young plantations leads to an abnormally high density of predators, which in turn influences the more vulnerable upland species on neighbouring areas (Reed, 1985).

The future for game in the uplands is bleak if current trends continue. Nevertheless, a slight change in the tax incentives for afforestation, replacement of the headage payment for sheep with a support system which would discourage over-grazing, reduced sporting rates and an improvement in game management practices could alter the economic equation in favour of moorland and game conservation; in simple terms, a fiscal package which embraces multiple land-use. The object of any such policy should be to maintain multiple land-use in the uplands, with sheep production as the primary land-use but in a manner that would be environmentally sympathetic and acceptable to the relatively new but important land-use – tourism.

1.5 Conclusion

This chapter sets the scene for the rest of the book; the subject of management in an ecological context is introduced and summarised in relation to changes in agriculture and land-use.

It should be clear from these introductory remarks that conservation requires management inputs, preferably based on an ecological understanding of the species and its environment. Furthermore, conservation cannot be carried out in isolation, it needs to embrace the countryside as a whole – an approach that requires a new environmental policy. For historical reasons, active wildlife conservation will depend on aspects of gamebird management although both require a sound scientific foundation based on ecological principles.

2 Population Changes in Gamebirds

Stephen C. Tapper

2.1 Introduction

Game management has twin objectives: first, to manipulate environmental characteristics so the habitat supports the optimum game breeding stock, and second, to ensure the maximum production of young birds to maximise the harvestable yield. To this end, game manager and scientist alike must measure their successes and failures with reliable and repeatable techniques which can be applied in a variety of situations.

This chapter is about these techniques which are both the foundation of most game research programmes and the basic tools of the game manager; techniques such as census methods used to measure spring and autumn stocks, and the use of bag records to examine long- or short-term historical changes.

2.2 Censusing gamebird populations

In principle, assessing the stock of a game species is no different from making a population estimate for any animal. For an ecologist, the method is usually a compromise between some statistically ideal approach and what is actually possible, practical, and cost effective. Most species of bird are diurnal, highly visible, and often advertise their presence. Thus, techniques used in monitoring gamebird numbers have much in common with those used for other birds. On the other hand, mammalogists often have to rely on mark and recapture methods to make population estimates; techniques which are not necessary for ornithologists. Catching and marking gamebirds, although frequently used for research where the fate of individuals needs to be known, is rarely employed in making estimates of population size. Instead population estimates are based either on the number of birds seen or in some cases the numbers heard calling.

For most bird species, counting procedures and sampling methods have been developed, tested and used to assess the size of national bird populations in several countries – see Robbins (1985) for a review of North American surveys and counts. In Britain, some of the first detailed censuses started in 1928 when E. M. Nicholson initiated a national census of herons and, later, rooks. Since these early days the British Trust for Ornithology has organised special surveys which have mapped the breeding and winter distribution of birds (Sharrock, 1976; Lack, 1986) and used territory mapping in the Common Bird Census to establish changes in the breeding densities of woodland, farmland and scrubland species. This complements a Nest Record Scheme which has provided information on annual production and breeding success of a wide range of bird species. Other schemes have included counts of estuary birds and systematic mist netting at selected sites to monitor the condition and age structure of over-wintering bird populations (see Hickling, 1983). The Wildfowl Trust have also used counts at specific sites on predetermined dates to establish numbers of over-wintering waterfowl (Owen, 1983). Despite some of the early work, most of these censuses and surveys have developed since the last War.

Censuses of gamebirds have a longer history, born not out of an interest in the species but a desire to improve numbers for sport. By the end of the 19th century, driven game shooting had become a highly fashionable sport in Britain with a distinct emphasis on the number shot (Walsingham and Payne-Gallway, 1895). Game managers were routinely making assessments of game stocks to establish the shooting potential of areas and instigating programmes of research to develop new management techniques (e.g. Lovat, 1911). In many instances, the census methods used in game research were developed from what had already been established and practised by keepers and others during the last century.

Some censuses are designed to give an accurate count over a small area, either because the area monitored is small or because it is a sample of a much larger area. Other methods rely on counts from unspecified areas to determine an index of population size, although these methods have been more widely applied in North America than in Britain.

2.2.1 Census techniques used in North America

Management of North American game is organised on either a state- or province-wide basis and the regional Fish and Wildlife Department determines the length of seasons and bag limits in different regions, depending on the results of surveys it has conducted. Under this system, the department must obtain estimates of game abundance which are comparable both with other areas and with previous years. An absolute estimate of the total population is not usually necessary and an index of abundance will usually suffice. Such methods have been in operation for many years, and Leopold (1933) gives examples for pheasant, bobwhite quail and ruffed grouse counts. Leopold (1933) emphasised that it was not the total number of birds seen that was important, but the relative numbers between areas. Since Leopold's time these methods have been elaborated and the analyses refined. The techniques are now established as part of North American game management and the options open to American game biologists when choosing a census appropriate to their species have been reviewed by Overton (1971).

A notable census method, developed by King (*in* Leopold, 1933), is the strip census. The simplest form of this technique involves walking a transect of specified length and noting the distances at which birds are observed. The transect width is then calculated as a function of the average distance between the observer and when the birds were first seen. Since gamebirds are cryptic and flush when approached, it is the flushing distance which is important and determines the width of the transect. Complications arise when the flushing distance varies with weather or cover, and particularly when not all birds react in the same way. For example, birds close to the observer tend to be flushed whereas only a proportion of the more distant ones flush and are noted. Hence, careful trials are needed before applying this method.

Roadside counts have proved useful for censusing North American gamebirds as they are both rapid and cheap. In some states pheasants have been censused extensively using this method. However, a wide range of factors affect these counts and they have to be standardised in relation to weather, season and time of day.

Another approach, widely used in North America, is to count the number of calls heard. Mourning doves call, pheasants crow, ruffed grouse drum and indeed most gamebirds produce a call that can be counted and used to estimate abundance. Various standard procedures based on listening at sampling stations for specified lengths of time have been developed and a range of correction factors applied to discount the effects of weather on the bird's calling behaviour. However, the most important consideration in using this method is to determine the social functions of the call before assuming they are good indicators of abundance. For example, it is well known that one crowing pheasant will stimulate another to start calling; thus there is a danger that at low densities some birds will be silent and it may be necessary to play back a recorded call to start all birds crowing.

2.2.2 Census techniques used in Britain

In Britain, game shooting traditions are quite different from those of North America (see also Section 8.1) since the landowner owns the rights to take the game on his land. For most gamebird species (including pheasant, partridge and grouse) shooting seasons are specified in the various game laws enacted in the 19th century, and for other species (including woodcock and snipe) they are qualified in the Wildlife and Countryside Act (1981). Only for this latter group can the Government alter the seasons without the consent of parliament and this is only when winter weather is thought to be adversely affecting survival. As a consequence, central and local governments take no responsibility for game management and landowners have the initiative to both develop the game stock and regulate harvesting pressure (see Chapter 8). This has resulted in game being intensively managed on individual estates. With some species, like partridges, where the birds are very easily seen at some times of the year it is feasible to census all the birds on an estate. For other species, such as the red grouse, the dense heather habitat makes total censuses difficult and sample counts have to be conducted. The census methods used for red grouse, pheasant and grey partridge have evolved along differing lines but the main aims are the same: to provide an estimate of the breeding stock at the beginning of the year and an assessment of production in the autumn or late summer prior to shooting. These three species illustrate the level to which game managers and scientists can routinely monitor gamebird populations in Britain.

RED GROUSE

The heather vegetation on most grouse moors consists of a mosaic of different aged stands so visibility varies and direct counts are usually unreliable. Where grouse are being intensively studied, territorial displays and disputes can be seen amongst resident males and it is possible to use territory mapping to assess the density of spring and autumn populations. In this way, Jenkins *et al.* (1963) were able to map the territories of grouse over a series of years (Fig. 2.1). However, they did find it necessary to have some of the cocks tagged for ease of identification, and to conduct long periods of observation to count the females and non-territorial birds.

Jenkins *et al.* (1963) also used transect counts to make comparable estimates of spring and autumn densities on a number of areas. Dogs, either setters or pointers, were used to find all the grouse within the transect area. Experience was essential for both man and dog since some hens were reluctant to flush in spring and could be missed; however, good observers with well trained dogs could produce consistent results. They checked their methods by, first, repeating the census at different seasons and second, against other counts made from a vehicle. Repeated counts showed a coefficient of variation of 22% at low densities but only 9% at higher densities. The same method was used in July and early August to assess production. At this time of the year immature birds are with their parents in covies and both the

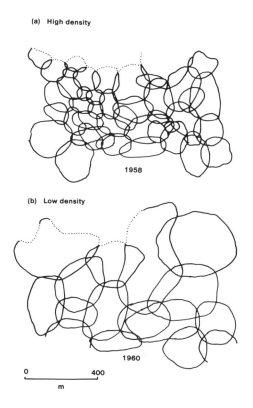

Fig. 2.1   Red grouse territories mapped as a population census in two years (a) when density was high; and (b) when density was low. (*After* Jenkins *et al.*, 1963.)

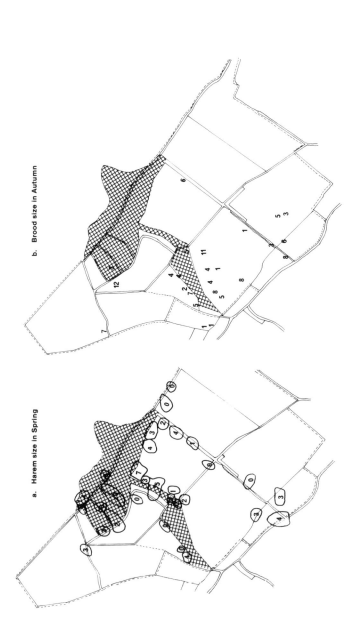

Fig. 2.2 Spring and autumn censuses of pheasants. A spring territory map (a) of dominant males is shown with the number of females in each harem indicated. The autumn count (b) shows the locations of all females and the size of their broods. Hatching indicates woodland (*Data from* D.A. Hill (unpublished).)

young and adult birds could be distinguished and counted as they were flushed. Consecutive counts as the young grew also enabled them to establish chick survival rates.

For the manager of a game resource, this method can be simplified a little by conducting spring counts on sample areas of 100 ha (250 acres) that are defined by recognisable topographical boundaries. Counting starts on the down-wind side and the observer walks back and forth across the area with the dogs quartering the ground ahead of him. As birds are flushed their sex is checked and landing place noted so they are not double-counted. In summer the count proceeds in a similar fashion but the average covey size is also recorded, usually as the ratio of young to adult birds, as a measure of breeding production.

PHEASANTS

The pheasant is the most numerous of British gamebirds but is one of the most difficult to census accurately. Although territorial males are very prominent as they strut about in the spring, they represent only a proportion of the males. The non-territorial males and the females are usually secretive and difficult to record accurately. The accepted technique used on farmland, without large blocks of woodland, is to scan each field or open area with binoculars on spring evenings and to count and map all territorial cocks (Fig. 2.2). Territorial males are identified as those with a harem of females, displaying by crowing and wing drumming; any cocks living in woodland rides or coppice that have not been seen can usually be detected by sound. Non-territorial males are discounted from the estimate of the breeding population. Females are shyer than males, but harems of females will remain within a few yards of their chosen mate and while he is displaying they can be counted. Even, so a proportion of hens will be missed and this can be corrected for by multiplying the average harem size by 1.3 (Ridley, 1983).

An autumn census to estimate production is carried out in August or September, when broods tend to be on cereal stubbles, around corners of woods and along hedgerows. This census can either aim to find all broods, or to estimate breeding production from a sample of 20 to 30 broods. It is also possible to estimate chick survival from the brood sizes in a similar way to the methods employed for partridges (see below).

GREY PARTRIDGE

The spring census is a pair count conducted between mid-March and the end of April. In a normal year, partridges in covies will have dispersed by March. Most pairs will have already chosen their nesting areas but not the actual nest site; in most cases any birds which are going to leave or move onto the study area will have already done so. On arable farmland with a high proportion of cereals a complete spring census is possible from counts made at dawn and dusk in good weather conditions. Crops are short at this time of the year and feeding pairs are readily seen with binoculars. The autumn count can either be a sample of the young and old seen while driving a vehicle around a selection of cereal stubbles or a complete count of all the autumn stock.

Fig. 2.3 The spring pair count of a high density mixed partridge population on a farm in Norfolk.

If the autumn count is a sample, then an accurate spring census (Fig. 2.3) is essential in order to estimate the autumn population. A complete autumn census can however be used to estimate the previous spring breeding stock; male survival of paired birds is high and those counted in September provide an accurate estimate of spring pairs. The few that are lost are balanced by the few unpaired males that have survived (Potts, 1986).

2.2.3 Population parameters estimated from count data

Gamebird censuses were initially designed to assist keepers and land managers to monitor their stocks and assess the potential harvest that could be taken from a population. They now provide the foundation of most gamebird research programmes. Jenkins *et al* (1967) used repeated counts of red grouse on intensively studied areas to show at what season most losses occurred. They identified particular periods of heavy loss between autumn and spring which they attributed to the effects of territorial birds excluding other individuals that either dispersed or died. These censuses were used primarily to document changes in numbers and they derived other population parameters such as breeding success and mortality directly from data obtained from monitoring nests and finding corpses.

Potts (1986) used the autumn census of grey partridges to estimate losses throughout the year on an extensive study area (29 km^2) in southern Britain. Few young in the autumn covies indicated small broods and low chick survival, probably caused by starvation. Many old pairs with no broods (incorrectly termed barren pairs) indicated poor nesting success which was attributed mostly to egg predation by corvids; while single, old males indicated predation of females usually during incubation.

Partridge counts can be used to estimate the survival rate of chicks. Given that grey partridges have an average clutch size of 13.8 eggs per nest, the chick survival rate (CSR) can be estimated from the mean brood size (x):

$$CSR = x/13.8 \qquad (2.1)$$

Potts (1986) used the geometric mean of brood size (brood sizes are first converted to logarithms, averaged and then converted back to whole numbers). However, the above formula was not appropriate when average brood size was less than 10, because some parents lost all their chicks and the adults appear as failed pairs. It is not obvious which pairs fail as a result of nest predation and which from zero chick survival. However, individual marking and radio-tracking studies have shown a relationship between brood size below 10 and CSR:

$$CSR = -7.81 + 7.81x \qquad (2.2)$$

and

$$CSR = 3.07 + 5.89x \qquad (2.3)$$

The first of these equations was calculated by Green (1984) and the second by Rands (1986a). Potts used a more complex curvilinear relationship, but all three methods give similar results (Potts, 1986).

Another important parameter that can be derived from these counts is nesting success: the percentage of pairs that successfully hatch a clutch. Potts (1986) terms this the brood production rate (BPR). This is defined by:

$$BPR = ((Tc/CSR)/13.8)/Ma \qquad (2.4)$$

where Tc is the total number of chicks counted and Ma is the number of adult males counted in August.

Having calculated these parameters it is possible to study how they are affected by factors such as population density or food supply. For example, Potts (1980) found that chick survival in grey partridges was independent of partridge density but was related to chick food supply. Similarly, Hill (1985) found that pheasant chick survival was related to insect abundance and in radio-tracking studies was able to confirm this by monitoring the survival of individual broods and their diet. Other parameters can be density-dependent, for example both hen losses and egg losses in grey partridges can be related to nesting density (Potts, 1980, 1986) yet this density-dependence was less marked or absent on farms where keepers were employed to control predators. Once these relationships have been found they can be confirmed as causal by experiment. For example, in red grouse Hudson (1986b) used the young to old ratio from summer counts as a control group to compare with the breeding success of experimental birds with reduced parasite burdens (Section 5.3.2). In another experiment, Rands (1986a) used counts of partridges and pheasants to demonstrate that reduced pesticide use in cereal fields increased chick survival (Section 6.3.1).

Our ability to readily census gamebirds quickly and efficiently without having to resort to labour-intensive capture and mark techniques has given the game biologist a significant advantage over other vertebrate ecologists studying more secretive animals. Intensive methods such as radio-tracking play an increasing role in the detailed investigations which are needed to develop and test ideas. The ultimate step of developing management techniques requires extensive studies and often relies on the census methods outlined here.

2.3 Bag records as indicators of population fluctuations

In the 1930s, The Bureau of Animal Population at the University of Oxford began studies which considered patterns of animal abundance. Cycles in numbers were first scientifically examined when researchers, led by C.S. Elton, realised that variations from year to year were not always random but for some species followed a distinct rhythm. At that time true census data over long time periods had not been collected for any animal population. Hunting, shooting, and trapping statistics were ideal sets of data, even though it was realised that they could never be a true reflection of population density. The best information to emerge during this period were the records of fur bearing mammals trapped for the Hudson's Bay Company in northern Canada. This information came from an area of land undisturbed by agricultural change or game management. The Hudson's Bay records of lynx trapped in the Mackenzie River region remain some of the best long-term information for any wildlife species.

Middleton (1934) was the first to use bag records from Britain in an attempt to detect cycles. He analysed these data which showed an approximate 6-year cycle in red grouse numbers and evidence of cycles in woodcock, partridge, and brown hare populations. Mackenzie (1952) examined grouse data from a selection of over 50 moors and his work remained the most comprehensive survey of red grouse bag data until the 1980s. Grouse bag records usually cycled with a period of 5–6 years, but this varied from one region to the next and in some cases from 3–10 years. There was variation in peak years on different moors, though many were well synchronised. He suggested there were periods of 2–3 years when most populations would peak and any synchrony was brought about by severe environmental factors which influenced all neighbouring populations. Williams (1954) carried this analysis one stage further and plotted the proportion of red grouse data sets which showed peaks in the same year. This indicated not only that the data were highly periodic, but also that in peak years only slightly more than 50% of the populations actually reached a maximum.

Although these early analyses were interesting they failed to test the significance of the fluctuations in a rigorous statistical manner. Thus, when Cole (1951) suggested that the existence of cycles was unproven and some time-series bore a remarkable resemblance to data read directly from a book of random numbers, he brought into question the actuality of such cycles. In a further paper, Cole (1954) even suggested that some of the treatments, like the sliding averages used by Middleton (1934), actually tended to create cycles in data sets where they had not existed before. To a very large extent the subject foundered, and ecologists turned their attention instead to properly gathered field data derived from ecological studies of fluctuating populations.

2.3.1 Techniques for examining population cycles in bag records

The lack of interest in long-term records since the mid-1950s was unfortunate because the basic type of analysis to examine such data

Plate 2.1   Records of the numbers of birds shot when systematically recorded from a large number of areas can provide valuable data on population trends and patterns of population change.

had already been established. Moran (1949, 1953) showed that statistical methods could distinguish random from non-random series and had demonstrated their use with some of the data given by Mackenzie (Moran, 1952). Although the methods were not complex, they were extremely arduous to perform on the existing calculating machines and consequently few researchers used the techniques.

Meanwhile, statisticians continued to develop the techniques of time-series analysis for studies outside biology and were greatly helped by the widespread introduction of computers. By the mid-1970s time-series analysis was well established and several major reference works had been published (e.g. Kendall, 1973; Box and Jenkins, 1974). As a result, ecologists began to return to the original series and re-analyse them with the new methods using computers (Bulmer, 1974; Finerty, 1980; Potts, *et al*, 1984; Williams, 1985).

The main purpose of applying time-series analysis was to test the idea that population fluctuations are not random and, if cyclic, to show the extent and period of the cycles. The basic statistical tool is the correlogram; aptly named since it is based on the correlation coefficient and results are presented as an X,Y graph. The correlogram is based on the following principle: if a series is random then data points will be independent and there will be no association (correlation) of points. However, if there is a cycle running through the series, there may be a fairly close correlation between points adjacent to each other and a good correlation could be expected between pairs of points separated by an interval equal to the length of the cycle.

To construct a correlogram, all possible data points are used to calculate correlation coefficients for increasing time-intervals. For short intervals the maximum number of pairs will only be a few shorter than the entire series, but for larger intervals the number will diminish until the interval becomes as long as the series, at which point there will be only one pair. Obviously performing correlations at such large intervals is meaningless, so it is usual to make calculations only up to one-third of the length of the entire series. Hence to detect a 10-year cycle, at least 30 years of data are required and preferably longer. Although the method is little more than a repeated series of correlation calculations it would be very tedious to perform by hand. A series of 100 years introduces nearly 3000 data pairs; a good sample, but one that requires a computer.

To understand the significance of data sets that exhibit cycles it is instructive to compare correlograms with those produced from contrived sets of data. First, a random series of numbers which fall within a random normal distribution are generated: in other words, the data vary about a mean with a characteristic bell-shaped distribution (e.g. Fig. 2.4a). For this series the expected correlation coefficients will be zero at all time intervals. However, this is not actually the case since there is always variation about the base line. Therefore a belt of

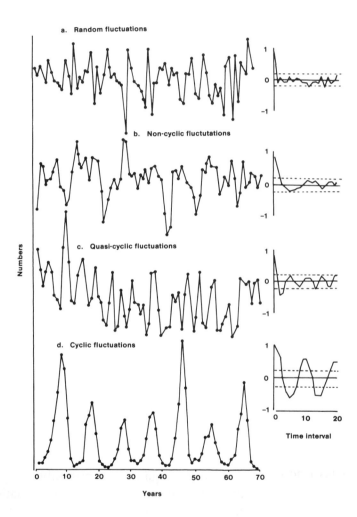

Fig. 2.4 Four types of time-series and their correlograms: (a) a random series based on random-normal deviations around a constant mean; (b) a random series but with one year dependent on the next; (c) a quasi-cyclic series with an average period of about 5 years; (d) a cyclic series with a period of 9–10 years. The correlograms (right) show correlation coefficients from +1 to –1 for time intervals of between 1 and 20 years. Dotted lines indicate the band outside which coefficients are statistically significant.

significance is imposed around this axis to contain this natural variation; most coefficients falling outside this belt will be significant, with 95% confidence limits.

Most animal populations do not vary in a random manner since numbers in one year will have at least some influence on numbers in the following year. This contribution can be simulated with random normal variates by averaging neighbouring points so that each value depends in part on the value in the previous year; a hypothetical non-cyclic gamebird is shown in Fig. 2.4b. If a long period cycle is created by using an algebraic function with random error terms it might appear as Fig. 2.4d. In this case the correlogram shows a clear wave pattern with high correlation coefficients occurring at time intervals equivalent to various multiples of the cycle length. Notice that the correlogram does not damp down with increasing time intervals. This is a model of a truly cyclic series; Nisbet and Gurney (1982) call these phase-remembering quasi-cycles because in reality these cycles are not quite as pure as a sine wave, where coefficients would always approach +1 and –1 in the correlogram. There are other possibilities: an intermediate form where there is some variation in the wave length of the cycle as well as random error terms. These are phase-forgetting quasi-cycles (Fig. 2.4c). The correlogram of these data shows a significant wave form but the coefficients gradually diminish and the correlogram is said to be damped.

Gamebird data often show trends in the series and these will swamp any short-term variation in the correlogram and make the detection of cycles difficult. The removal of trend is largely a matter of empirical judgement, since the distinction between a varying trend and a fluctuation is arbitrary. For a linear trend, a least squares straight line could be used and the correlogram calculated on the residuals, but non-linear trends require another approach. Two methods which are commonly used are:

(1) Calculating a polynomial trend and then subtracting it from the original data to produce a trend-free series.
(2) Subtracting each value in the series from the one next to it.

This latter procedure is called differencing and is extremely easy to apply; however, it can alter the appearance of the series considerably and could affect subsequent analysis of short-term fluctuations.

Fitting a polynomial to the data is the most usual way of obtaining trend. These can be made to fit almost any series and are calculated using a moving average process with a number of elements having different weightings; a good description of this approach can be found in Kendall (1973). Another simpler way of calculating the trend on game bag records is to use a simple unweighted moving average of five

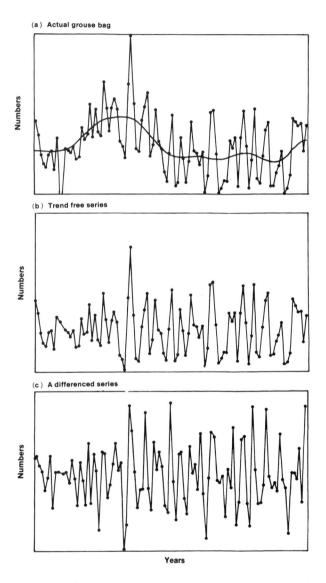

Fig. 2.5 Two methods for detrending a time-series: (a) the original series with a smooth curve calculated by a moving average process; (b) a detrended series derived by subtracting the smooth line from the original series; (c) a trend-free series produced by differencing the original series.

elements and repeatedly run it through each successive series (Potts *et al.* 1984). With each pass the series becomes smoother and smoother until eventually it is virtually a straight line. Just how often the averaging process needs to be done is a matter of preference, but 10 runs produce a smooth curve which follows the changing level of the fluctuations. A series of bag records for a Yorkshire grouse moor and the trend line which was fitted to it are shown in Fig. 2.5a; a series derived by subtracting the trend from the original is shown in Fig. 2.5b. This trend-free series should have a mean of zero and have the appearance of the original series with long-term changes ironed out. By comparison a series which has been differenced (Fig. 2.5c) loses much of the appearance of the original. Once the detrending has been accomplished, calculation of the correlogram can proceed.

2.3.2 Regular fluctuations in gamebird numbers

Time-series analysis of bag records for a number of lowland species are shown in Fig. 2.6. In the woodcock records from Northern Ireland there is very little trend so the series is not altered substantially by detrending. The correllogram has the first five coefficients very close to the base line indicating no relationship between the bag in one year and any of the subsequent five years; the coefficients at lags greater than five years are either not significant or may be taken as spurious. Most woodcock series show a similar pattern and can be considered random. This is not surprising since most woodcock shot in Britain are migrants from Scandinavia, and the extent to which they occur in Britain and Ireland will depend largely on winter weather (Tapper and Hirons, 1983). A re-examination of Middleton's (1934) woodcock data shows these are also non-cyclic and so his assertion of a 9-year cycle is likely to be due to his treatment of the data.

Resident lowland game populations can be expected to behave differently since bag records will reflect changes in the local populations. However, like the woodcock, many partridge and pheasant series are also random; this is probably because bag records are not a true reflection of population levels. Some series do show a significant coefficient at an interval of one year, as shown by the partridge series in Fig. 2.6b. This does not indicate cycling but simply a small measure of dependence of numbers in one year on numbers in the next. Many pheasant series show much less variation than other species since the practice of hand-rearing birds has reduced both the variation in numbers and the relative importance of wild birds.

Some upland game species like black grouse do show a clear cyclic pattern (Fig. 2.7a). Unfortunately the substantial decline in this species during the early part of the century means that most series have a large downward trend in the data which reduces the sensitivity of the correlogram. However, the significant coefficients at 2, 5, 7, 10, and 12 years clearly indicate a cycle with a period of about 5 years. This series is quasi-cyclic but it is possible that if overall numbers had not fallen then it might have approached the truly cyclic kind. Other black grouse

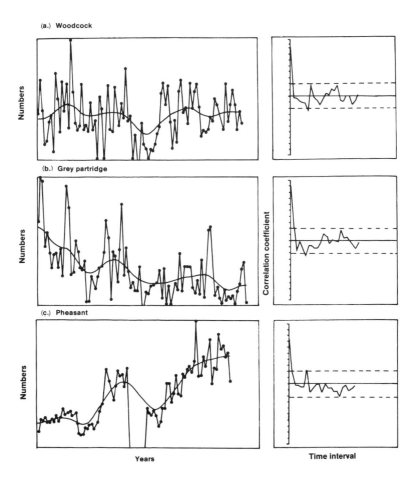

Fig. 2.6 Time-series analysis of lowland game: (a) a woodcock series showing almost random fluctuations; (b) a partridge series which is random but with a significant correlation at a time lag of 1 year; (c) a pheasant series showing less annual variation than the partridge series, but with a similar correlogram.

series show a period of about 4 years while some show a weak 3-year cycle.

Red grouse series are also quasi-cyclic. In Scotland, like the black grouse, there is considerable variation in cycle length, although 6 years appears to be the average. Williams (1985) in a re-analysis of Middleton's (1934) and Mackenzie's (1952) data confirmed this; and more recently, Barnes (1987) analysed data from 75 Scottish moors and found evidence of quasi-cycles ranging in period from 4 to 18 years

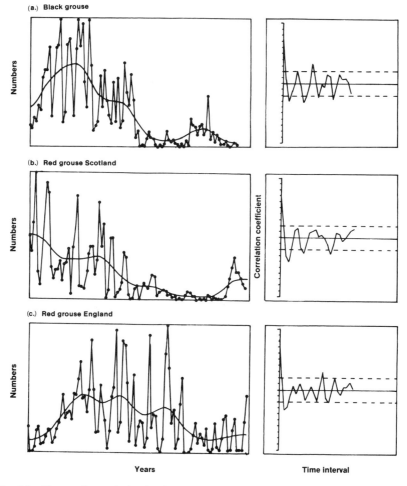

Fig. 2.7   Time-series analysis of upland game. (a) a black grouse series from Scotland showing quasi-cycles with a 5-year average period; (b) a Scottish red grouse series showing quasi-cycles of about 6 years; (c) an English red grouse series showing quasi-cycles with a period of around 5 years.

with an average of 6. There is also a tendency for the length of cycles to increase the further north the population is: 4 years in the Peak District, 5 years in the North Pennines and Southern Uplands and 6

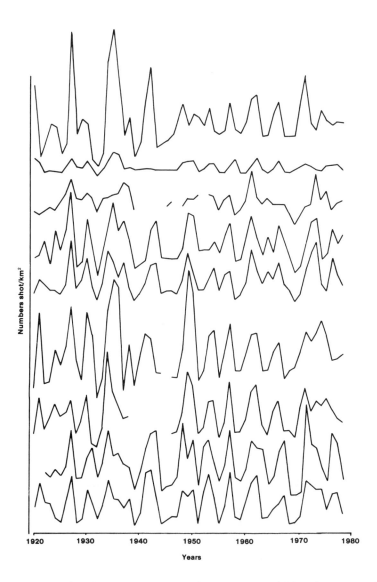

Fig. 2.8 Quasi-cycles may be synchronised between neighbouring moors. Nine Peninne moors arranged from North–South (top–bottom) and plotted as the bag per km², showing how some cycles are well synchronised (e.g. 1957 peak year) whereas others are not (e.g. 1967).

years in the Northern Highlands. A typical series for the Highlands is shown in Fig. 2.7b and for the Pennines is shown in Fig. 2.7c. The correlograms are heavily damped, demonstrating quasi- rather than true cycles. It is important to note that these quasi-cycles tend to lose their predictability with time so it is difficult for game managers to predict when a population will crash.

Quasi-cycles appear to be common in bag records of grouse and where they occur, neighbouring populations are often in close synchrony (Fig. 2.8); probably because weather affects populations in the same way. Not all English grouse moors have cyclic bag records, some 20% of the larger ones show no evidence of quasi-cycles (Potts *et al.*, 1984). In England the drier moors show no evidence of cycles and the data are like those of a typical lowland gamebird (Hudson *et al.*, 1985; Section 5.5).

In summary, time-series analysis of bag records is useful to the game biologist since it defines the pattern of annual variation in gamebirds and produces a precise description of these changes. Any mathematical simulation model which attempts to account for these changes must be able to reproduce the effects found in a correlogram. For lowland game, the average density and the causes of the random annual variations are the main problems. For grouse, the model must explain why quasi-cycles occur in some populations and not in others, why there is variation in cycle length and why they are shorter in one part of Britain compared to another.

2.4 Bag records as indicators of population trend

Examination of bag records provides a useful way to monitor trends in the abundance of game species. Since the data indicate the number shot as opposed to the number alive, they only provide an index of density. However, a continued fall in survival, breeding production or an increase in dispersal will lead to an overall population decline and such changes will be reflected in the bag records. In an analysis of fluctuations, the trends in numbers are removed before proceeding, but for long-term changes it is the trend itself which is of most interest.

Records from individual estates are not very useful on their own since they inevitably reflect the changing interest of the landowners in shooting and the differing performances of a succession of keepers, as well as a whole multitude of factors peculiar to any one shooting estate. The best way to overcome this individual variation is to use a large sample of estates. In some European countries, where all hunters have to report total numbers of game killed to obtain their game licence, it is even possible to use the total national bag rather than a sample. This approach is exemplified by Denmark where the well organised system of bag returns from individual hunters has been in operation since 1940. These data have provided a barometer of game abundance over 40 years (Strandgaard, 1964; Strandgaard and Asferg, 1980). In Britain no such legal requirement exists and non-government organisations, such as the Game Conservancy, have had to rely on information volunteered by estate owners and keepers.

In Britain, the introduction of pesticides into farming together with the loss of game habitats and the decline of many game and predatory bird species drew attention to the importance of monitoring animal populations as part of a general conservation effort. In 1961 the Game Research Association set up the National Game Census to monitor game bag records. Over 600 farms and estates submit annual returns of all game shot on their shoots. This bag record scheme now provides the only source of baseline data on game abundance in Britain and helps game research by highlighting the changing performance of different species.

Before looking at trends in detail, it is essential to understand some of the limitations of the National Game Census scheme. These limitations are:

(1) The sample is non-random, being based on a largely self-selected group of enthusiasts.
(2) The sample represents some of the best managed and most intensively shot areas of ground, which are not always typical.
(3) When game shooting becomes impractical contributors may drop out of the scheme, so some declines in bags may be underestimated as an increased emphasis is placed on the remaining, probably better, areas.
(4) Regional differences in shooting traditions cause regional variation in bags which are not a reflection of game numbers, e.g. the need to protect arable crops from pigeon or rabbit damage leads to greater pressure on these species in some areas.
(5) A change in shooting pressure on one species might affect the bag of another which can lead to unpredictable trends that are not a reflection of game abundance.

It is important to be fully informed about how the data were collected and the factors which could have affected the bag.

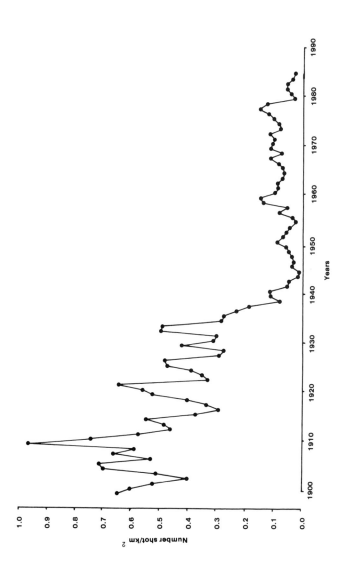

Fig. 2.9 Combined bag records of black grouse from 58 estates which have near complete sets of data from 1900 to the present. Numbers per km² of grouse moor.

2.4.1 Changes in the numbers of grouse shot

Black grouse have shown a gradual decline over the last 25 years but the recent reduction represents only a fraction of the loss that has taken place this century. Barnes (1984) has showed that the decline in bags during the early part of this century was severe (Fig. 2.9). In Scotland the decline appeared to commence earlier in northern areas and seems to be associated with a general contraction of the species range that started during the 19th century. The pattern for this species is similar in many other European countries, and its cause is not well understood.

The national trend for red grouse shows only a small reduction in recent years, but there are significant regional differences (Fig. 2.10). The more productive grouse moors in the North of England, in particular the central Pennines (Hudson, 1986a), show no clear trend but the Scottish data indicate a progressive decline since the mid-1970s. Barnes (1984) noted that the Scottish decline had been a reduction from a post-war level which itself was considerably below the bags attained at the turn of the century and the years between the Wars.

Fig. 2.10 National Game Census bag records of red grouse from English and Scottish moors.

Similarly, even though the North of England populations would seem healthy, longer-term data does suggest that even these were higher in pre-war populations (Hudson, 1986a). The cause of the decline in Scotland has yet to be determined but in England and Wales, Hudson (1986a) has shown that loss of the heather acreage as a result of over-grazing and the reduction in the number of keepers have been sufficient to account for the fall in bags observed.

The decline in red grouse recorded from moorland areas is an underestimate of the total loss. There are many upland areas which were formerly grouse moors which have been afforested or turned into grass through over-grazing. Furthermore, some moors have shown a gradual loss of red grouse habitat which is not always recorded, so providing an underestimate of the decline.

2.4.2 Changes in the number of partridges shot

Annual spring censuses have shown a severe reduction in breeding numbers of grey partridges since the last War and this is reflected in the

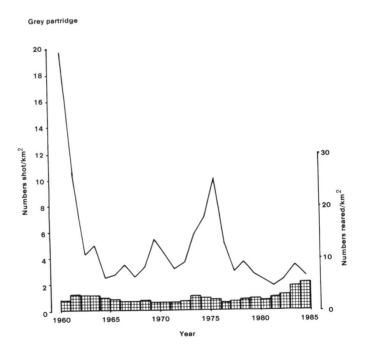

Fig. 2.11   National Game Census bag and rearing records for grey partridge.

bag records (Fig. 2.11). Pheasants and red-legged partridges have now replaced the grey partridge as the main lowland quarry species. The decline of this species has been well documented and has occurred throughout its range in Europe, Asia and in North America where it was introduced (Potts, 1986). Although a range of factors have contributed to this decline, it was the widespread use of herbicides in cereal farming, which reduced broad-leaved weeds and led to the loss of certain insect species eaten by the chicks, that initiated the decline. The contribution made by reared birds to the bag in Britain is, so far, quite small.

There has been a dramatic increase in the number of red-legged partridges shot over the last 25 years (Fig. 2.12). This has probably been due to two changes:

(1) The disappearance of grey partridges brought about a general reduction in partridge shooting from which the red-legged partridge has benefited. This is because red-legged partridges were probably over-harvested (Potts, 1986) as a consequence of greater vulnerability to shooting mortality than grey partridges. The red-

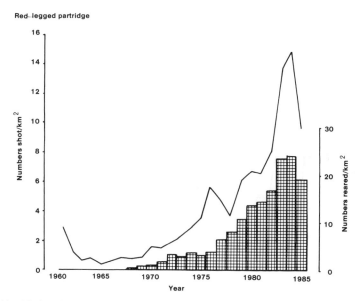

Fig. 2.12   National Game Census bag and rearing records for red-legged partridge.

legged partridges fly lower, more slowly, and consequently are more likely to be shot (Section 8.3.1).

(2) The increase in the number of red-legged partridges reared and released. This species, like other *Alectoris* species, is easily raised in captivity and an increase in this activity has also led to the species increasing its range beyond the eastern counties where it was first established.

2.4.3 Changes in the number of pheasants shot

The numbers of pheasants shot per acre is now greater than has previously been recorded (Fig. 2.13). Hand rearing has always been popular for this species and even in Edwardian days the large estates reared many thousands of birds to be released (e.g. Turner, 1955). Much of the lowland woods of Britain have been designed to hold and

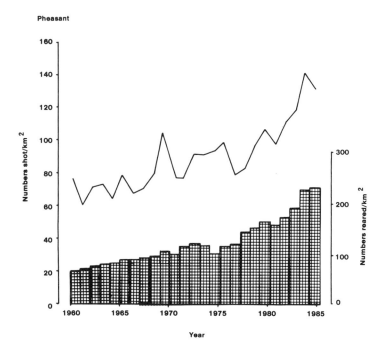

Fig. 2.13   National Game Census bag and rearing records for pheasant.

present pheasants in a sporting manner (Coles and Vandervell, 1977); a trend which continues to be developed today (Gray, 1986). During the Second World War pheasant rearing was banned and bags were consequently low, but since 1953 rearing programmes have rapidly expanded. With the introduction of poultry rearing technology, pheasant rearing is now cheaper and requires less manpower than before. However, the wild breeding pheasants have probably suffered as a consequence of the introduction of relatively tame birds which contribute little to stocks. Game managers have also tended to invest in winter coverts, designed to prevent birds dispersing and provide a challenging shot when flushed, as opposed to nesting and chick rearing habitats which would improve the production of birds from the wild population.

2.4.4. Changes in the number of woodcock shot

Unlike all the foregoing species which are resident game, woodcock

Fig. 2.14 National Game Census bag record for woodcock.

migrate to this country from northern Europe. Many birds do breed in Britain but most that are shot probably come from Scandinavia. Although the bag records for this species show an upward trend (Fig. 2.14) it is unlikely that this represents an increasing population. Many woodcock over-winter in the western coastal districts of Britain (e.g. The Lizard, Cornwall) and in such areas specialised woodcock shoots have developed; the bag records from these shoots do not show an increasing trend. The year-to-year variation can be related to the severity of the winter. Within Britain for instance, central districts shoot more woodcock in mild winters, whereas in severe winters the coastal shoots do better (Tapper and Hirons, 1983). However, the vast majority of woodcock are not taken by specialist shoots but are killed during normal pheasant shooting days. The large increase in pheasant shooting has led to an increase in the number of woodcock shot and when the effects of this are removed from the data the trend is lost.

2.5 Management implications

For the game manager the use of census methods and the recording of game bags should be an essential procedure carried out systematically at the appropriate season. A regular census will provide the most accurate assessment of the game stock and will enable the optimum level of harvesting to be organised on each management unit or beat (see Section 8.4). The counts will also indicate dispersal of birds, which in turn may suggest ways in which the habitat can be improved to improve conditions for stock on areas where game is sparse. As already discussed, the game biologist can use autumn counts of partridges to calculate key mortalities in the birds' life cycle and there is no reason why the manager or keeper should not use the same data to indicate how the game production might be increased on each area of the estate. The presence of a large number of cock birds in the autumn indicates predation on incubating hens, which could suggest that predator control has been ineffective. Similarly, a large number of failed pairs suggests that either egg predators have taken many nests or nesting habitat is poor. Small brood sizes suggest a low chick survival rate; keepers commonly blame this on the weather but this is only partly true, as it is the weather's effects on the chick's insect food supply which are normally crucial. Thus for partridges and pheasants small broods should be taken as indicators of starvation more than anything else. Trials of reduced pesticide use on field edges could be set up to see if brood sizes can be improved in subsequent years (see Section 6.4).

Annual censuses of this kind will also show if some new management practice is adversely affecting the game and may indicate the cause of additional losses. Some alterations in farming, such as the introduction of a new crop, change in the rotation, or removal of livestock, could all affect game survival which would be first noticed after a close examination of the autumn count. The introduction of hand reared game for the first time could also be assessed in this way.

Gamebird counts are not always easy to carry out and there are many factors which lead to problems in getting an accurate count. In some instances, if farming practices can be altered it may be possible to accomplish counts much more efficiently. Rolling cereals early in spring allows counting vehicles to be driven over crops and increases the visibility of partridges. Cutting stubbles short and refraining from burning allows time for an accurate post-harvest count to be conducted.

Over longer periods of time and on an extensive scale, bag records may provide a useful indicator of game management techniques. Where woodland has been renovated and altered for shooting, the bag record will probably be the only real indicator of success. Historical records may provide a useful clue as to the potential of moorland for improvement in grouse stocks. For species such as red grouse, where total counts on a moor are not feasible, the bag record or the drive itself will often give the manager the best guide as to the consequences of a change in management. Finally, because bag records are easy to keep over long periods they may be better indicators of sustained change in population or productivity than counts carried out over a few years, where the effects of natural annual variation cannot be discounted.

2.6 Conclusion

For the scientist, census methods are ideal for monitoring population changes in game species. However, they are inevitably short-term exercises in comparison to the long-term changes that affect the countryside. For this reason it is vital to maintain a long series of data to monitor any change in abundance. Bag records serve this purpose well since they have been widely collected, and continue to be recorded in detail. Computers and sophisticated forms of analysis make these data more valuable now than they have been in the past. For most purposes there is no prospect of census data ever replacing bag data and it behoves shoots to record as much detail as possible relating to their bag records to obtain the maximum benefit to the long-term conservation of game species.

3 Population Biology and Life-History Variation of Gamebirds

Andrew P. Dobson, E. Robin Carper, and
Peter J. Hudson

3.1 Introduction

This chapter considers further aspects of the population biology of gamebirds and discusses how some of the patterns observed might have evolved through the process of natural selection. Ecologists usually consider such studies under the general heading of 'life-history strategies'. Essentially, the studies aim to ascertain how different species maximise their lifetime reproductive success, defined as the total number of offspring produced within its lifetime, that survive to the age of first reproduction. As this is determined by a variety of different facets of the species' ecology, many life-history studies are concerned with whether there are consistent trends in the way that survival and fecundity rates vary between and within species.

The study of how natural selection has tuned the survival and fecundity of different species is particularly important in the case of managed populations. Many aspects of management aim to increase or decrease certain population parameters in relation to those that have evolved for the species in the unmanaged state. For example, hen pheasants are caught and placed in laying pens where they produce large numbers of eggs which are then incubated artificially (35 eggs per female is not uncommon). Such a level of egg production is much greater than the average clutch size recorded for 'wild' pheasants. Management of wild populations also tends to increase population densities to levels far greater than in the unmanaged habitat. On some estates red grouse have been recorded at densities of 115 pairs km^{-2}, while in the natural state density is probably closer to 3 pairs km^{-2} (Hudson and Watson, 1985). In biological terms management may be thought of as a subtle form of experimental manipulation that reveals more about the population biology of the species. For example, populations which are harvested at different intensities may be used to determine whether increased mortality leads to increases in fecundity or changes in the rates of dispersal.

3.1.2 Single population studies versus comparative studies

Two complementary approaches may be made when studying life-history variations. One approach is to obtain data from a long-term study of a single species where information is gathered throughout the life of as many individuals as possible. Studies of this type tend to emphasise differences between individuals in their net lifetime reproductive success: a classic study of the sparrowhawk in the south of Scotland showed that a high proportion of the population's recruitment is undertaken by only a few individuals (Fig. 3.1).

Although long-term studies of gamebirds have been conducted (Jenkins *et al.*, 1963; Potts, 1980, 1986; Watson *et al.*, 1984; Hudson, 1986a), none has collected data on lifetime reproductive success. Detailed observations of individual gamebirds over a long period of time would be invaluable in providing this data.

When limited amounts of long-term data are available for a population, specific aspects of life-history theory can be tested by undertaking carefully designed experiments. Such experiments have been particularly important in examining the factors determining clutch size in birds. However, to truly monitor evolutionary changes in bird populations fairly unique circumstances are usually required; for example, the small gene pools of Darwin's finches in the Galapagos Islands have enabled Grant (1986) to undertake some of the classic studies of micro-evolution in bird populations. Nonetheless, even these studies required relatively long periods of time, of the order of five to ten generations for the species studied.

In the absence of a detailed long-term study or manipulative experiments, a comparison of the available life-history data for a range of species is often useful. Such an approach enables us to correlate interspecific variations in survival and fecundity with other aspects of species' ecology, such as variations in the types of habitats used or the mating and feeding strategies of different species. Provided a series of sensible but rigorous statistical procedures is followed when undertaking these multi-species comparisons (see Clutton-Brock and Harvey, 1984), the life-history strategies of different species may be compared. This occasionally permits more quantitative speculation on how natural selection may have operated in tuning the observed life-history parameters in a single species or population.

In this chapter we shall adopt both strategies. Initially we shall consider the key life-history variables in turn and give examples from detailed studies of single species. We shall then make some larger inter-specific comparisons using a set of data for European ducks and gamebirds.

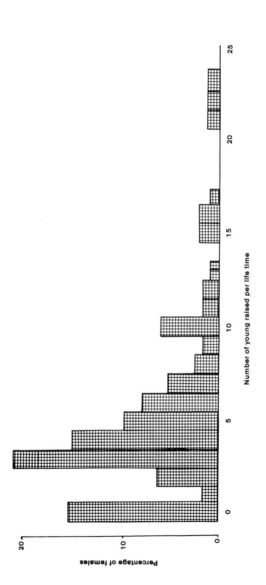

Fig. 3.1 Lifetime reproductive success in a population of sparrowhawks (*after* Newton, 1986). The histogram shows the percentage of females which produce different numbers of offspring; about 50% of the offspring are produced by 15% of the population.

3.2 Clutch size

Ornithologists have investigated the adaptive significance of clutch size for many years. Lack (1948) proposed that the number of chicks the pair could feed determined the number of eggs a female laid. He suggested that the survival of individual chicks declined with clutch size so that larger clutches do not always lead to larger numbers of chicks fledging. However, observational studies into clutch size of birds have found that the average clutch size is often lower than that which produces the most fledglings: for example, most red grouse lay a smaller clutch than the level which produces the maximum number of chicks (Fig. 3.2). Cody (1966) pointed out that increases in predation on larger clutches may be a factor which tends to reduce clutch size. Later, Charnov and Krebs (1974), in a paper that builds on the work of Williams (1966), suggested that as increased production of offspring may lead to increased mortality in the mother so the 'optimal' clutch size may be less than that suggested by Lack. Where some cost to the parent accrues with increased reproductive effort, selection will favour the clutch size that maximises lifetime productivity of the parent. This is not necessarily the one that maximises the number fledged within one season and in general will tend to be less than this value (Fig. 3.3).

Unfortunately few data unequivocally support the survival-fecundity interaction which is required for the Charnov/Krebs model of clutch size determination. Although the most common brood size in many species is less than the brood size that produces the maximum number of young per season, this only provides circumstantial evidence that such an effect may be operating. In altricial species (those with young born naked, blind and dependent on parents for food), the increased cost of large broods to the parents is apparent: more young mean, quite simply, more mouths that must be fed and more work for the parents. Although this factor is certainly an integral part in determining the 'optimal' brood size, the long-term effects of repeated seasonal stress from relatively larger broods is difficult to assess. While such observational studies provide interesting data, only experimental manipulations of clutch size can be used to rigorously compare the different hypotheses. Unfortunately, studies that have artificially increased clutch sizes in passerine species have given equivocal results about compensatory reductions in survival (DeSteven, 1980; Nur, 1984). However, an elegant study by Bryant (1979) clearly shows that double-brooded female house martins (*Delichon urbica*) have lower survival than single-brooded females. This suggests that the time the birds devote to breeding may be an important component of the effort

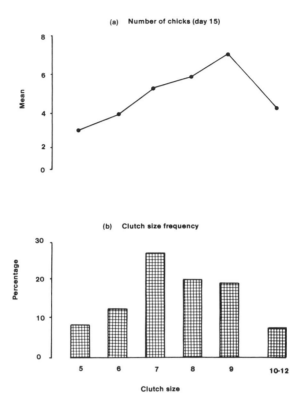

Fig. 3.2 Frequency distributions of clutch size and brood size for red grouse. The lower graph is the percentage of clutches of different sizes observed in the population while the upper graph shows the mean brood size produced relative to clutch size; the most productive clutches were of 9 eggs. (*After* Moss *et al.*, 1981.)

they put into rearing any individual clutch (see Section 3.6).

If determining the ultimate consequences of increased parental effort is complicated in altricial birds, it is even more so in birds such as gamebirds with nidifugous young (those that leave the nest soon after hatching; see Winkler and Walters, 1983). Since the parents do not feed their young, the increased energetic costs to the parent are either relatively low or must come from some other aspect of brooding which may be still more difficult to assess. For example, there may be costs to the parents in protecting the chicks from predators (Safriel, 1975), the physiological demands of producing more eggs (Inglis, 1977; Ankney and MacInnes, 1978) and, of course, having to incubate them. In a study on canada geese, Lessells (1986) manipulated the numbers

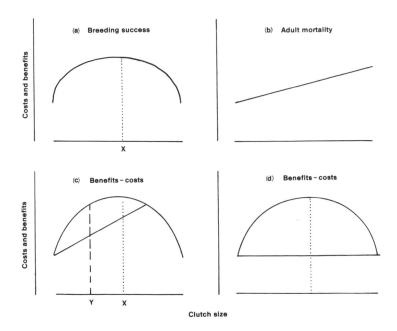

Fig. 3.3   Trade-off between clutch size and adult survival.
(a) Relationship between breeding success (benefit) and clutch size; Lack's hypothesis predicts that the commonest clutch size (X) is also the most productive.
(b) The costs of breeding increase with clutch size.
(c) Combining the benefit curve and the cost function, the greatest net benefit occurs at Y, a clutch size less than X.
(d) If the costs of breeding are independent of clutch size, X and Y coincide. (*Modified from* Charnov and Krebs, 1974, and Perrins and Birkhead, 1984.)

of goslings in broods to study the effects of brood size on both the goslings and the adults. Her study found no detrimental effects on the offspring (measured by gosling growth, survival and age at first breeding) or on adult over-wintering survival. However, the females with larger broods moulted later, weighed less, and bred later the following season, although this did not affect their clutch size in the second year. Lessells concluded that the number of eggs laid was determined by some factor other than the fitness consequences of brood size, such as the female's reserves before laying. In addition, as Lessells acknowledges, the study was done on a population of sedentary geese. Most populations in North America migrate, and the consequences of lighter weight and delayed moulting may be more significant for migrant populations (Barry, 1962).

In addition to the energetic demands on the parents that may limit clutch size, there are also physiological constraints on the number of eggs a female can lay. Prior to breeding, females have a given store of reserves which they can invest in egg production, either a few large eggs or many small ones. Many studies of gamebirds have stressed the importance of chick survival in the first two weeks of life, and it seems reasonable to suppose that chicks which hatch at an advanced stage with good yolk reserves are going to survive relatively well (Ankney, 1980). Therefore, the clutch size laid will also be a result of a trade-off between the amount of food reserves available to the hen and the size of egg which produces a chick with good survival chances. In this respect, we may expect to see large variation in clutch size and/or egg size in relation to female condition and the available reserves (Ankney and Bisset, 1976; Ankney and MacInnes, 1978). Variation in egg size within a species tends to be small and in some gamebirds, like the red grouse (Moss *et al.*, 1981) and the willow ptarmigan (Erikstad *et al.*, 1985), the size of the eggs does not vary with clutch size. One interpretation of this finding is that birds will lay the size of egg that provides the optimal chances for the chick's survival (Smith and Fretwell, 1974). Eggs tend to be larger in second than in first clutches (Parker, 1981; Erikstad *et al.*, 1985), possibly because the chicks will be hatching after the optimal time and additional yolk reserves may help the chick to survive through the first few days of life.

Predation may also have a role in influencing the clutch size of birds with nidifugous young (Perrins, 1977). Clutch sizes may be lower in birds suffering high predation during laying and incubation simply because females take longer to lay larger clutches and the longer the eggs are in the nest, the more vulnerable they are to predators. Robertson and Hill (1987) used data from two nest record schemes and found that 10% of pheasant nests were lost per day during laying and 2.8% per day during incubation.

In many gamebird species, clutch size is also dependent upon the age of the parent, with birds breeding for the first time having lower clutch sizes than older or more experienced birds (Fig. 3.4). As hatching and fledging success may also be a function of parental experience, analyses of factors affecting clutch size should take care to allow for these variables. This may be particularly important in populations where survival and recruitment vary erratically due to environmental or meteorological conditions, as these lead to variations in the proportion of birds of different ages in the population.

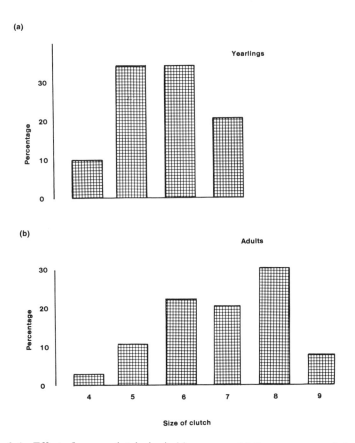

Fig. 3.4 Effect of age on clutch size in blue grouse: (a) the percentage of clutches of different sizes laid by yearling birds; (b) the clutch sizes of adults. (*From* Zwickel, 1975.)

3.3 Survival

Survival is much harder to measure than fecundity in wild populations of most bird species. Although excellent textbooks exist which describe methods for estimating the values of these life-history traits (Southwood, 1978; Caughley, 1977; Brownie *et al.*, 1978), the data are often fraught with statistical biases, and few field experiments ever produce data of sufficient quality or quantity to satisfy the statistical assumptions of these techniques. Nevertheless, it is important in any study of population dynamics to obtain some indication of the survival rates of birds of different ages (Fig. 3.5). Although we occasionally obtain estimates of the mean or maximum life expectancy of a game species, we rarely obtain any information about how different hunting

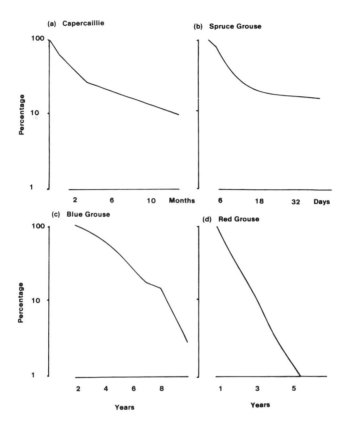

Fig. 3.5 Survival curves of four species of game birds. The upper two graphs show survival over the early months of life. The data for the capercaillie are from Linden (1981), those for the spruce grouse are from Smyth and Boag (1984). Note that in both cases 80 to 90% of birds born die within the first year of life. The lower two graphs show survival curves for birds that have survived to start reproducing. The data for blue grouse are from Lewis and Zwickel (1982), those for red grouse are from Jenkins *et al.*, (1963).

rates or variations in meteorological conditions affect survival.

3.3.1 Adult survival

In most bird species, adult survival is usually assumed to be fairly constant. Although there are several flaws in this assumption, particularly for long-lived birds, it is extremely difficult to detect senescence in studies of gamebirds, as few individuals survive to old age. However, the greatest changes in mortality rate occur over the first year of life, initially starting fairly high and then declining to some lower level (Fig. 3.5). The quantity of data available to estimate the mortality rate at any age similarly declines exponentially, and estimates of mortality for immature birds are often heavily biased due to differences in recovery rates of birds in the different months of their first year of life. Although maximum life expectancy is sometimes used as an index of longevity in studies of gamebirds, it is important to realise that estimates of this parameter increase systematically with the quantity of data used to estimate it; this can create a large systematic bias and make common species appear longer-lived than rare species. Conversely, although larger quantities of data may be available to estimate mortality from managed populations, the increased mortality due to hunting may produce a steeper mortality curve. (Compare Fig. 3.5c and d, for lightly exploited blue grouse and heavily exploited red grouse.)

3.3.2 Additive and compensatory mortality

The effects that hunting has on a population are not well understood. Perhaps the most fundamental question that still remains is whether hunting mortalities act in an additive or a compensatory manner. That is to say, does hunting kill birds in addition to the number that normally die over the winter, or does the hunting simply kill off the excess that would have died during the winter and thus lower or compensate for winter mortalities?

Many studies suggest that hunting acts in a compensatory manner, but such results can be misleading. Since management practices strive to maintain populations at maximum densities, much of the over-winter mortalities are due to starvation or dispersal off the range. In such cases, hunting may tend to act in a compensatory manner by alleviating the mortalities from overpopulation. However, hunting kills may appear to be compensatory in what would otherwise be an increasing population: the hunting may not lower the spring breeding density from the previous year, but the population will certainly not grow as a protected population would.

In general the level of compensation is likely to be variable, with low levels of hunting mortality usually compensated for and higher levels of mortality only occasionally so. A more quantitative answer requires a more detailed knowledge of how population density affects rates of

Plate 3.1   The first 20 days of life for gamebird chicks are critical. They must (a) grow rapidly and (b) avoid predation. Chick mortality through starvation and predation can reach 90% and is therefore a major determinant of lifetime reproductive success.

recruitment and adult survival. This is discussed in the next section.

3.3.3 Chick survival

In a number of gamebirds, mortality over the first year of life can be in the region of 80 to 90% (Fig. 3.5). The critical stage for most species is within the first 20 days of life, a time when growth rate is greatest and when the chicks must develop thermogenesis (Pedersen and Steen, 1979) and become capable of avoiding predators (often by flight). Studies on various gamebirds indicate that two factors are believed to play a significant role in influencing chick survival: first, the influence of maternal nutrition on the quality of the egg and second, the role of insects in the diet of chicks. Poor female condition can be influenced by poor nutritional state or heavy parasite burdens. It has been suggested that maternal condition influences the quality of eggs laid, which in turn causes annual changes in chick survival (Siivonen, 1957). In a study of red grouse, Jenkins et al. (1965) collected clutches of grouse eggs from the wild and reared them under bantams. The proportion of chicks reared in captivity was correlated with the ratio of young to old birds reared in the wild, suggesting that egg quality was an important factor influencing chick survival. However, Hanssen et al. (1982) believed this method inadequate for testing egg and chick quality in the willow ptarmigan and so looked at annual variations in the chemical composition of eggs. They found that chick survival was not related to any discernible measure of egg quality but to June temperatures and the level of predation, influenced in turn by the abundance of lemmings (Hanssen and Utne, 1985). In an analysis of chick survival in clutches from captive and wild red grouse, Moss et al. (1981) came to the conclusion that over 50% of the observed variation in chick survival was related to intrinsic differences amongst hens; however, it is still not clear whether this is due to genetic or environmental effects on the mother.

Although intrinsic factors may play a role in influencing chick survival, it is clear that extrinsic factors, and in particular food quality, are important to survival as well. In a wide range of studies, workers have found associations between the abundance of insects in the chicks' diet and survival (Cross, 1966; Potts, 1970, 1973, 1980, 1986; Green, 1984; Hill, 1985; Rands, 1985, 1986a; Hudson, 1986a). The importance of the insects on the chicks' diet has been demonstrated experimentally in grey partridges (Cross, 1966; Potts, 1980, 1986) and red grouse (Hudson, 1986a). Workers were unable to rear chicks

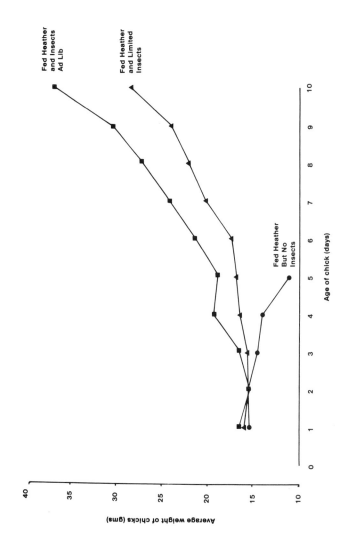

Fig. 3.6 The growth of captive red grouse chicks fed differing quantities of insects. Chicks provided with heather alone did not gain weight and died within 6 days, while chicks provided with insects grew well and survived. (*After* Hudson, 1986a.)

successfully on the adults' diet, and chick growth and survival were improved when insects or some other nutrient-rich supplement was provided (Fig. 3.6). By extrapolating from research on poultry, Wise (1982, 1985; see also Moss, 1985; Potts, 1986) demonstrated that the sulphur-based amino acids, cystine and methionine, were likely to be the limiting nutrients in chick growth. As these are in relatively low concentrations in the adults' diet, the chicks would be required to eat incredible quantities of the adults' food in order to survive and grow. Insects carry relatively high levels of methionine and cystine (four times that of wheat and more than 15 times that of heather), and it seems reasonable to suppose that eating insects will benefit chick growth and survival. Thus, although many intrinsic and extrinsic factors play some role in determining chick survival, a gamekeeper can at least partially reduce chick mortality by providing an abundance of preferred insects.

3.4. Density-dependence and recruitment

Studies of the factors determining clutch size, fledging success and survival of individuals within a population have found that many of these parameters are dependent upon the density of the population in different years. In most species where data on clutch size and fledging success have been collected over a range of population densities, we tend to see a negative relationship between population density and per-capita recruitment (Fig. 3.7).

The survival of immature birds through their first winter is also likely to be dependent upon the density of adult birds in the population. These relationships can be important in regulating the size of the population from year to year. Where relationships between simple measures of recruitment and population density appear equivocal, it is important to appreciate that more subtle mechanisms may be determining how density affects rates of recruitment to the population. For example, as density rises, the prime habitats may be used first, forcing additional birds into marginal habitats which are less productive. This will tend to decrease the average per-capita rate of recruitment and may be a very powerful density-dependent mechanism in populations that live in heterogeneous habitats. In a study of partridge, Rands (1987b) found the relationship between recruitment rate and density varied from one farm to the next due to variation in available nesting habitat. As the goal of habitat management on many game estates is to maximise the areas of suitable

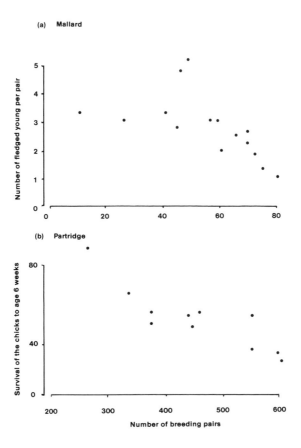

Fig. 3.7 Effect of density on different parameters of fecundity or recruitment in mallards and grey partridge: (a) shows the decline in the number of young fledged per pair as the number of breeding pairs increases (*after* Hill, 1984a); (b) shows the change in survival of chicks to age six weeks in a population of grey partridge. (*After* Blank *et al.*, 1967).

breeding habitat for different species, it is important to bear in mind that altering the mosaic of habitats will also tend to alter the shape of the recruitment function.

3.4.1 Mechanisms of population change

In ecology, the debate about the relative importance of the mechanisms that regulate population size has tended to centre on relatively few species; the grouse and ptarmigan have been one such group. Some of the mechanisms, such as the role of predation and parasitism, are discussed in their respective chapters (see also the review by Angelstam, 1987). These explanations can account for cycles observed, often operating through the effects of breeding production (Bergerud *et al.*, 1985). However, as Watson and Moss (1987, and references therein) point out, a fall in a population can occur after breeding success is high. A number of theories have arisen to explain this observation.

One theory is that variations in summer productivity (influenced by extrinsic factors such as resource abundance and meteorological conditions) lead to changes in the yearling to adult ratio in the following spring (Smyth and Boag, 1984). As density is increasing, many young are recruited to the population; and since yearlings often have smaller clutches than adults (Zwickel, 1975; Smyth and Boag, 1984; Fig. 3.4), the recruitment rate drops, and population density falls. However, in Zwickel's study, although the difference in productivity between yearlings and adults was significant, the proportion of young in the population corresponded neither to the average clutch size produced nor to the average number of chicks per female.

Moss and Watson (1985), on the other hand, attribute the regular changes in red grouse densities to intrinsic cycles in the levels of aggression which limit territory size and hence the breeding densities of this species. Aggressive behaviour, they argue, is selected against as density decreases; presuming that neighbours are most likely to be kin, giving them room to breed increases the individual's inclusive fitness. However, at greater densities, when pre-territorial summer emigration is high, the likelihood of neighbours being kin is much less (Green, 1983), and aggression is selected for. Some support for this theory has been provided by removal experiments (Krebs, 1971; Watson and Jenkins, 1968). When territorial individuals are removed, they are often replaced by others who subsequently breed. This suggests that there are birds both available and capable of breeding, an important prediction of the spacing behaviour theory. Even so, it is necessary to know more about the degree of relatedness between individuals in the population and whether the replacement birds would have bred or not, had the removal experiment not been conducted.

The major difficulty with the spacing behaviour theory is distinguishing cause and effect: any factor that is operating to increase the population density is likely to bring a corresponding increase in visible displays of aggression; thus, the levels of aggression could be a response to, not responsible for, the fluctuating densities.

The controversy between intrinsic and extrinsic factors has tended to obscure the fact that the two hypotheses are by no means mutually exclusive. Chick production, adult mortality (in most studies, a measure of dispersal and deaths in the study area), territory establishment and weather all influence spring densities. The problem of determining which mechanisms are important to population regulation may best be examined by considering a simple, general model of a bird population.

3.4.2 A life-history model for gamebirds

A suitable model for the dynamics of a hypothetical bird population is illustrated in Fig. 3.8. Essentially, the model assumes that the numbers of birds in year $t+1$, will equal the number of adult birds that survive from year t, plus the numbers of birds that are born in year t that survive to age one. The functions $f_1 (N_t)$ and $f_2 (N_t)$ represent the possible effects of population density on survival and recruitment. Note that it is quite possible for either of these functions to equal unity at all population sizes if density has no effect on either survival or fecundity. However, that both of these functions will equal unity is unlikely, as this would imply a totally unregulated population. Similarly, it is important to realise that when $f_1 (N_t)$ equals unity, there can be no compensatory mortality from hunting. The degree of compensatory mortality depends entirely on the shape of this function; if it has a strong negative slope then compensation is likely, if it has only a weak negative slope then compensation is only going to be minor. The other diagrams in this figure illustrate how different shaped density-dependent functions may be produced by different biological mechanisms such as limitations of food supply or finite numbers of breeding territories. The figures illustrate idealised hypothetical cases; in reality the shape of these functions will be moulded by a mixture of these different functions. Notice that in general management always tends to reduce the slope of these density-dependent relationships (e.g. by increasing the amount of food available or by increasing the numbers and quality of breeding territories).

It is also important to realise that there may be some interaction between fecundity and survival in individual birds (as is discussed in the section on clutch size above). This would require the inclusion of a third function $f_3 (E_t)$ which modifies adult survival as fecundity changes (Fig. 3.9). If this effect is significant, we may see an apparent positive interaction between adult survival and density in a system

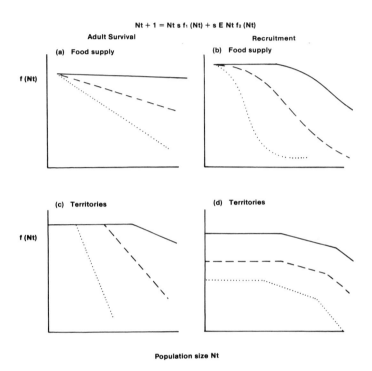

$$Nt + 1 = Nt\ s\ f_1\ (Nt) + s\ E\ Nt\ f_2\ (Nt)$$

Fig. 3.8 Simple model of population dynamics of a game bird species and the factors that determine the shape of potential density-dependent factors. Two functions are assumed to be potentially operating: $f_1\ (N_t)$ determines the influence of population size, N_t, on adult survival; $f_2\ (N_t)$ determines the influence of population size on production and survival of young birds. The graphs sketch out how various biological and management options affect the shape of these functions. The graphs on the left depict how (a) food supply and (c) number of available breeding territories affect survival. In (a) decreasing supplies of food are indicated by increasingly broken lines, whereas in (c) the number of available territories decreases as the lines become more fragmented. Note that in (a) increases in population density give a steady decrease in survival, essentially because there is less food per bird. In (c) survival is assumed constant until all the available territories are full after which it declines so that sN_t always equals the number of territories.

The graphs for the number of young birds produced in any year again depict idealised cases for the effects of (b) available food and (d) numbers of territories. The conventions of increasing fragmentation of the line with diminishing resources follows that of (a) and (c). In (b) increasing population density leads to steady decline in recruitment, while in (d) recruitment remains constant until all territories are taken, when recruitment declines. The lines of different slope depict the possible case of more marginal habitats being used for nesting once the best quality areas are full.

where only the fecundity term was strongly linked to density. In a system where population density affects both survival and fecundity, increased costs of reproduction associated with increased fecundity may countermand the benefits of increased survival at low population density. Unravelling the relative strengths of these different interactions requires a lot of data from experiments conducted at a range of population densities.

$$Nt + 1 = Nt \; s \; f_3 \; (Et) + s \; E \; Nt \; f_2 \; (Nt)$$

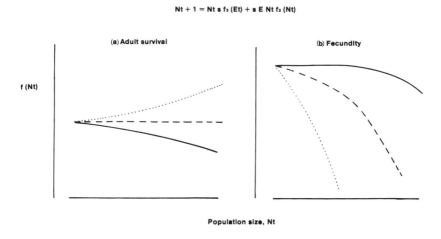

Fig. 3.9 The effects of including in costs to increased reproduction on the model of game bird population dynamics. The function f_2 (N_t) is the same as in Fig. 3.8. An additional function, f_3 (E_t), assumes that increased levels of fecundity lead to reductions in survival. The curves again illustrate different intensities of density-dependent relationship and the curves in (a) correspond to those in (b). Thus when recruitment is only weakly linked to density (solid line), reductions in fecundity at high population density hardly affect survival. In contrast when fecundity is tightly linked to population density (dotted line), the large reductions in fecundity as population density rises lead to increases in survival.

3.4.3 Problems with determining the shape of recruitment curves

Determining how clutch size and fledging success vary with population density is probably the most important task if a population is to be managed efficiently. However, the data necessary to ascertain the shape of this curve need to be collected over a wide range of population densities. As the most efficient type of management will tend to maintain the population at some constant density, these data are often hard to obtain. Populations that are recovering from severe environmental perturbations, such as a bad winter, or those that fluctuate over a wide range of abundances, such as many grouse species, are likely to give more useful information about the shape of these functions than populations which remain relatively constant. Thus, until these data are collected and more is known about the relative intensity with which density-dependent effects operate on survival and fecundity in populations of gamebirds, we will be unable to make anything other than speculative guesses about whether hunting operates additively or compensatorally to other sources of mortality. As changes in management will alter the shape of these functions, populations should be monitored especially accurately at times when management practices change; it is then that much useful information may be gained about the relative strength of the wide variety of different mechanisms that may contribute to population regulation.

3.5 Dispersal

Statistical and logistic problems plague attempts to estimate dispersal rates in wild animal populations. Here we have problems not only in determining the shape of the frequency distribution of dispersal distances for a species but also in estimating the extent of dispersal and differentiating between animals which have dispersed out of the study site and those that have died and decomposed or have been eaten. Although studies involving radio-telemetry may help to reduce some of the problems in this area, obtaining large sample sizes or assessing just how much the telemetry techniques bias the estimates will still be hard.

3.5.1 Natal and breeding dispersal

Two types of dispersal are usually recognised: natal dispersal – the distance between where an animal is born and where it breeds – and breeding dispersal – the distance between where an adult breeds in successive breeding seasons (Greenwood, 1980). In general, females tend to disperse further than males (Fig. 3.10; Greenwood, 1980), and natal dispersal distances are greater than those between breeding seasons.

Breeding dispersal may be affected by either reproductive success in the previous breeding season or population density. In the former case, unsuccessful breeders tend to disperse further than successful breeders, which tend to renest at a site where they have previously been

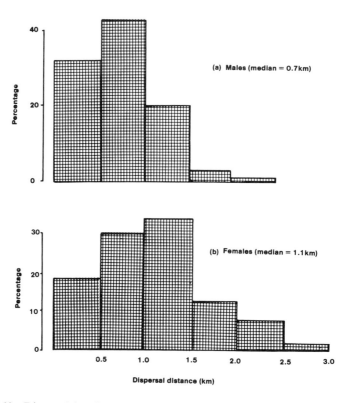

Fig. 3.10   Dispersal data for male and female blue grouse; (a) data for males, (b) data for females. In both cases frequency distributions are illustrated for the distance moved by birds from where they were radio-tagged as juveniles to where they were found breeding in the next breeding season. (*After* Hines, 1986.)

successful. Dispersal may also be higher when population density is higher, but note that this may also be because breeding success is lower and because birds have to move further to locate an available territory. The evidence to support this is somewhat varied. Hines (1986) found dispersal was not density-dependent in blue grouse and, in a re-analysis of the data presented by Jenkins *et al.*, (1963), found that dispersal in red grouse, too, was not related to density. However, more recent studies by Watson *et al.*, (1984) have suggested that dispersal in red grouse may indeed have a density-dependent component.

3.6. Interspecific comparisons

To examine variations in survival and fecundity at higher taxonomic

Table 3.1   Nested analysis of variation in selected life-history variables at different taxonomic levels in European ducks and gamebirds. The figures given are the percentage of variation in the data at each taxonomic level.

Variable	Species	Genus	Family	Order
Female body weight	11.89	62.18	0.00	25.93
Adult mortality	6.88	45.67	0.00	47.45
Clutch size	13.87	57.28	28.84	0.00
Egg weight	6.16	37.35	0.00	56.48
Incubation time	21.82	45.14	0.00	33.04

levels, we collated data on these variables for the European gamebirds from Cramp and Simmons, 1977, 1980. Analyses performed at both the species and generic levels, as nested analysis of variance, suggested that this was where the majority of variation in the data lay (see Table 3.1). The main results, presented in Table 3.2, tend to confirm those of

Table 3.2   Relations between different life-history variables for European gamebirds and ducks. Parallel regressions were fitted to the data for each group, but no significant difference was detected between the slopes. Figures given in each case are the correlation coefficient, r, the slope of the major axis regression, b, and in parentheses, the sample size. Statistical significance is indicated as follows: *** = $p <$ 0.10, ** = p 0.05, * = p 0.01, n.s. = no significant correlation, F.wght = female weight.

Variables	Genus		Species	
Clutch size × log F.wght.	r = −0.568 b = −11.6	** (18)	−0.590 −10.5	*** (30)
Adult survival × log F.wght.	r = −0.499 b = −66.2	* (14)	−0.669 −47.5	*** (24)
Clutch weight × log F.wght.	r = 0.89 b = 0.15	*** (18)	0.91 0.14	*** (30)
Log clutch weight × log F.wght.	r = 0.86 b = 1.01	*** (18)	0.87 0.98	*** (30)
Log egg weight × log F.wght.	r = 0.97 b = 1.81	*** (20)	0.97 1.87	*** (48)
Log incubation time × log F.wght.	r = 0.70 b = 0.26	*** (19)	0.72 0.26	*** (47)
Log incubation time × log Egg wght.	r = 0.63 b = 0.12	*** (19)	0.69 0.13	*** (47)

a similar analysis of North American gamebirds (Zammuto, 1987). Both mean clutch size and annual survival decline with increases in body size, suggesting that larger birds not only are longer lived but also tend to lay fewer eggs per season. No interactions are apparent between clutch size and mortality once the effects of body size are removed (Table 3.3). An interesting interaction appears to emerge between reproductive effort and body size. In general all the species tend to lay total clutches whose weight is approximately equal to 35% of their total body weight. However, larger species tend to lay smaller numbers of eggs and so lay disproportionately larger eggs. As the slope between incubation time and female body size has a slope less than that of the relation between incubation time and egg size, and both have slopes less than unity, this suggests that larger species may be reducing incubation time *relative to their body size*, by laying fewer, larger eggs. This may mean that time is as important a constraint on fecundity/survival interactions as energy. Larger birds may therefore lay fewer but larger eggs in order to speed development and reduce the length of time for which the parents must care for the eggs.

Although part of this analysis contrasts with that of Zammuto (1987) in finding no pay-offs between survival and fecundity, the data are of a very heterogeneous quality and much better estimates of survival and juvenile mortality would be required before the analysis could be said to give other than speculative results. In addition, it is important to bear in mind that the patterns we see at the interspecific level are not necessarily representative of those at the intraspecific. Where detailed studies have been done on individual populations, for example the sparrowhawks studied by Ian Newton (1986, Fig. 3.1), those individuals with the highest annual fecundity and lifetime reproductive success were those that lived the longest. Analysis of these data gives a positive relationship between survival and fecundity.

Table 3.3 Partial correlations between mortality, M, clutch size, CS, and female body weight, F.wght. In each the correlation between two variables with the effects of the third removed are given at the species and generic level. Levels of significance indicated as in Table 3.2.

Variables	Genus	Species
Log (F.wght) × M – CS	–0.372 n.s.	–0.370 n.s.
Log (F.wght) × CS – M	–0.506 *	–0.475 **
CS × M – Log (F.wght)	0.311 n.s.	0.375 n.s.
Sample size	14	19

3.7. Conclusion

Both ecologists and the managers of game estates are concerned with determining the factors which maximise the lifetime reproductive success of gamebirds. The analysis of how life-history parameters such as clutch size and survival are tuned in gamebirds will obviously benefit from more studies where management is used, or considered, as a controlled experiment. The two models outlined in Figs. 3.8 and 3.9 suggest that really quite complex and carefully designed experiments have to be undertaken if we are to understand how fecundity and survival interact with each other in any particular habitat to produce the observed variations in life-history variables. Carrying out these experiments not only aids estate managers who are concerned with producing a constant yield of birds for sportsmen to hunt, but also allows biologists to answer questions about the evolution of life-history strategies in birds.

Although the interspecific comparisons of life-history data raised some interesting points, a further analysis would benefit from additional information. Here, as with the single species studies, it would be interesting to know if the costs of reproduction, required by the Charnov and Krebs (1974) model of clutch size, are paid in energetic units or in time units. Essentially we need to know whether the constraints on the numbers or size of eggs laid are due to energy lost for survival or whether the length of the breeding season restricts breeding effort in any individual season. It seems likely that the answer to this question will best be determined by manipulative field experiments. Joint interactions between game managers and ecologists may be most useful in addressing this problem.

4 Predators, their Ecology and Impact on Gamebird Populations

Jonathan C. Reynolds, Per Angelstam and Steve Redpath

4.1 Introduction

Before the 20th century, predation was universally regarded as a major factor controlling the numbers of organisms in nature. Scientists, naturalists, and game managers alike believed that since predators killed their prey they must reduce prey numbers. More recently, ecologists have shown that the influence of predators on prey populations may not always be straightforward, and have developed a more sophisticated understanding of the relationship between predator and prey. To begin with, did predators control their prey, or were predator numbers controlled by their food supply? In some situations, such as the relationship of lynx and snowshoe hares in Canada, the numbers of both prey and predators followed one another in cycles of abundance (Elton and Nicholson, 1942), apparently because each successively controlled the numbers of the other. Both mathematical models and laboratory populations of invertebrate predators and prey (e.g. Huffaker, 1958) could produce similar effects, but only under special circumstances. Errington (1946) proposed that predators may in fact be unimportant in the control of prey density. He observed mortality in muskrats (Errington, 1943) and in bobwhite quail (Errington, 1945) and saw each population as having a surplus number of individuals, whose death was assured, regardless of the means. The ultimate cause of death was, he thought, being surplus to the capacity of the environmental resources that muskrats or bobwhite quails use. More recently, field studies have shown that the importance of predation actually varies from one system to the next and in some instances can indeed have a major impact on prey dynamics (Sih *et al.*, 1986) when the capacity of the environment to support a prey species is influenced by the abundance of predators.

Predation is just one of an array of interrelated factors which can influence the dynamics of gamebird populations – others include parasitism (Chapter 5) and habitat quality (Chapter 6). It is also a very complex process in itself, being founded on the individual behaviour of sophisticated organisms. Consequently, in order to understand the impact predators can have, it is frequently valuable to use models, both to simulate the dynamics of populations and to explore the theoretical considerations influencing individual behaviour. Such general models provide an important insight into the processes involved in complex field situations.

The aim of this chapter is to review our current knowledge of predation on gamebirds and to show how generalised models have enabled us to clarify many of the issues involved. Ways in which gamebird managers can influence the effect of predators are examined and various methods in addition to predator removal are considered and evaluated.

4.2 How predators operate

When hunting, predators have to make a number of decisions: where to hunt, what to feed on and how to catch prey. Various models have been developed to describe realistic problems of this kind and are collectively known as Optimal Foraging Theory. These models have proved successful at predicting the behaviour of the predators both in the laboratory and the field. Optimal foraging models assume that natural selection has favoured heritable variations in foraging behaviour which increase individual feeding efficiency for some currency like energy or nutrient intake, and has resulted in strategies which tend to maximise feeding efficiency. The problem of testing optimal foraging models lies in identifying and quantifying the costs and benefits of different alternative strategies so that the optimal solution can be predicted. It is still very difficult to test these models quantitatively in the field because of the difficulty of assessing all the costs and benefits arising in natural situations.

4.2.1 Where to hunt

Potential prey items, be they nesting partridge, wildebeest on the African plain, or worms in a field, invariably have an uneven distribution in the environment. Since some patches will contain more prey than others, the predator is confronted with the problem of first choosing a patch containing many food items, second, making a 'decision' on how long to forage there, and third, what to take. At first glance, the answer may appear to be that the predator should select the most productive patch and stay there. However, the presence of the predator will deplete the food resource and at some point another patch will become more productive than the first (Fig. 4.1); moving to another patch, on the other hand, will incur costs of time and effort. What should the predator do?

A broad solution of optimal foraging theory to the predator's dilemma is proposed by the Marginal Value Theorem (Charnov, 1976). This proposes that to maximise its rate of food intake, a predator should leave a patch when this rate falls (due to either consumption or disturbance) to the average value for the environment as a whole. In reality predators have to sample the habitat, through trial and error, to find the prey items and the relative profitability of different patches.

A similar problem faces predators when they have to feed their young. Now, in addition to weighing the energetic cost of moving between patches against the improved rate of prey intake gained by moving, they must also consider the energetic cost of a return trip from the breeding site to the feeding area. This feature of foraging is referred to as Central Place Foraging because the predator's behaviour is restricted by its breeding site (a central place). Modelling predicts that the amount of food brought back to the breeding site will depend on how far the predator has to go to hunt (Orians and Pearson, 1979). The further a predator has to travel to feed, the larger the load that must be

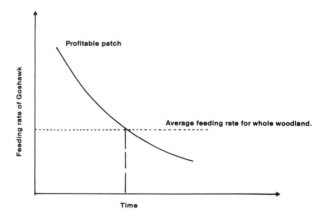

Fig. 4.1 Schematic illustration showing that a predator (eg. goshawk) hunting in woodland should leave a profitable patch (eg. a pheasant release pen) when the feeding rate falls to that of the rest of the woodland.

brought back to the young. This means that predators are restricted, in the breeding season, to limited areas around the breeding site where they can hunt. To be successful, therefore, they must choose areas to breed in which will contain enough prey items to feed themselves and their young. This is a serious problem for many of the large mammalian and avian predators as they and their young can rapidly deplete an area of food and the adults are forced to feed further and further from their breeding sites.

It is difficult to express general models like these, or their solutions, in a way which holds equivalent meaning for all predators. For many of the vertebrate predators that hunt gamebirds, the total consumption over several patches may only be one item, while the chances of a kill in any given patch will decline rapidly through disturbance by the hunting predator. The decision for the predator is not then concerned with its rate of intake, but with how long to forage fruitlessly in each patch. Furthermore, it may assess the profitability of the patch not in terms of its success, but in terms of the numbers of prey detected but not captured. Finally, patch use by predators is likely to be interrelated with the question of which prey types to hunt (next section): for example, a fox foraging for a couple of hours in open pasture has clearly made a decision to hunt invertebrates such as beetles or worms rather than nesting gamebirds. Clearly, predictions of what specific gamebird predators should do require special modifications of the general Optimal Foraging Model.

4.2.2 What to hunt

Besides choosing where to hunt, a predator also has to decide which types of prey items to eat. When only one type is available, the number of individual prey eaten by a predator in response to prey density is described by the predator's functional response curve (Holling, 1959). At a relatively high density of prey, the predator will encounter items so frequently that its search time falls to virtually zero and it spends almost all its time handling and consuming prey. At this density the predator will have reached its maximum rate of food intake and any further increase in prey density will not result in a greater rate of consumption.

Although different predators exhibit variations in the shape of the functional response curve (e.g. Fig. 4.2), they all share two common features: an initial increase in predation rate with prey density and a maximum predation rate above which increased prey density has no

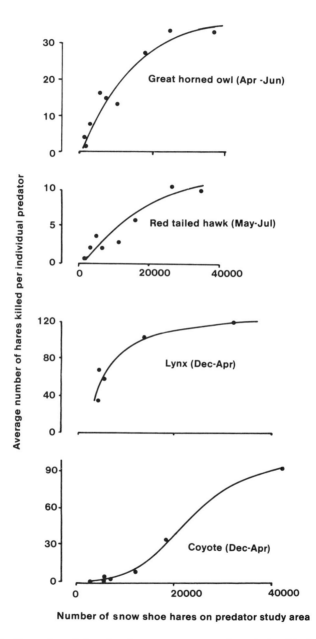

Fig. 4.2 Examples of functional response curves; the relationship between the density of snowshoe hares and the number of individuals eaten by various predators. (*After* Keith *et al.*, 1977.)

effect. Differences between systems lie in the shape of the rising part of the graph which depends on characteristics specific to the predator, its prey, and its environment: in particular the searching efficiency of the predator and the time spent handling the prey.

Functional response curves have an inherent problem: they only examine the predators' response to variation in density of one prey type, whilst in natural conditions the majority of predators will eat a range of prey types. In such cases Optimal Foraging Theory suggests that the predator should selectively take the most profitable prey type. The profitability of each prey type depends on its basic value (energy, nutrients, etc.) relative to the cost (energy and time) of searching for and handling the item. Consider a simple situation where a predator is hunting nesting gamebirds, of which just two species are available, one larger than the other and thus more profitable. Theory suggests that the predator will take the larger nesting birds whenever it comes across them, but will only take the smaller species when the larger species is scarce. If we considered a series of situations where the larger type was increasingly common, we would expect the predator to switch at some point from being a generalist (taking both species) to being a specialist on the larger species alone. In natural conditions, it is unlikely that a predator will totally specialise on a single gamebird species, though there is plenty of evidence that diet width is indeed related to the abundance of preferred prey. Studies in Finland found that as much as 70% of the diet of goshawks consisted of various grouse species (Sulkava, 1964); further south, where grouse were less common, they made up only 28% of the diet (Höglund, 1964). For weasels in southern Britain (Tapper, 1979), voles were the principal food, but the inclusion of birds in the diet increased as vole numbers declined.

The general optimal foraging model allows us to see how an individual predator might improve its efficiency by changing its range of food items – its diet width – in different situations. Three broad rules emerge:

(1) When the time taken to handle (i.e. locate, chase, catch and eat) prey is short compared with the search time, predators should be generalists, since they lose little search time whilst handling each prey item. Conversely, if handling time is long, relative to search time, then predators should specialise in profitable prey types.

(2) In a relatively unproductive environment where the encounter rate for all prey types is low, a predator should have a broader diet. In a more productive environment where profitable prey types are common, predators can be expected to specialise.

(3) When certain prey types are considerably more profitable than others the predator should specialise; and when the difference is not great, it should generalise. Relatively less profitable items should be ignored no matter how common they are.

The functional response of a predator to a prey type will therefore depend on the abundance of other prey, with predators tending to select the more profitable prey types. The shape of the curve describing the overall response of predators to one type of prey is crucial in determining the impact of predation on that prey population. Only in the case of a response curve where the consumption rate accelerates as prey density increases will predation tend to limit prey numbers. In other words, any increase in prey density will be met by an increase in the proportion of the prey population killed (e.g. coyote in Fig. 4.2). Such a response curve is likely to occur when a generalist predator switches its attention between prey types, depending on their relative abundance.

These deductive or *a priori* models, founded on foraging theory, have uncovered the salient features which influence how an individual predator behaves. Before considering how these behaviour patterns affect the dynamics of the prey population it is necessary to examine the factors that influence the overall density of predators.

4.2.3 The numerical response and territorial behaviour of predators

Besides responding behaviourally to changes in prey density, predators may also respond numerically: the density of predators may vary in relation to prey density (Fig. 4.3). This response has two components: firstly, high prey densities attract predators, causing them to aggregate in the area. This is observed in over-wintering predatory birds which often concentrate where there is a plentiful food supply (e.g. Kenward *et al.*, 1981; Keith and Rusch, 1987). Secondly, predators breed more successfully within an area with high prey density (e.g. Trautman *et al.*, 1973; Hewson and Kolb, 1975; Lindström, 1983).

The density of many vertebrate predators is partly regulated by the predators' own social system and territorial behaviour, which space out individuals or social groups. For example, foxes maintain quite strict territorial boundaries (Fig. 4.4), although both territory size and the number of individuals per territorial group vary between geographical areas according to the availability of prey (Macdonald, 1980; Kruuk and Macdonald, 1984). The degree of territorial exclusion

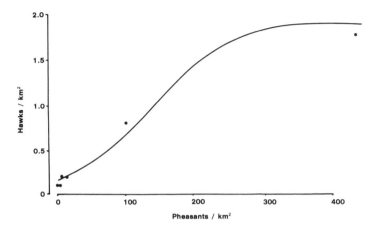

Fig. 4.3   An example of the numerical response of predators; an increase in goshawk density with increased pheasant density. (*After* Kenward, 1986.)

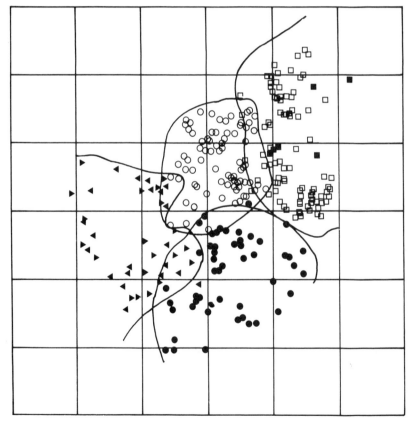

Fig. 4.4   Location of 5 radio-tagged foxes during a three-month period in the autumn of 1985 in Dorset showing the exclusive nature of territories. (Reynolds and Tapper, unpublished.)

varies greatly between predator species, and in some predators, such as the hen harrier (Balfour, 1962), territories can overlap, suggesting that the costs of defending a territory outweigh the benefits of having a competitor-free space. The lower the degree of territorial exclusion, or the greater the flexibility of the predator's social system, the greater the capacity of the predators to respond numerically to variations in prey density.

The density of predators in an area can also be influenced by the profitability of adjacent areas. Habitats where prey are abundant will have high predator densities and may serve as a source of dispersing predators which recolonise or increase the density in less profitable adjacent areas. For example, it has been suggested (Hewson and Leitch, 1987; Christiansen, 1979) that predation on moorland game-birds by foxes may be increased through dispersal of foxes from nearby forest plantations, where a plentiful vole supply ensures good reproduction (Hewson and Kolb, 1980). Such effects have important consequences for game managers, which will be discussed later.

4.3 Predator avoidance

Gamebirds have evolved certain adaptations, both morphological and behavioural, which enable them to avoid a variety of avian and mammalian predators. Passive avoidance involves methods of avoiding detection by predators. The most obvious of these is camouflage. The majority of gamebirds are ground-nesting, and this makes them particularly vulnerable during incubation. Females, which are solely responsible for incubation and guarding the young, are clearly under enormous selective pressure to remain inconspicuous, and have evolved cryptic colouration. Similarly, all gamebird chicks are cryptically coloured. Adult males, on the other hand, have to balance the benefits of predator avoidance with the cost of not attracting a mate and, in polygamous species in particular (Chapter 7), tend to be more brightly coloured. The avoidance of detection in sitting hens appears also to extend to scent emission: sitting hens are much harder for a trained dog to find than at other times, probably because the birds close their caeca, which are responsible for much of the scent emission (Hudson, 1986a).

Active avoidance of predation includes a variety of distraction displays to lure the predator away from the young (e.g. Bergerud, 1970; Pederson and Steen, 1985), whilst increasing the risk of predation on themselves. These can range from a direct attack on the predator, to feigning broken wings to attract predators away from the young.

During winter, snow cover can make some gamebird species more conspicuous and therefore vulnerable to predation. The formation of flocks is generally thought to decrease vulnerability and to allow more time for each bird to feed, since there are effectively more eyes to detect predators. The costs and benefits of this are discussed in more detail elsewhere (Krebs and Davies, 1984). Similar effects may also occur at leks.

Although most predator avoidance behaviour is undoubtedly instinctive, there is growing evidence to suggest that some is learned, or at least modified through experience. Thus, hand-reared pheasants were more prone to predation than wild birds except when incubating (Robertson and Hill, 1986). Experience with adult birds may therefore give chicks an advantage which hand-reared birds do not obtain.

4.4 The dynamics of predator–prey interactions

Prey populations are influenced by various processes which can function either in a density-dependent or a density-independent manner. All density-dependent factors tend to have a regulatory influence on populations, whereas density-independent processes tend to be destabilising although the final determination of numbers will be a combination of both sets of factors. Predation, as we have seen, is almost always density-dependent: it is positively related to prey density through both the functional response and numerical response of the predators. We now examine the circumstances that result in predators limiting the density of prey.

If a prey population is allowed to increase in the absence of predators it can be expected to rise to a level set by other limiting factors such as food availability or parasitism. When predators are introduced to this population both populations will tend towards a new equilibrium. Mathematical models of predator–prey dynamics suggest that the level of this equilibrium is dependent upon two features:

(1) The rate at which the prey population increases.
(2) The hunting efficiency of the predator.

Both an increase in the prey rate of increase and a decrease in the predator hunting efficiency will lead to a rise in the equilibrium level. In this simple situation we can see that predators can limit their prey when they are efficient and when prey have a low rate of increase relative to the rate of predation.

Such models are based on a number of assumptions. For example, they do not include any variation between individuals in the prey and predator populations, whereas in reality individuals differ in many respects. Introducing such realism to the models can have profound effects, both on the position of the equilibrium and also on the stability of the interaction.

4.4.1 Selective predation

Individuals within a prey population differ in condition and age, and these two factors make a great deal of difference to the vulnerability of the prey. If predators selectively remove sick, weak or malnourished prey, then predation is regarded as being compensatory to other forms of mortality and will have a minor effect on prey numbers. Some studies have shown that certain individuals are selected. For example Hudson (1986a) showed that predators selectively caught red grouse with high parasite burdens. Other studies, however, have shown that prey victims do not differ from the rest of the prey population. In the willow and black grouse, Angelstam (1984) found no difference in body size or body weight between surviving birds and those killed by predators. From these studies it would seem that predators select weak individuals when they are available and when healthy prey are relatively invulnerable. Vulnerable individuals, though, need not be weak or sick. They may be just one class of individuals which are predisposed to predation. For example, incubating gamebirds are far more vulnerable to mammalian predators than are other individuals at that time of year. It is obviously important therefore in a field study to examine which prey are selected, as the type of selection may influence prey dynamics.

4.4.2 Compensatory mortality

When prey density increases above the number which the habitat can sustain, then those individuals which do not get a nesting site or territory are in effect surplus and if they die, the mortality will not affect prey numbers in the next generation. The ultimate cause of death was being one of a surplus, hence predation was not additive to natural mortality but compensatory (see discussion of compensatory mortality in Chapter 8). This is an important point as it means that even though a high rate of predation may be observed on a prey population, it may be having no effect on overall density. For predators to play some role in regulating prey numbers predation must be additional to natural mortality: in other words prey are killed which would otherwise have reproduced.

4.4.3 Stability

A population is regarded as being unstable if its density fluctuates significantly in either a regular or a random fashion. A stabilising process is one which reduces such fluctuations. Several features of the predator–prey relationship favour stability:

(1) density-dependent predation
(2) generalist predators
(3) habitat diversity
(4) self-regulation

1. DENSITY-DEPENDENT PREDATION
As a result of both the functional response and the numerical response of predators, predation accounts for a smaller proportion of a prey population at low prey densities than at high densities. This is extremely important, for it means that predation will tend to control prey numbers when they increase and relax when prey numbers decline. In this way predation will tend to maintain the prey population around an equilibrium level, though it is also important to realise that predation is only one of many factors acting to determine population density levels. Some of these factors will also be density-dependent and stabilising, and will tend to support the stabilising effect of predation. Others may be density-dependent but destabilising, or density-independent, and act to negate the stabilising effect of predation. Acting alone, predation can only regulate prey numbers if at some prey density it outstrips the rate of increase of the prey population. Nevertheless, the actual density at which any equilibrium occurs depends on all factors impinging on the population, not just the density-dependent ones.

2. GENERALIST PREDATORS
As discussed in Section 4.2.2, only when the predators' rate of consumption increases with prey density in an S-shaped curve will predation tend to limit the increase of prey numbers. Although such

relationships may occur in the numerical response of specialist predators, they are particularly characteristic of the functional responses of generalist predators. Predation relaxes as prey density falls again, since the generalist predators switch to other prey types. Naturally, the stabilising influence is absent at prey densities beyond the concave part of the density-dependent relationship, since the increase in consumption rate no longer matches the increase in prey density. Also, the stabilising influence must be counteracted if switching behaviour lags behind changes in prey density, or if individuals within a generalist predator population become life-time specialists (Potts, 1986, mentions individual crows, snowy owl, merlin, sparrowhawk, and badger becoming partridge specialists).

Not only their impact on any one prey type, but the numbers of generalist predators too are stabilised by there being a variety of prey types available.

3. HABITAT DIVERSITY

Diversity and spatial variation in the types of habitat available to the prey population are also likely to enhance the stability of a prey population. One reason for this is that diverse habitats contain a range of prey types amongst which generalist predators can choose. Another reason is that predation will be lower in certain habitats than in others – because the habitat structure affords protection, because prey densities there are too low to interest predators, or because the predators are attracted to other habitats for quite different reasons – so that some habitats will act as 'refuges' against predation and 'sources' of prey production which can disperse to surrounding habitats.

4. SELF-REGULATION

Self-regulation occurs when a population is limited by competition between its members for resources, either directly (exploitation), or through territoriality or some other social system (interference). Theoretical studies of predator-prey interactions predict that when either the predator or the prey population are so regulated, the stability of the system will be increased. Erlinge *et al.* (1984) suggested that the regulation of real predator populations in southern Sweden through territorial behaviour was partly responsible for the prevention of significant fluctuations in rodent numbers.

To summarise, the importance of predation in influencing the size of a prey population depends on the way predators operate. Predators respond to the density of each prey type in two ways: the functional response of the individual predator, and the numerical response of the predator population as a whole. If the combination of these two is an effective response to changes in prey density then predators can limit prey numbers. Predation, however, is only one of many factors affecting prey population dynamics, and its regulatory effect may be counteracted or supported by others. Various common features of vertebrate predator–prey interactions favour stability in prey numbers; but the role of predation in determining the density around which this stabilising influence operates depends on its importance relative to other factors.

4.5 The impact of predation on gamebird populations

4.5.1 Observations of field populations

The rate of predation on a gamebird population can be estimated by studying either the losses from the prey population or the proportion of prey items in the predator's diet. These types of study have inherent difficulties and only provide a minimum estimate of predation rate. In neither case is it possible to discern whether the mortality caused by predation is either compensatory or additive.

The extent of predation on gamebirds has been estimated in a number of studies (Dumke and Pils, 1973; Trautman et al., 1973; Linden and Wikman, 1983; Pils and Martin, 1978; Erlinge et al., 1984; Sargeant et al., 1984). However, it is important to note that measured predation rates frequently relate to specific seasons, or stages of the birds' life-history, and this often makes it difficult to make comparisons between studies or, more importantly, to make an estimate of the effect of predation on the prey population. Despite this, it is clear that predation rates cover a wide range of values, and those studies that have considered the causes of this variation have generally found predation rates to be strongly related to gamebird density. Nevertheless, measured predation rates do not necessarily provide an estimate of the effects of predation on a gamebird population, as in some cases there can be a compensatory effect in the survival or productivity of the prey as a result of the predation.

Observations have shown that, for many grouse species, nest predation is an important source of loss in productivity (Myrberget, 1972, 1984a,b, 1985a,b,c; Johnsgard, 1973; Zwickel, 1975; Angelstam, 1979, 1983; Redmond et al., 1982; Storaas et al., 1982; Angelstam et al.,

1984, 1985). Potts (1980, p.10) summarised information about nest loss rates of grey partridge in various parts of the world and found that around 60% was attributable to predators where there is no mowing.

4.5.2 Experimental studies

Since measurements of predation rate do not reveal the effects of predation on a prey population, a number of studies have manipulated predation rate and monitored its effect. In most of these experiments predator numbers have been severely reduced within a given area and the performance of the prey population there compared with a similar area where predators have not been removed.

1. EFFECTS ON BREEDING SUCCESS

In a planned experiment, Chesness *et al.* (1968) investigated the effects of nest predation on pheasant production in southern Minnesota. Nest predators were reduced in one area by trapping, and pheasant nesting success there compared with an untrapped area. The net result of the experiment was a two-fold increase of pheasant chick production in the trapped area. Nest predation rates were back to normal within a year after predator trapping had ceased.

In an attempt to stop the spread of rabies northwards from Germany into Denmark an intensive campaign of fox control was run between 1964 and 1974 in a belt of land stretching from coast to coast of southern Jutland (Jensen, 1970). Fox densities were dramatically reduced following gassing of earths and the introduction of a bounty for each fox shot. The effect of this fox removal was a 50–100% increase in the bag of hares, partridge and pheasants within the fox removal strip. No such increase occurred in the sporting bag from adjacent areas without fox removal. Game bags returned to normal levels on the cessation of the rabies scare in 1975, but when intensive fox removal was once again applied in 1979, the same effects were repeated (Fig. 4.5).

To eliminate the influence of confounding factors and demonstrate clearly the effect of predation, a number of studies have added a refinement to the technique by conducting the experiment twice. After running the experiment once, treated and untreated areas are exchanged and the experiment repeated. In a study on duck nesting success, Balser *et al.* (1968) removed all mammalian nest predators from an experimental area and doubled the proportion of nests that were successful. Reversal of treatments between the two areas also led to a reversal in nesting success, demonstrating clearly that nesting

Plate 4.1 Predator–prey relationships are complex but there is substantial evidence that the fox can have a significant impact on some gamebird populations.

success was suppressed by the action of the mammalian predators.

The impact of predation on breeding production is therefore particularly important in the management of gamebirds since chick production constitutes the major part of the post-breeding harvest. Whether such benefits can affect overall density, however, is a separate issue.

2. EFFECTS ON BREEDING DENSITY

Two studies have shown that removing predators did result in higher breeding densities. Duebbert and Lokemoen (1980) found that intensive control of duck predators by means of poison baits, trapping and shooting led to an increase in both hatching success (63% to 93%)

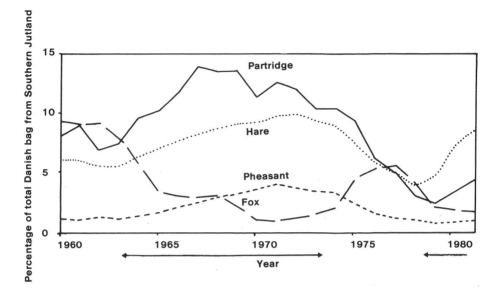

Fig. 4.5   Annual game records from Southern Jutland during changes in fox control. Intensive fox control to prevent the spread of rabies took place between 1964 and 1974 and again from 1979 onwards. (*After* Jensen, 1970.)

and breeding density (from 7 to 35 nests per km²). Marcström *et al.* (1986, 1987) also found an increase in breeding density of black grouse, capercaillie, hazel hen and willow grouse on two islands off the Swedish coast, when foxes and pine martens were reduced. On the treated island, hens were on average 2.2 times more productive than on the untreated island. Densities of adult grouse declined on untreated areas and increased on treated areas. The effect of predator removal was most obvious for counts of capercaillie and black grouse at the lek. Capercaillie increased 1.7 times and black grouse 2.5 times, corresponding to an annual increment of 28% and 26% respectively. However, this increase in breeding density was less than the increase in chick production, presumably because winter losses or dispersal had been greater.

Often, as in Marcström's study, the effects on the breeding density are not as profound as those on breeding production. One possible reason is that the removal of predation increases the importance of other factors, such as food supply, parasitism or territorial limitation, in regulating the population. When production is increased, more birds disperse away from the predator control area as it approaches its equilibrium density. For the grey partridge, Potts (1986) regarded spacing behaviour in relation to nesting habitat as the factor most important in determining over-winter loss. Here the effects of nest predation did carry through to the partridge breeding population in the following spring.

Alternatively, the small effects of predator removal on subsequent breeding density could be the result of increased mortality from some other factor. This could be caused by an increase in other predators, as suggested by the experiments of Parker (1984) and Trautman et al. (1973), or by the increase in factors such as parasitism or habitat deterioration (Kie et al., 1979). Consider a population regulated by various processes: if one of these regulatory factors (in this case predation) is suddenly removed, then the prey population will shift to another equilibrium level determined by the remaining processes. Such an alteration is likely to affect the long-term stability properties of the interaction and as a consequence may increase the rate of mortality on the population.

These manipulation experiments demonstrate clearly that predators are often responsible for depressing the breeding success of gamebirds although the benefits to the size of the population tend to be relatively short-lived after the removal effort ceases. Many of the experiments did not find any large improvement in spring breeding density nor do they reflect the long-term effects on gamebird population dynamics of reducing predation. They do show that removing predators will alter the effects of other factors influencing the prey and that removing only a part of the predator population, even the most important part, may have a smaller effect on predation rates than expected since this may provoke increased, compensatory consumption by the remaining predators.

4.6 Predation and cyclic fluctuations in gamebird densities

Many gamebird species, particularly those at northern latitudes, undergo cyclic fluctuations in density. In northern parts of Fennoscandia, for instance, grouse populations undergo regular 3–4-year population fluctuations (Siivonen, 1948, 1952, 1954a,b, 1957; Moksnes, 1972; Myrberget, 1986; Hornfeldt, 1978; Angelstam et al., 1982, 1984, 1985; Hornfeldt et al., 1986). By contrast, grouse populations further south on the European continent are generally non-cyclic (Ruwet, 1982; de Franceschi, 1982; Ellison et al., 1982; Ellison and Magnani, 1985). The majority of red grouse populations in Britain are quasi-cyclic (Potts et al., 1984; Hudson et al., 1985) lacking the regularity of more northern grouse cycles.

As discussed in Chapter 2, a lot of the data used to analyse cycles have been based on autumn bag records, influenced greatly by variations in the production of young, and there are few long-term data on spring density. However, a 13-year series of spring counts of black grouse in central Sweden (Angelstam, 1983) exhibited a pattern with a 3–4-year cycle in breeding density, albeit with much lower amplitude than autumn density.

Various hypotheses have been put forward to account for these cycles, and they can broadly be divided into intrinsic (self-regulation) and extrinsic mechanisms (e.g. parasitism or predation). Watson and Moss (1979) presented a general explanation for population cycles in grouse species, which suggested that changes in behaviour caused increased mortality and/or dispersal. For the red grouse in northern England, however, Hudson (1986a,b) has shown that parasitism is the likely cause of the cycles; but changes in the behaviour of the grouse may be a consequence of parasite burdens.

Scientists in Fennoscandia also tend to favour extrinsic factors as a cause for cyclic fluctuations (for reviews see Angelstam *et al.*, 1985; Myrberget, 1986). Apart from explaining the tendency to cycle any hypothesis about these cycles must also explain:

(1) The fact that tetraonid and small rodent population cycles are coupled in time (Hagen, 1952; Moksnes, 1972; Myrberget, 1972, 1986; Angelstam, 1983; Angelstam *et al.*, 1984, 1985; Storaas *et al.*, 1982).
(2) The time lag of one year between spring densities of small rodents and grouse (Angelstam, 1983; Myrberget, 1984a, 1986).
(3) Changes in the period and tendency of populations to cycle (Angelstam *et al.*, 1984, 1985; Hudson *et al.*, 1985).

Hypotheses involving intrinsic factors have failed to explain the system of regular population fluctuations among boreal grouse species in Fennoscandia, whereas temporal and spatial variation in predation pressure could explain all the above facts (Angelstam *et al.*, 1985).

Analysis of data on a black grouse population in boreal forest in Sweden (Angelstam, 1983) and a willow grouse population in northern Norway (Myrberget, 1984b) showed that total annual losses were closely correlated with summer losses. Nest predation varied from 10% to 63%, and from 7% to 78%, respectively. The lowest predation rate occurred at peaks in small rodent numbers and the highest when small rodent numbers declined.

It was suggested that cycles in gamebirds occurred because of the compounded predation pressure from a generalist predator community which varied its diet in relation to the availability of the main prey item, the small rodents. The predators switched to eating grouse (the alternative prey) when small mammals were scarce and reverted to their main prey as they became more common (Angelstam *et al.*, 1984). In boreal forest, the nest predation causing this pattern appears to be performed by all generalist predator species in approximate proportion to their relative densities (Angelstam, 1986).

Recently Lindström *et al.* (1987) performed an experiment in which a community of generalist predators was supplied with superabundant food during a population decline of small rodents. A small but significant reduction in nest predation on grouse resulted. This suggests that predation is a necessary, though perhaps not a sufficient, explanation of the decline in grouse reproduction in years when predators shift from small mammals to grouse eggs and chicks.

In southern Scandinavia, where grouse do not cycle, habitat diversity is greater, caused by the fragmentation of the boreal forest, and this is thought to account for the relative stability (Angelstam *et al.*, 1984). As discussed in Section 4.4.3, habitat diversity leads to a more complex array of food items available to generalist predators and thus to more stable population levels which are not dependent on the populations of small rodents. Further support for this hypothesis comes from a study by Andren *et al.* (1985) which found that predation on dummy nests was more constant in the south than in the north.

Although nest predation is the proximate reason for the fluctuations in black grouse spring density in boreal Sweden (Angelstam, 1983), and for willow grouse in northern Norway (Myrberget, 1985b, 1986), the ultimate reason may be an entirely separate factor. For example, the vulnerability of hen birds to predation may vary with underlying changes in plant food quality (Angelstam *et al.*, 1984, 1985; Brittas, 1984; Myrberget, 1986) which may in turn cause poorer distraction displays (Mercer, 1969; Bergerud, 1970; Jenkins *et al.*, 1963, 1967). Other workers have also found that in years with poor chick production hens were flushed from the nest more easily than in good years and this may have influenced the rate of nest predation (Angelstam, 1983). Pedersen and Steen (1985), however, found that differences between years in the occurrence of distraction displays were not correlated with changes in body condition or chick production, suggesting that changes in food were of little importance in these years.

In summary: various hypotheses have been proposed to explain the existence of regular fluctuations in gamebird density. Extrinsic factors are often sufficient to explain these cycles, with intrinsic factors only becoming important when densities are high. In boreal Fennoscandia, nest predation from generalist predators has been proposed as the reason for the 3–4 year cycle, although the ultimate reason for the increase in predation may be related to some other factor such as food quality. In southern Scandinavia, where populations do not exhibit these fluctuations, a wider prey base resulting from habitat fragmentation is thought to be the cause. This provides the predators with a more constant food supply and stabilises the interaction.

4.7 Management and predation

Of all the factors influencing gamebird populations, predation is the most obvious and is frequently suggested as being the major limiting factor. Darwin (1859) summarised this when he wrote: '...there seems little doubt that the stock of partridges, grouse and hares on any large estate depends chiefly on the destruction of vermin.' Game managers have tended to subscribe to this view (see Tapper et al., 1982), whilst ecologists have sometimes regarded predation as unimportant. One reason for these opposing views is that game managers are interested primarily in the harvest of gamebirds from an area of land, which depends largely on autumn numbers. Ecologists, however, tend to study the causes of variations in spring numbers at the onset of breeding. The experiments discussed in this chapter emphasise the influence predators have on breeding production, whilst the effects on breeding density are frequently less significant.

As stated in Section 4.4, predators can be expected to limit prey numbers when they have a high hunting efficiency relative to the prey population's rate of increase. The aim of the game manager should therefore be to decrease the hunting efficiency of the predators and maximise the prey's rate of increase. Habitat quality should be an important feature of land management, ensuring that the gamebirds have ample food to produce large broods (see Chapter 6). For example, heather burning on freely drained moors is an important part of red grouse management, providing hens with a nutritious food supply (Watson and Miller, 1976; Hudson, 1986a).

4.7.1 Reducing predation

In this section we examine various ways in which predation can be reduced. Many of the proposed ideas may have important implications for management procedures, but at the present time they are based only on theoretical considerations and have yet to be properly tested in the field.

The most obvious way of reducing predation is to remove the predators and this has been a traditional feature of shooting estates in the British Isles. Such control over large areas and long periods can be so effective in reducing populations of carnivorous mammals (Langley and Yalden, 1977) and raptors (Moore, 1957) that it actually limits their geographical distribution. Whilst the precise effect of predator control on prey breeding densities remains unclear, discontinuation of predator control and the subsequent increase of common predator species is suggested as one important reason behind declines in partridge and wild pheasant (Tapper et al., 1982; Potts, 1986) as well as red grouse (Hudson, 1986a) populations in Britain.

Removing predators can be very labour-intensive. In the predator removal experiment by Chesness et al. (1968), the cost of removing predators averaged $21 (at that time) per individual predator taken and $4.50 for each extra chick hatched in the trapped area compared with the untrapped 'control' area. In Norway, an 80% reduction in hooded crow density during a 3-year period on an area of forest of only 55 hectares involved shooting 130 adult crows, destroying 20 nests, and laying out poisoned eggs – a total effort of 469 man-hours or 3.7 hours per crow shot (Slagsvold, 1978). Duebbert and Lokemoen (1980) showed that poison was a more effective method of control and one man using strychnine-poisoned baits could effectively control mammalian predators on a 259 km² area. The use of poisoned baits is now illegal in many countries for ethical reasons.

Antifertility agents could conceivably offer a labour-efficient and ethical means of reducing predator populations. Unfortunately, field testing of the chemical diethylstibestrol against foxes in North Dakota, which initially appeared promising (Linhart and Enders, 1964; Balser, 1964), failed to reduce reproductive performance. Controlling predators in isolated patches will be ineffectual compared with control over larger areas (Potts and Vickerman, 1974). Hudson (1986a) has shown that the mean annual bag of grouse per unit area in northern England was correlated with the density of gamekeepers within and around an estate. Keeper density accounted for 11% of the variation on bag between moors, but this increased to 27% when the density of keepers within 5 km of the moor was considered. Thus, moors surrounded by keepered moors were more productive than isolated moors. This presumably results from immigration of predators from outside source areas. For a country shooting estate in Britain, we might expect the fox density to be somewhere in the region of 1–4/km². However, a gamekeeper often kills as many foxes as 6/km². Similarly there are many instances where raptors have been shot by gamekeepers, only to be quickly replaced by other individuals (Newton, 1979). (Newton, 1979).

Apart from removing predators, there are alternative methods which can reduce the efficiency of predators. This efficiency can be measured both as a change in individual behaviour and a change in overall number (Section 4.2), so management could aim to alter these factors. There are four main ways in which the environment can be altered so as to lessen the effects of predators on gamebirds:

(1) Altering habitat
(2) Increasing predator interference
(3) Feeding predators
(4) Changing prey behaviour

1. ALTERING HABITAT

Since habitat features are involved in determining the vulnerability of prey, changing these could in some instances lead to a longer-term and more cost-effective solution than killing or otherwise removing predators. Kenward and Marcström (1982), for example, offers practical suggestions for reducing goshawk predation on pheasants by increasing cover around feeding sites and removing nearby tall trees on which goshawks could perch.

Where only a small proportion of habitat is used by the gamebird (e.g. hedgerows for grey partridge), the effects of the predators can become concentrated. Increasing the area of this habitat, in the case of the partridge by providing wider hedgerows or banks, could therefore decrease the predators' hunting efficiency.

The amount of cover available for nesting birds is also an important factor. In Dakota, Duebbert and Kantrud (1974) examined duck nesting success in relation to habitat differences and predator control (Table 4.1). They showed that when predators were not removed, the density of duck nests was six times greater in idle agricultural ground with good nesting cover than on actively farmed land. Controlling predators on the idle land produced a 23-fold increase, showing that improved habitat quality, in combination with predator control, can vastly increase the potential harvest.

2. INCREASING INTERFERENCE

The exclusivity of territories (Section 4.2.3) in many territorial predator species implies that residents actively defend them against incursions. If the way predators defend their territories can be determined, then predators may be 'fooled' into believing that an area is occupied. For example, foxes are known to mark their territories with scent. If scent could be applied in a persistent form around an area

Table 4.1 Effects of predator removal on duck nesting success on two habitats in South Dakota (Duebbert & Kantrud 1974).

Treatment		Idle land	Farmed land
Predators removed	nests/km^2	299	12
	nest success	92%	84%
	ducklings/ha	22	0.7
Predators not removed	nests/km^2	84	14
	nest success	68%	51%
	ducklings/ha	4.7	0.5

of land, it might be possible to prevent foxes from setting up territories. Similarly, stuffed raptors at known nesting sites might prevent birds from nesting there. However, at the present time such strategies remain purely conjectural.

3. FEEDING PREDATORS

In generalist predators, whose predation at a critical time of year may have great impact on the production of young birds (e.g. predation on sitting hens), temporary alternative food sources may be an effective solution. An experiment to see if predation on capercaillie, black grouse, and hazelhens could be reduced by feeding predators during spring and early summer (Lindström et al., 1987) gave results which supported this hypothesis. It is possible that this temporary distraction of resident predators by feeding at critical seasons may well be more cost-effective than removing them, provided it does not encourage a build-up of predator numbers.

Another variation on this theme is to feed predators with gamebirds that have been treated with an emetic (a chemical which makes the predator sick). Experiments with treated insects have shown that birds quickly respond to these substances and avoid unpalatable prey types (Brower *et al.*, 1967). The more unpleasant the experience, the longer the prey was avoided. Feeding resident predators with unpalatable gamebirds may therefore have a significant impact on decreasing the rate of predation. Similarly, 'electric eggs' giving severe shocks to egg predators have been suggested.

4. PREY BEHAVIOUR

Hand-reared gamebirds are more vulnerable to predation than are wild-reared ones (Section 4.3). It may therefore be necessary to give captive-bred young gamebirds some experience in predator avoidance, for example by rearing them with bantams hens, before releasing them – an idea presently being tested at the Game Conservancy.

To summarise, the aim of game management is to achieve a maximum harvest, and predator control is necessary if this is to be achieved, though it should be conducted with the wider environmental considerations in mind. Predator control can be a very costly process and will often be ineffective unless performed over a large area. Reducing the hunting efficiency of predators by various means, or confusing their territorial systems, might provide alternative or supplementary management techniques.

4.8 Conclusions

Predation is only one of a set of processes that influence the dynamics of prey populations. The relative importance of predation within this set depends on a variety of factors, such as prey density, predator density, the efficiency of predators, whether or not they are generalists, and the availability of alternative prey. There can also be complex interactions between predation and other processes. Predation may therefore play a greater or lesser role in determining prey abundance in different circumstances. A number of common features of vertebrate predator–prey systems, though, lead us to expect that its general influence will be to stabilise numbers.

Both observational and experimental (predator-removal) studies provide strong evidence that predators can be highly effective at reducing the annual production of gamebird populations, whilst for various reasons the effects on breeding density are less dramatic. The reduction of predation within the bounds of ethical and conservation considerations is necessary if game managers wish to produce a maximum yield from their land, although this may have important consequences on the long-term stability of the gamebird populations.

5 The Ecology and Control of Parasites in Gamebird Populations

Peter J. Hudson and Andrew P. Dobson

5.1 Introduction

Parasitic agents are ubiquitous; the majority of living species are parasites of one form or another, and there can be little doubt that this group of animals has been remarkably successful in exploiting other living organisms. It is therefore somewhat surprising that few ecological studies have concentrated on the role of true parasites in regulating animal numbers, while at the same time there have been extensive studies on the biology of the parasitoids (Hassell, 1978, 1981). The lack of detailed studies is reflected in the majority of contemporary ecological texts, with some recent exceptions (May, 1981; Begon *et al.*, 1986). Most have chapters on the importance of predation and competition, but parasitism is usually considered a special case of predation where the parasite has little or no effect on the host population.

The parasite is often seen as benign, living in a fine balance with its host; if it becomes harmful and kills its host, it follows that the parasite will lose its home and die. Those parasites that maintain a harmless level of infection have traditionally been seen to be more successful and, in evolutionary terms, selected for. Epidemics, by their very nature, are considered the exception where the careful balance between host and parasite is temporarily disturbed and the effects of the parasite lead to massive host mortality. The parasite's actions are considered density-independent since the imbalance can be brought about by a wide range of factors such as climatic changes or human intervention.

A different perspective is put on the host–parasite relationship by the parasitologist, who almost by definition tends to see the parasite not as benign but as an organism which benefits at the expense of its host (Crofton, 1971; Whitfield, 1979). Epidemiologists who study the population behaviour of diseases (in many ways parasite ecologists) have tended to concentrate their studies on the biology of parasites of man and his livestock. Only recently have the principles of epidemiology and ecology been brought together and applied to natural animal populations. The synthesis of these two disciplines suggests that parasites operate in a density-dependent manner and are thus capable of regulating the size of the host population (Anderson and May, 1978, 1979; May and Anderson, 1978, 1979). Empirical evidence shows that the relative effects of parasites increase with density, decreasing the growth rate of the host population through reductions in fecundity and survival and thus acting in a way similar to predation or competition. In evolutionary terms the success of any parasite depends on transmission from one host to another, and the parasite that produces successful transmission stages will be at an advantage even if such action kills its host.

Although theoretical studies provide a sound framework and indicate that under certain conditions parasites can regulate the size of their host population, the extent to which they do so in natural populations is not yet clear. In the special case of managed as opposed to unmanaged populations, parasites are likely to be of greater importance. The traditional management procedures of habitat improvement and predator control are designed to increase population density; this will tend to increase the rate of parasite transmission, leading to a rise in parasite burdens. In other words, the removal of limiting factors such as predation and food quality may increase density but may also result in an increase in the importance of parasitism.

Parasites are deleterious to the survival and productivity of gamebirds; reducing their impact is an important objective of gamebird management in some areas. In the case of reared or rare species, management procedures can create artificially high densities which may result in parasites becoming established which would not have done so if the animals were in their natural, more dispersed state. In situations where the host has little or no previous exposure to the parasite the species may be particularly vulnerable if its resistance to infection is low. A further problem is that a managed population of animals may act as a reservoir for a disease which threatens humans or their livestock; for example, domestic poultry and gamebirds share a number of harmful parasites.

This chapter describes how parasites operate to influence individual animals, how these effects influence the growth rate of the population, and the implications of these for managing animal populations.

5.2 Parasite biology

Although the characteristics of parasitic agents vary greatly in their size, influence on the host and life-history, a number of general features may be detected, which form the basis for an understanding of the ecology of parasitism. This section outlines some of these general principles and provides the essential elements used in later sections to develop population models and methods of reducing the effects of parasites.

5.2.1 Parasite types

Defining the associations between host and parasite can become complex and there is a tendency for biological understanding to be lost in semantics. A simple and convenient division (proposed by Anderson and May, 1979) is to categorise parasites into either macroparasites (helminths and arthropods) or microparasites (viruses, bacteria and protozoa). This division is not just a reflection of size: the two types tend to have different life-history characteristics which can influence the dynamics of both the host and the parasite population. A general comparison between these, together with the actions of predators and competitors, is shown in Table 5.1. This division, by its very nature, is coarse but it serves to illustrate the differences between animal interactions and their effects on the encumbrant.

MACROPARASITES

Macroparasites tend to be the larger metazoan parasites including the worms (e.g. tapeworms, nematodes, flukes) and arthropods (e.g. ticks, biting insects). Their size makes it possible to estimate numbers of parasites per host, although total population estimates for a parasite are difficult since some utilise a variety of alternative and intermediate hosts to complete their life cycle. Generally, small numbers of macroparasites tend to have only a mild effect on their host, but heavy infestations can lead to a serious decline in condition, and death. An increase in the parasite burden is usually the result of infection and not parasite reproduction within the host. In comparison with other animals of their size, macroparasites tend to produce remarkable numbers of eggs and live for a relatively long time, in many instances nearly as long as their host. This long life expectancy, coupled with the host's failure to produce a strong immunological response to reinfection, often leads to fairly persistent infections.

Table 5.1 Comparison of some life history characteristics of macro- and microparasites with those of other regulatory agents

Life history characteristic	Microparasite	Macroparasite	Parasitoid	Competitor	Predator
Ratio of mean expected lifespan	$\ll 1$	< 1	~ 1	~ 1	> 1
Ratio of body sizes	much smaller than hosts	smaller than hosts	mature stages similar	similar size	larger than prey
Intrinsic growth rate of population	much faster than hosts	faster than hosts	comparable but slightly slower	similar or almost identical	usually slower than prey
Interaction with host individuals in natural populations	one host usually supports several populations of different species	one host supports a few too many individuals of different species	one host can support several individuals	individuals reduce the proportion of available resources	many prey items are needed to feed each predator
Effect of the interaction on the host individual	mildly to fairly deleterious	variable; not too virulent to definitive, can be intermediate	eventually fatal	not usually fatal	usually immediately fatal
Ratio between numbers of species at the population level	many species of parasite within each host individual	many species of parasite from each host population	most hosts harbour one or occasionally several parasitoids	several species may utilize one common resource	each predator uses several prey species
Degree of overlap of the two species ranges	occur as diffuse foci throughout host's range	occur as diffuse foci throughout host's range	usually present throughout host's range	ranges overlap but usually not entirely	range is usually greater than prey's

All ratios expressed as exploiter/victim.

MICROPARASITES

In contrast to the macroparasites, microparasites tend to be small with high reproductive rates within the host; viruses, bacteria and protozoa are all included in this group. Since reproduction occurs within the host, the host population can be considered as consisting of a few distinct groups: infecteds, susceptibles and immunes. The pattern of infection within a host tends to be transient; a rapid increase in the number of parasites induces a strong immunological response from the host leading to a decline in the level of infection and often leaving the host immune to further infection.

5.2.2 Prevalence and frequency distribution of parasite numbers per host

The distribution of macroparasites within the host population is usually measured as the proportion of the population carrying the parasite (prevalence) and the mean number of parasites per host within the host population (mean intensity of infection).

With microparasites, each individual host can be considered to be either infected or uninfected so the proportion of hosts infected is the

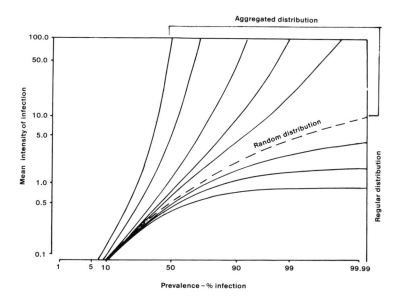

Fig. 5.1 Schematic relationship between prevalence and mean intensity of infection. Aggregated distributions have low prevalence and high intensity while regular distributions have high prevalence and low intensity. (*After* Anderson, 1982b.)

principal measure of the distribution of a disease. Presence or absence of the disease can be determined using a wide range of techniques. In some instances the presence of microparasites in the blood stream can be determined simply by a blood smear, although increasingly sophisticated indirect techniques are now frequently used. To detect the viral infection of grouse known as louping-ill, blood samples are taken and tested serologically for an immune response. This test reveals if the bird has been exposed to the disease rather than the proportion of the population currently infected. If the parasite is particularly virulent, only a few hosts will show a positive response to the test since the majority of infected hosts will have died from the effects of the parasite.

The presence of macroparasites is usually determined either from direct counts of the parasite (e.g. ticks) or indirectly by the identification of eggs or larvae in the hosts' droppings. Estimates of prevalence together with the mean intensity of infection provide a rough description of the parasite's distribution within the host population. However, to fully understand the nature of macroparasite infections we need to get some idea of the frequency distribution of the number of parasites per host. These frequency distributions fall into one of three categories, depending on the statistical relationship between prevalence and the intensity of infection (shown graphically in Fig. 5.1). These are basically:

(1) A random distribution: parasites are considered to be distributed randomly through the host population when the mean intensity of infection is approximately equal to the variance, and the distribution can be described by the Poisson distribution.
(2) A regular distribution: in this case most of the hosts have similar parasite burdens, i.e. prevalence is high and intensity is low. More formally the variance is less than the mean, and such a distribution may be described by the positive binomial distribution. Such distributions are rarely encountered.
(3) An aggregated distribution: here a few of the hosts carry a large proportion of the parasite population, prevalence may be low but intensity high and characteristically the variance is greater than the mean. The extent of this aggregation can be described by the exponent of the negative binomial distribution, k; the smaller the value of k, the greater the extent of aggregation.

In the majority of instances, parasites tend to have an aggregated distribution (Fig. 5.2). At first, the non-random distribution of the

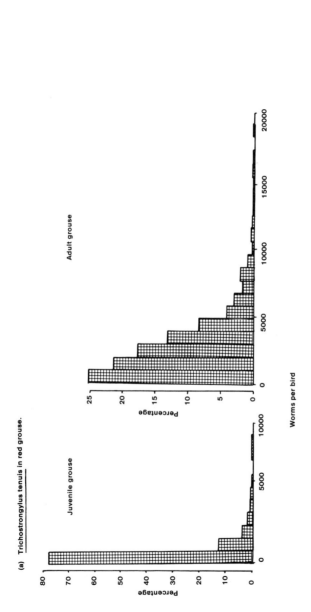

Fig 5.2 Two examples of aggregated frequency distributions of parasites: (a) the caecal nematode *Trichostrongylus tenuis* from red grouse, and (b) the sheep tick *Ixodes ricinus* on red grouse. Note that in the case of the nematode adults carry greater infections than juveniles while for the sheep tick, juveniles carry higher infestations. (*After* Hudson, 1986a.)

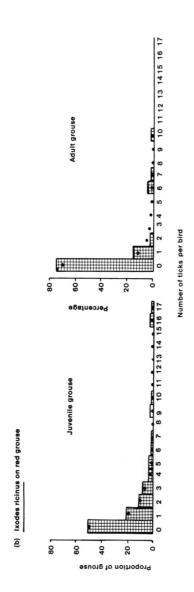

Fig. 5.2(b)

parasites through their host population may seem surprising. However, there are a large number of mechanisms that generate aggregated distributions; uneven distribution of infective stages, selective habitat use by the hosts, and variation in the immune response of individuals to the parasite will all tend to produce an aggregated distribution of parasite numbers per host (Anderson and Gordon, 1982).

The pattern of parasite distribution is unlikely to remain constant

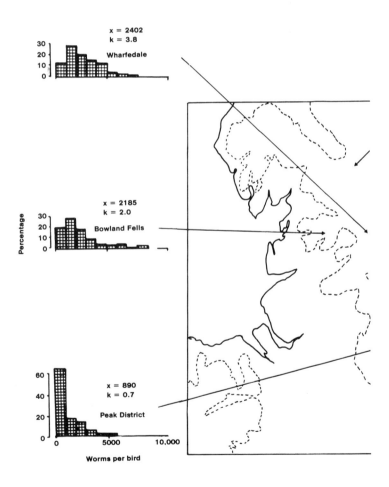

Fig 5.3   Changes in the frequency distribution of the caecal nematode *Trichostrongy-lus tenuis* in red grouse from various populations in northern England (after Hudson, 1986a). These reflect geographical variation in grouse density and rainfall.

since the various forces acting to produce an observed distribution will tend to alter both in time and space. For example, the variation in the distribution of the nematode *Trichostrongylus tenuis* in red grouse populations through northern England (Fig. 5.3) is a reflection of differences in the densities of grouse, rainfall and other factors influencing infection rate. Within a population there is also a tendency for the mean number of parasites per host to increase with the age of the host, which tends to change the distribution from an initially random one to an increasingly aggregated one (Fig. 5.4).

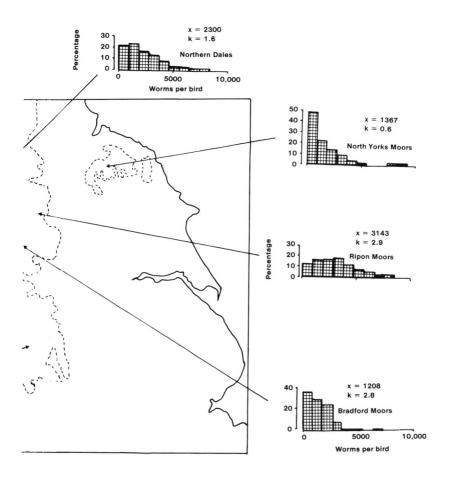

5.2.3 Transmission between hosts

A successful parasite is one that produces at least one offspring in its lifetime which infects another host, survives to maturity and subsequently produces its own offspring. This basic reproductive rate of parasites is often denoted by the symbol R. The object of many control programmes is to reduce the transmission rate and the value of R to less than 1 so the parasite population is reduced. In this respect, an understanding of the factors influencing the rate of transmission is essential for any management programme which aims to reduce parasite numbers.

Successful transmission depends on a number of factors. Above all, transmission is dependent on the availability of a susceptible host; the greater the density of these, the greater are the chances of success (see Section 5.2.4). Transmission also depends on the survival of the

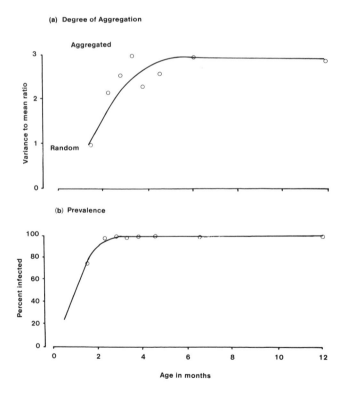

Fig. 5.4 Age-related changes in the pattern of distribution and prevalence of the caecal nematode *Trichostrongylus tenuis* in red grouse. (*After* Hudson, 1986a.)

infective stages and the rate at which these come into contact with the susceptible hosts. Since transmission is a critical part of the life-history of all parasites, it is perhaps not surprising to find that parasites exhibit a range of adaptations which prolong the period of infectivity and increase their chances of contacting a susceptible host. A number of parasites use an intermediate host in which they spend part of their life before reaching the definitive host and developing to maturity. These hosts often provide protection, act as a means of reaching the definitive host and in some instances enable the parasite to multiply, thereby increasing the chances of successful transmission.

Parasites sometimes take advantage of the behaviour of the intermediate host to assist transmission: for example, the malarial parasite takes advantage of the host-seeking behaviour of the mosquito to aid transmission to a suitable host. In other instances the parasite may alter the intermediate host's size, colour or behaviour to make it appear a vulnerable prey item to the definitive host and thus improve the chances of successful transmission. A tapeworm infection of wolves and dogs uses a herbivore such as moose, sheep and hare as an intermediate host. Within the sheep, the parasite invades the central nervous system and affects the animal's co-ordination, the sheep stagger about, become separated from the herd and fall easy prey. When the wolves eat the sheep they become infected by the parasite.

One well studied and interesting example (reviewed by Moore, 1984) is the effect of different species of thorny headed worms (*Acanthocephalans*) on the behaviour of their intermediate hosts, freshwater shrimps. Parasite transmission from the shrimp to the duck, the definitive host, is facilitated when the parasite causes the shrimps to swim to the surface of the water where they are eaten by dabbling ducks such as the mallard (Fig. 5.5). Another closely related parasite also infects the shrimps and causes them to move towards the light, but instead of moving all the way to the surface they stay in the mid-water where they are eaten by diving ducks such as scaup. Finally, a third species of parasite makes the infected shrimps move to the surface but causes them to dive when disturbed, making them vulnerable to both the dabbling and diving ducks.

5.2.4 Transmission rates, host density and time lags

In the simplest case, the rate of parasite transmission is directly related to host density. However, there is a minimum host density below which the value of R falls below one and the parasite reproduction fails to compensate for parasite mortality. This is usually termed the threshold for establishment. The actual host density at which this occurs varies from one parasite–host system to another. In general this threshold host density is low when parasites exhibit low pathogenicity, when the period of infection is long or when transmission efficiency is high.

Some host populations show large fluctuations in density; when at low density, it is possible that the parasites could become locally extinct. To avoid this the parasites exhibit a number of adaptations which keep infective stages viable for long periods of time, maintaining transmission efficiency and keeping the value of R above unity. This includes the production of a range of transmission stages, the utilisation of alternative hosts and the exploitation of infective agents: strategies which, in effect, produce transmission stages viable for long time periods and compensate for sudden and rapid changes in host density or even periods of total absence.

An interesting system which illustrates the point of transmission stages remaining viable for long time periods is the disease syngamiasis or gapes, a nematode infection of the respiratory system of gamebirds, common amongst reared pheasants. The parasite can be transmitted

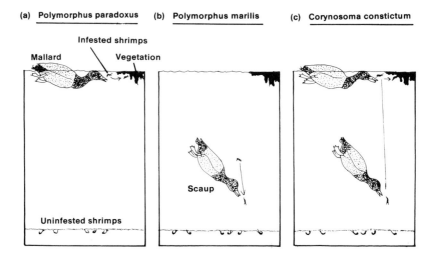

Fig. 5.5 The impact of three species of thorny-headed worms on the behaviour of their intermediate hosts, freshwater shrimps. Uninfested shrimps tend to avoid light and burrow deep into the mud at the bottom of the pond. Those infected with (a) *Polymorphus paradoxus* swim to the surface where they fall easy prey to their definitive host, the mallard. Those infected with (b) *P. marilis* swim in the mid-water and are eaten by scaup, while those infected with (c) *Corynosoma constictum* swim to the surface and dive, so are eaten by both species. When the shrimps are eaten by the ducks, the parasites mature and live in the intestines of the ducks. (*After* Moore, 1984.)

directly from one bird to the next as eggs or larvae and hence is easily transmitted at high densities. Removal of the hosts (e.g. from release pens) does not result in the local or immediate extinction of the parasite since the eggs of the parasite are eaten by earthworms where they can remain viable for several years before infecting a pheasant. Furthermore, the parasite utilises a number of alternative hosts such as starlings and rooks. Quite clearly the control of the parasite is difficult; earthworms take the egg stages deep into the soil, making treatment of the ground ineffectual, and the alternative hosts always provide an opportunity for reintroduction. The parasite succeeds with rapid transmission directly between individuals when their density is high, and is able to use the earthworm as a transport host and an insurance against periods of low host density.

Although macroparasites are usually considered host-specific, they are often capable of utilising alternative hosts and producing free-living stages which are fairly long-lived. This feature, in conjunction with the relatively long-lived adult stages and generally lower pathogenicity of macroparasites, makes their transmission threshold lower than that for microparasites. As such, we can expect to see macroparasites existing at much lower densities of hosts than microparasites.

Vectors, such as biting insects or ticks, can reduce the dependence of transmission rates on host density since in these cases the threshold density depends on the ratio of the densities of both the vector and definitive host. As an example, consider the sheep tick which transmits the louping-ill virus from sheep to grouse and ingests the virus during a blood meal on an infected host. The ticks' life cycle usually takes 3–4 years but may take up to 6, while still maintaining the disease in any short-term absence of hosts. Rapid changes in the host population will not greatly influence the success of the disease since its transmission is dependent not so much on the host density but on the rate at which the ticks bite. For ticks, the maximum could be twice a year (although once a year is more likely), making the biting rate of the ticks on infected hosts more significant than the abundance of the ticks.

The time lag between the production of transmission stages and the infection and subsequent effect of the parasite on the host can lead to cyclic fluctuations in numbers, such as those described in Section 2.3. Population cycles occur when the time delay is long compared to the response time of the host population. The length of the population cycles produced depends on the time lag, which in a directly transmitted nematode is a function of the life expectancy of the free-living stage in relation to the growth rate of the population (Dobson and Hudson, 1987). This delay in the density-dependent response of the population and the implications for population change have been discussed in detail in the ecological literature (see for example May, 1981; Begon *et al.*, 1986).

5.3 Direct and indirect effects of parasites

Quantifying the effects of parasites on their host is clearly important if we are to make decisions on the implementation of a costly control programme. Crofton (1971) proposed that an estimate of a parasite's lethal level, the number required to kill a host, was a possible starting

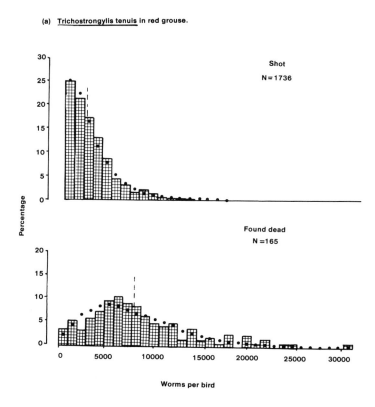

(a) **Trichostrongylis tenuis in red grouse.**

Fig. 5.6 The frequency distribution of parasites in a random sample (shot) of birds compared with hosts found dead and believed to have died as a result of the infection. The examples come from (a) red grouse infected with *T. tenuis* (after Hudson, 1986a) and (b) grey partridges infected with *Syngamus trachea* (after Potts, 1986). Birds dying of the infection naturally carry more parasites but comparing the two distributions allows one to estimate mortality rates within the population.

point. For many systems this is not realistic and so Anderson (1978) has suggested that a meaningful alternative is to measure the extent to which parasites suppress the growth rate of their host population. This includes both direct and indirect effects on the host's birth and death rate. Direct effects on the reduction of host survival or breeding production can appear obvious, but indirect effects on the vulnerability of infected individuals to predation and on competitive ability may also play a significant role.

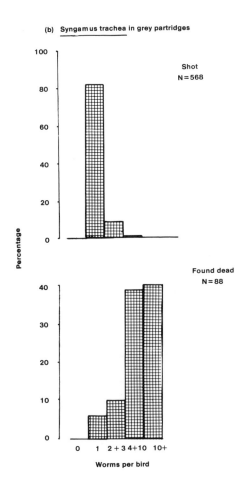

Fig. 5.6(b)

5.3.1 Direct effects on survival

The effect of macroparasites on host survival tends to increase directly with the number of parasites carried by the host. Determining what effect parasites have on the survival of their hosts is difficult in the wild and usually can only be determined under laboratory conditions. One indirect method of estimating mortality can be achieved by examining the parasite burdens of birds that have died from the infection with those in the wild population (Fig. 5.6). Anderson and May (1978) show that one way of quantifying these effects is to divide the natural growth rate of the host population by the mean parasite burden. In a system where the mean parasite burdens are high, the parasite is unlikely to be causing severe mortality, whereas a distribution with low mean parasite burden and a high proportion of hosts infected is indicative of a more pathogenic species. Even so, increased pathogenicity does not necessarily result in increased suppression of the host population; indeed, it can lead to the reverse (see Section 5.4).

The action of many parasites is influenced by a range of factors, not least of which is the nutritional state of the host. Parasites often compete directly for the host's food resources, so a host under nutritional strain is more likely to die from the effects of parasitism than a well fed host. Laboratory studies on a range of parasites have shown that parasites and poor nutrition have a synergistic effect; when the two act together the total effect is greater than it would be if the two acted independently. In a number of cases the parasite may actually cause the host to eat less. This type of anorexic response can obviously compound the problem, since the host, should be compensating for the parasite-induced loss of nutrients with an increase in food intake. Heavy parasite burdens coupled with protein deprivation can also lead to a reduced immunological response in the host, thereby improving the conditions for parasite survival and reproduction and magnifying the effects of the parasite. Such an effect was shown in a study on avian malaria: Brooke (1945) found that parasite burdens in pigeons fed on a poor diet grew faster than in those on a good diet since the poorly fed birds were unable to launch a strong immunological response.

The effect of poor nutrition and reduced immunological response of the host can be confounded further when competition between hosts for food increases with host density. With certain assumptions, Anderson (1979, 1981) has shown that an increasing pathogenicity of the parasite with host density produces two stable equilibria, one with high host density and low parasite burdens and the other with low host density and high parasite burdens. Disturbance from the equilibrium with high host density can result in a switch to the lower equilibria with high mortality and a crash in the host population. In some instances this crash can be initiated by active or inadvertent management techniques. In Missouri, wildfowl populations were managed intensively to produce high densities; during water pumping the birds became even more concentrated and in some instances this has led to nutritional stress and an outbreak of avian cholera (Petrides and Bryant, 1951; Vaught et al., 1967).

5.3.2 Direct effects on reproduction

Parasites can reduce the reproductive output of their host population either directly by reducing the survival of offspring or indirectly by reducing the condition of the mother and her ability to care for the offspring. A number of examples fall into the first category, one of the most interesting being the lungworm/pneumonia complex frequently recorded in sheep and deer.

The parasitic nematode that causes the disease lives inside the lungs of sheep and deer where it seems to cause little harm but becomes a problem when grazing density is high and the animals are under nutritional stress. In the bighorn sheep of North America, the parasite is considered one of the most important factors influencing changes in population size. In British Columbia, mortality rates of up to 95% have been recorded in some populations of bighorn sheep (Buechner, 1960; Price, 1980), and in 1941, large areas of the Banff National Park were cleared of sheep after an outbreak of the disease. The lungworm (*Protostrongylus stilesi* and *P. rushi*) itself may have little effect, but it predisposes the lungs of its host to bacterial and viral infections which can lead to pneumonia and death. The lambs of bighorn sheep are particularly susceptible to the disease when stressed, and since the parasite can be transmitted directly from the mother to the unborn lamb via the placenta (vertical transmission), prevalence and mortality can be very large.

In contrast to the direct effects of the lungworm/bacteria system, the nematode parasite *Trichostrongylus tenuis* of red grouse reduces the condition of the mother and her ability to produce and raise offspring. In a series of experiments, Hudson (1986a,b) demonstrated that reducing parasite burdens in hen grouse resulted in an increase in hen weight gain before incubation, in the number of eggs laid, in hatching success and in the subsequent survival of the chicks (Fig. 5.7). The efficacy of the treatment varied from year to year but was greatest in

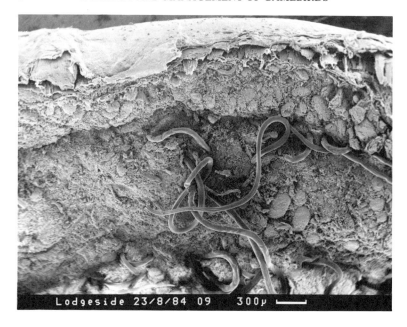

Plate 5.1   An electron micrograph of *T. tenuis* parasites burrowing into the caecal mucosa of red grouse (a). The parasites cause severe damage to the guts and reduce the condition (b) and productivity of female grouse.

years of high parasite burden, with a seven-fold improvement in overall production in one year.

5.3.3 Indirect effects of parasites on hosts

Since parasites generally reduce the condition of their host, it is reasonable to expect this to influence other aspects of their life. Individuals in poor condition may be more vulnerable to predators and less able to compete for resources such as food, territories and mates (see Sections 6.3 and 7.2). We have already seen how the effects of a parasite can be increased in malnourished hosts, but the reverse can also happen: the parasites can cause malnutrition by reducing the hosts' competitive ability and status.

Observations on red grouse (Jenkins *et al.*, 1963) found that grouse without territories had greater parasite burdens than grouse with territories. Infection rate is high before territorial aggression commences (Hudson, 1986a), suggesting that the effects of the parasite may be to reduce the condition and the ability of the cock grouse to successfully compete for a territory. Such an effect could preclude the grouse from the primary habitat, forcing them into areas where food quality is poor and so exacerbating the effects of the infection.

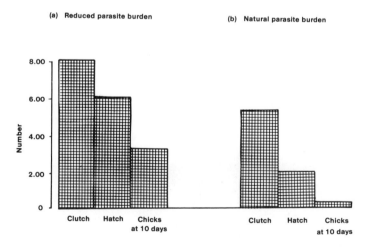

Fig. 5.7   The breeding production of hen red grouse with (a) experimentally reduced parasite burdens and (b) natural infections in 1983 (after Hudson, 1986a,b). The experiment demonstrated that parasite burdens of hens significantly reduced breeding production.

Reduced condition caused by parasites could also make the host slower, weaker and thus more vulnerable to predation. In one of the classic studies of predation Murie (1944) found that 26% of dall sheep

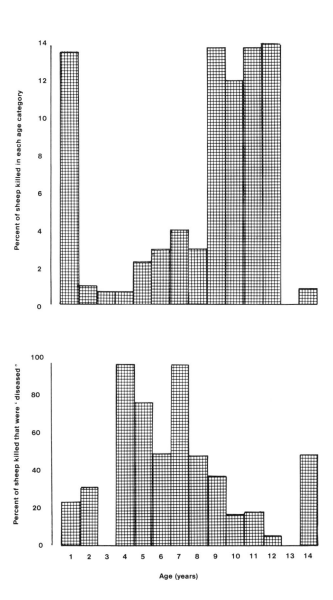

Fig. 5.8   The age distribution of dall sheep killed by predators at Mount McKinley Park (*after* Murrie, 1944). The predators tended to kill (a) a large proportion of the relatively weak young and old sheep whereas (b) the middle-aged sheep killed tended to be diseased.

killed by predators showed signs of severe infections of the jawbone. He suggested that the infection influenced the grazing efficiency of the animals, so reducing their condition and making them vulnerable to predation by wolves. Overall, the old and young sheep were caught by the wolves because they were probably slower and weaker (Fig. 5.8), while most of the breeding sheep (2–8 years old) caught were diseased.

A slightly different situation has been proposed for red grouse infected with the caecal nematode *T.tenuis*. Just prior to incubation hen grouse stop producing caecal faeces, which leads to a reduction in scent emission. This is presumably an adaptation to reduce the chances of being detected by a predator. By searching for incubating hens with trained dogs, Hudson (1986a) found that hens with reduced worm burdens were less likely to be found by scent than hens with natural infections. In this example the hens appear more vulnerable to predation not because of the debilitating effects of the nematodes but because of their interaction with physiological mechanisms.

Although parasites can predispose their hosts to predation, it is interesting to speculate how management techniques can influence the relative effects of predators and parasites. In the absence of predators, a proportion of infected individuals would die from parasites, although these losses are likely to be less than the combined effects of parasites and predators. In at least three instances, workers have proposed that by reducing predators the significance of parasites in the regulation of the host population has effectively increased (Kie *et al.*, 1979; Hudson, 1986a; Potts, 1986).

5.4 The theory of parasitism: the effects on the host population

The description of parasite biology together with a summary of their effects on individuals provides a reasonable insight into how parasites can operate, but it is not clear what the consequences are at the population level. One approach which improves understanding is to feed these features into a mathematical model and subsequently change certain aspects of the model to make predictions of when a parasite can regulate its host population and under what conditions the host population can escape these regulatory effects. The major assumption within these models is that we examine a simple system where predators, food quality and other competitors show no regulatory effects unless the parasite population is removed. At first glance this assumption is unrealistic, but since the objective is to obtain insights into the mechanisms of the host–parasite relationship, such simplifications help to clarify our understanding.

The following models which describe the dynamics of host–parasite populations were developed by Anderson and May (1978, 1979), May and Anderson (1978, 1979), and are based on the biological characteristics of the parasite–host relationship already described. This is a brief and simple review; more details on the mathematics involved and exceptions to the general patterns described are presented in the primary papers.

5.4.1 Macroparasites

Changes in the population of any animal can be considered as simply the sum of the additions from birth and the losses from death. In the host population there will be natural birth and death rates influenced by factors other than parasitism (e.g. predation, food availability), although in the system we are to consider the parasites alone will influence any changes in these rates. The population of parasites living within the host population will also be subject to certain birth and death rates influenced by the densities of both host and parasite populations. The parasites' birth rate consists of two components: the production of the transmission stages and the rate at which these infect the hosts. The parasites' death rate consists of three components: losses through the natural death of the parasite, losses through the natural death of the host, and losses caused by the parasite killing the host.

An example of the interaction of the two populations is summarised diagrammatically in Fig. 5.11, page 123. The important feature to note is that the dynamics of both populations are linked together, so any changes in the parasite population will have consequences for the host population and vice versa. Analysis of the model predicts that the parasite population will regulate the host population at a stable equilibrium. This means that any changes in either the host or parasite population will lead to the two populations returning to the equilibrium level. However, this stability will only exist if the birth rate of the parasite is large in comparison with the birth rate of the host; if it is small, then the host population grows faster than the parasite population and escapes the regulatory effects of the parasite.

The size of the equilibrium population is influenced by the distribution of the parasites within the host population and the pathogenicity of the parasite (the parasites' influence on host death rate). Parasites with a moderate pathogenic effect will tend to depress the size of the host population further than the relatively harmless or highly pathogenic parasites (Fig. 5.9). This may seem paradoxical until one considers that the death of a host leads to a fall not only in the number of hosts but also in the number of parasites and the rate of parasite transmission. When the pathogenicity of the parasite is moderate, parasite burdens tend to increase, leading to mortality and suppression of the host population. When pathogenicity is high, hosts tend to die with only small parasite burdens and consequently parasite transmission is low; this leads to a small parasite population and a relatively large host population. At the absolute extreme, highly pathogenic parasites kill their host almost immediately, transmission is very low, and the parasite population may fall to extinction with no suppression of the host population. When the objective of a management programme is to increase a population it is not necessarily the highly pathogenic species that must be controlled but more usually the parasites of moderate pathogenicity.

The extent of suppression of the host population also depends on the degree of parasite aggregation within the host population (Fig. 5.9). When parasites are highly aggregated a small proportion of the host population carries a large proportion of the parasites; any loss of the heavily infected hosts leads to a loss of a larger proportion of the parasite population. Overall, this results in relatively little effect on the

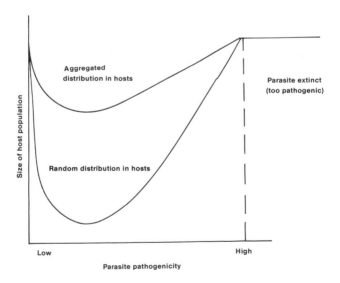

Fig. 5.9 The effect of macroparasite pathogenicity and pattern of distribution on the host population. Moderately pathogenic species and species distributed in a random fashion tend to reduce the size of the host population the most. (*After* Anderson, 1979.)

host population. Hence, when parasites are aggregated within the host population they have less effect on the host population than when the parasites are distributed at random.

5.4.2 Microparasites

The structure of the model for microparasites differs fundamentally from that described for macroparasites, since individuals within the host population are considered rather than the size of the parasite burden within the host. The host population consists of three basic categories depending on an individual's previous exposure to the parasite; hosts are considered susceptible before infection, infecteds after infection (during which period they are also infectious) and finally immune when they develop an immunity. As an epidemic moves through a host population the density of susceptible hosts is reduced as the infecteds become immune, so reducing transmission rates and the prevalence of infection.

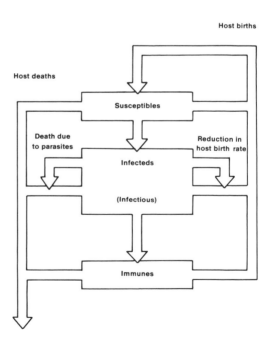

Fig. 5.10 A generalised representation of a host population infected with microparasites showing different host classes and the flow of hosts from one class to the next. Perpetuation of the disease within a host population requires a continual production of susceptibles either through birth or recovery from infection.

The basics of the model for the host–microparasite interaction are presented in Fig. 5.10. The model need not include all the features shown here; in some infections the parasite kills all the hosts so that immunity never develops, in others, immune hosts can become susceptible again. Analysis of these models shows that the parasite will only cause an epidemic when the density of susceptible hosts is sufficiently high. When transmission rate is so low that, on average, each infected individual fails to infect one susceptible ($R<1$) then the parasite will no longer persist in the population. If this rate is greater than 1, then the disease will spread through the population of susceptibles, eventually converting them all to infecteds and, those that survive, to immunes. In the absence of new susceptibles the disease will eventually die out. Perpetuation of the disease can only occur if hosts become susceptible once again or, as is more often the case, susceptible young individuals are added to the population. The probability of an infection becoming endemic depends on the size of the population and the recruitment rate of susceptibles.

Microparasites will regulate the growth of their host population only when the death rate of infected hosts is greater than their reproductive rate. If this condition is not satisfied, then the higher birth rate of the hosts will lead to an increase in the population until some other limiting factor checks its growth. The extent to which the parasite reduces the size of the host population depends on the pathogenicity of the parasite. As with the macroparasites, it is the moderately pathogenic diseases which regulate the host population rather than the highly pathogenic or the comparatively innocuous diseases.

5.5 An example of the influence of a parasite on a host population: the grouse–*Trichostrongylus tenuis* system

The basic epidemiological models summarised in the previous section provide a sound theoretical framework which can be applied to any parasite–host system to improve understanding and as an aid to developing an integrated and effective control programme. Workers that have applied the model have usually been studying human, livestock or laboratory parasite–host systems (e.g. Anderson, 1982a; Anderson and Crombie, 1985; Keymer, 1982, 1985; Wilson *et al.*, 1982). The few cases from natural animal populations include the fascinating study on the spread of rabies across Europe (Anderson, 1982c), tuberculosis in badgers (Anderson and Trewhella, 1986) and the role of the parasitic nematode *Trichostrongylus tenuis* in red grouse populations. We shall consider in detail only the gamebird system.

The parasitic nematode inhabits the blind-ending caecal sacs of the red grouse and has a direct life cycle with no intermediate hosts (Fig. 5.11). Infections occur in other gamebirds (Cram and Cuviellier, 1934), and Potts (1986) has suggested that it once played a significant role in the population dynamics of grey partridges. Since red grouse live on heather moorlands, not usually inhabited by other gamebirds, the system involves the red grouse as the only host.

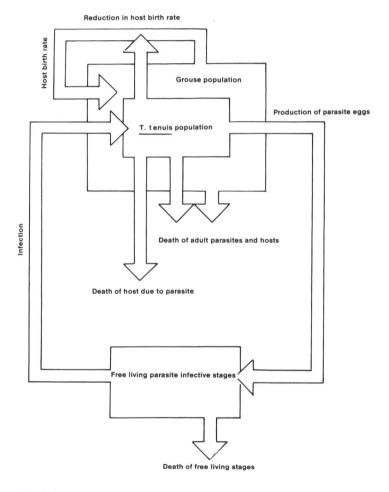

Fig. 5.11 Schematic representation of the life cycle of a macroparasite, in this instance *Trichostrongylus tenuis*, showing the interaction of the parasite and grouse population.

The life-history of the parasite and its interaction with the grouse were first studied in detail at the turn of the century (Lovat, 1911). Wilson (in Lovat, 1911), who conducted much of the work, believed the parasites caused the sharp fall in numbers in a straightforward density-dependent manner through their effect on host mortality. As the numbers of grouse increased so did the number of infective stages on the heather, leading to an increase in the level of infection until the parasites reduced the condition and survival of the grouse. However, Lord Lovat who edited the volume did not see the changes in grouse numbers simply as a host–parasite interaction; he felt that food quality was the factor that weakened the birds and predisposed them to infection. Unfortunately, Wilson was unable to comment or investigate this further since the report was published while he was in the Antarctic on Captain Scott's ill-fated journey to the South Pole. Further studies on the population biology of grouse between 1956 and 1961 in Glen Esk (Jenkins *et al.*, 1963) provided some evidence to support Lord Lovat's suggestion. They found a poor association between parasite burdens and condition between years and from observations concluded that the grouse that died with high worm burdens were surplus to the population, and it was the social position of the birds that predisposed them to heavy parasite burdens. Further investigations by another Wilson (1979) led Potts *et al.* (1984) to propose that the parasite could cause the cyclic changes in grouse bags recorded in the north of England through its effect on breeding production. Detailed epidemiological studies (Hudson *et al.*, 1985; Hudson, 1986a, b; Hudson and Dobson, 1988; Dobson and Hudson, 1987) have suggested that the parasite can cause the observed regular cycles in population density.

Certain aspects of the *T. tenuis*–red grouse system have already been described. As with many parasites the nematodes show an aggregated distribution (see Fig. 5.2), although the degree of aggregation is relatively low, partly as a consequence of the high parasite burdens. Production of the egg stages is dependent on the intensity of infection, with a general fall in egg production per worm with high worm burdens (Hudson, 1986a). The survival of free-living stages is dependent on wet conditions, and some initial studies indicate adult worm life expectancy is only a little less than that of adult grouse.

There is evidence to suppose that the parasites reduce both the survival and fecundity of the red grouse. The work of Jenkins *et al.* (1963) suggested that non-territory-holding males had higher parasite burdens than territory-holding males, indicating that the parasites may have some general effect on the birds' ability to hold territories.

However, as both Lovat (1911) and Jenkins *et al.* (1963) have suggested, the parasite induced mortalities were insignificant in causing the regular crashes. Hudson (1986a,b) examined the effects of parasites on the breeding production of wild hen grouse and demonstrated that the parasite had an effect on all indices of female reproduction (Fig. 5.7). According to the simulation model developed by Potts *et al.* (1984), these sub-lethal effects on fecundity are sufficient to cause regular crashes in grouse numbers.

Given the information about parasite distribution and the effects of the parasite on red grouse breeding success and survival, the system (Fig. 5.11) has been modelled (Hudson *et al.*, 1985; Dobson and Hudson, 1987) following Anderson and May (1979). Analysis of the model suggests that there are three important features influencing the system:

(1) The life expectancy of the free-living stages.
(2) The parasites' effects on grouse breeding.
(3) The parasites' effects on grouse survival.

When the the life expectancy of the free-living stage is long and the parasites' effect on grouse breeding production is greater than their effect on host survival, the model predicts that grouse numbers will cycle. However, these fluctuations can become unstable. When a term describing the limiting effects of territorial behaviour at high density is included the model produces stable limit cycles. The cycle length, or period, is mainly determined by the relative value of the life expectancy of the free-living stages of the parasite and the intrinsic growth rate of the grouse population. With the productivity seen in the north of England, the model produces cycles with a period of 4 to 5 years (4.8 recorded in England; see also Sections 2.3 and 9.2.2). When the growth rate of the population is low (perhaps because of low clutch size and chick survival) the cycle length is longer, a situation reflected in the 5–7-year cycles seen in Scottish populations. Decreases in the survival rate of the free-living stages also tend to increase cycle length, though very low values ultimately lead to the parasite being unable to sustain itself in the host population.

The model suggests two ways in which the effects of the parasite on the red grouse could be reduced by a control programme. Each of these seeks to reduce the size of a specific parameter in the host–parasite association: first in the life expectancy of the free-living stages and secondly the parasite burden within the population of hen grouse.

The free-living larvae are particularly susceptible to drying conditions, thus draining or reducing the humidity of the moors is one possibility. However, the efficacy of draining a moor to reduce humidity is likely to be limited. Many areas with rainfall above 1.3 metres per annum have a blanket covering of peat which tends to act like a sponge preventing any significant reduction in the level of the water table. On some moors which lie at the edge of a blanket-bog, drainage could convert them into the equivalent of freely drained heather moorland, and it is conceivable that this would reduce humidity and larval survival. However, drainage will also have other ecological consequences which may be disadvantageous to the grouse. Chemotherapy to reduce the mean worm burden is an alternative approach which has met with some success, and this is discussed in Section 5.7.1.

5.6 Parasites and the structure of ecological communities

The introduction or elimination of a parasite from a host population can influence the interaction of a wide range of species in the community. One of the most devastating examples of a parasite changing a whole community of animals occurred in Hawaii after avian malaria was introduced into the bird population and reduced the number of endemic bird species on the island by more than two-thirds (Van Riper, 1986).

In the Serengeti, changes in the incidence of the viral disease rinderpest have dramatically changed the structure of the community of wild herbivores living in the area (Sinclair, 1979, and summarised by Dobson and Hudson, 1986). The result has been a rapid increase in wildebeest and buffalo, followed by an increase in the lions and hyenas that prey on them. Any future changes in the incidence of vaccination and the spread of the disease could have serious repercussions on an important and spectacular wildlife resource.

One example from gamebirds provides an analogous situation to the virus infection in the Serengeti. Red grouse can become infected with the viral disease louping-ill when they are bitten by the sheep tick. On the North York Moors, there has been a steady fall in grouse numbers associated with a fall in the breeding production of grouse and an apparent increase in the incidence of louping-ill. The increase in the louping-ill is associated with a change in the competitive interaction between bracken and heather. The bracken vegetation produces a thick mat layer; this provides a good habitat for ticks and is currently replacing the heather food plant of the grouse. Since the bracken provides a better habitat than the heather for the ticks, it has been suggested that the spread of bracken has led to a spread of ticks and increased the incidence of louping-ill in grouse. Theoretically, the virus cannot be maintained by the grouse alone, and since sheep are the only other hosts which provides a viraemic response, a vaccination programme similar to that instigated against rinderpest could lead to the control of the disease and an improvement in the grouse population.

Clearly, the influence of parasites on the host population can have serious repercussions on the whole community and important implications for conservation and management.

5.7 The control of parasitic infections

The object of most control programmes is to reduce the deleterious effects of a parasitic agent below the point where it is causing financial loss or environmental damage. In epidemiological terms the object is to minimise the value of the basic reproductive rate (R). If this is kept below 1 the parasite population will be reduced.

The control of parasitic infections of man and his livestock often involves a programme of chemotherapy, vaccination or sanitation. In wild animal populations the application of sanitation techniques (e.g. removal of dung) or the direct treatment of individual animals is usually impractical. In such conditions the control programme tends to rely on indirect methods. This section reviews some of the principles and techniques of parasite control.

5.7.1 Chemotherapy

Chemotherapy is the application of a chemical to the host, often orally, which reduces the mean parasite burden. Such an approach is common in the control of macroparasite infections of humans and livestock, since it is both cheap and provides instant relief. However, such a control programme is only of short-term benefit, for all treated animals are immediately susceptible to reinfection. Long-term reduction of the average parasite burden will usually require continual treatment. The rate of reinfection and the frequency at which treatment must be repeated is dependent on R, in effect a measure of the force of reinfection to which treated individuals are exposed (Anderson, 1982a).

If the object of the control programme is to eradicate the parasite, the proportion of the population that will have to be treated per unit time is dependent on the value of R (Fig. 5.12). One of the problems in many epidemiological studies is to obtain a value for R, as this is likely to vary with environmental conditions. In the example of *T. tenuis* in red grouse, shown in Fig. 5.12, the estimated value lies between 5 and 10, indicating that if the object of chemotherapy was to eradicate *T. tenuis*, then just about every individual within the population would have to be treated. Such an objective is clearly impractical. A more realistic approach would be to reduce the parasite burden to an acceptable level determined by economical or environmental conditions. With the red grouse, an average burden of less than 2000 worms should make only a mild impact on the grouse population, although the proportion of the population that needs to be treated is dependent on the initial parasite burden (Fig. 5.13).

Part of any control programme should include the regular monitoring of parasite burdens. In this respect an interesting feature to note (Anderson, 1982a) is that whereas the parasite burdens fall exponentially with the increase in the proportion of the population treated, the prevalence of the parasite infection often remains quite high until the rate of treatment reaches the critical value for parasite eradication. That is to say, measures of parasite prevalence alone do not provide a good measure of the impact of control.

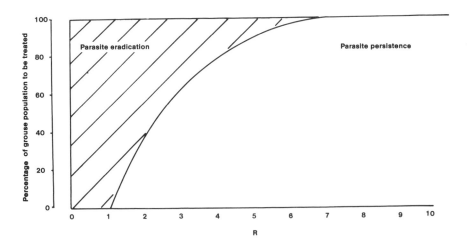

Fig. 5.12   The proportion of a host population that needs to be treated to eradicate a parasite with respect to R, the parasite's basic reproductive rate. This example is based on *T. tenuis* in red grouse, where R lies between 5 and 10; eradication of this parasite would require treating the whole population. (*Based* on Anderson, 1982a.)

These calculations also assume that all treated individuals are caught at random, but since the parasite is not distributed at random within the host population, a more efficient approach is to selectively treat only the most heavily infected individuals. The greater the degree of aggregation (i.e. the larger the value of k), the more efficient this method will be. In the grouse–*T. tenuis* system, the efficiency of treating the same number of individuals, but just the heavily infected individuals, increases the effects of chemotherapy by a factor of 4.

A common method of applying chemotherapy in reared and released gamebirds is to include the chemical in the birds' feed. For example, in the control of gapes in pheasants, an anthelmintic is often mixed with food and administered over a period of 14 days. Similarly, in the control of the lungworm in bighorn sheep the anthelmintic is mixed with fermented apple mash and fed to the wild sheep. The possibilities for indirect chemotherapy are wide and have not been investigated in detail. For gamebirds one possibility for the future could be to incorporate the chemical in a grit pill similar to the boluses used for control of gut parasites of cattle. These could be introduced into the gizzard of chicks, where they slowly release an anthelmintic which prevents infection.

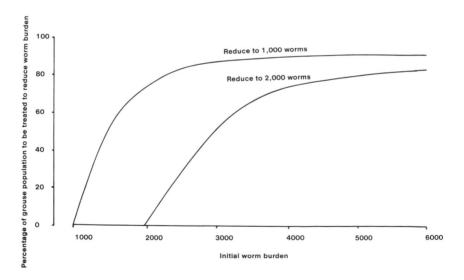

Fig. 5.13 The proportion of a grouse population that needs to be treated to reduce *T. tenuis* burdens to an acceptable level (R taken as 5).

5.7.2 Immunisation

Vaccines designed to immunise hosts against macroparasites have been investigated in detail within recent years but have met with limited success. One method currently being used is the introduction of irradiated (damaged) larvae into the host: these stimulate an immune response from the host and provide the host with protection against a natural challenge. Such a vaccine against gapes for poultry has been developed, although this has not widely been applied to gamebirds. Other successful vaccines include one against lungworm in cattle and another against hookworm in dogs.

For the microparasites, immunisation is currently the principal method of control. Once again the objective is to reduce the value of R to less than unity; when R is large, a large proportion of the population must be vaccinated to eradicate the disease (Fig. 5.14). Vaccination programmes along these lines have been used successfully in the control of a number of human diseases such as smallpox, measles and rubella.

The immunisation of wild animals is usually impossible since it involves the capture and treatment of individuals. In some instances, such as the control of rinderpest in the Serengeti and the control of louping-ill in grouse, the immunisation of livestock can lead to a significant reduction in the prevalence of disease in wildlife.

Vaccination has also been used in the control of the spread of rabies

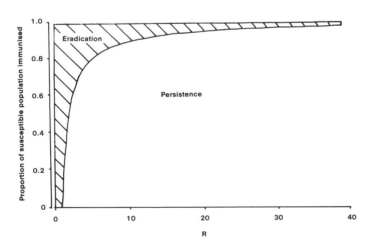

Fig. 5.14 The proportion of the susceptible host population that must be immunised to eradicate a microparasite infection with respect to R, the parasite's basic reproductive rate.

through the fox populations in Europe, an approach that has become particularly attractive since numerous other attempts to stop the spread of the disease through culling foxes have proved immensely difficult. The development of an oral vaccine which, when placed in a sausage bait and eaten by the fox, provides immunity, has been tested with varying degrees of success. Even at low fox densities vaccination is possible and in combination with a culling programme could prevent the spread of the disease. However, the degree of success does depend on the behaviour of the foxes, which changes with both density and food availability (MacDonald, 1980).

5.7.3 Environmental control and vector-borne diseases

The removal of transmission stages through environmental management is one of the most efficient ways of controlling parasites in the long term. In wild animals, such an approach is particularly effective when a vector is involved. As previously discussed, the value of R is dependent on the ratio of vectors to hosts, and reduction in the density of vectors would be an efficient way of reducing the incidence of the disease. Control of the vector is achieved through the removal of environmental conditions necessary for the vector's existence. Some of the best examples of this include the removal of areas of stagnant water in which mosquitoes (vectors of malaria) breed and the selective drainage of areas containing snails (intermediate host of the liver fluke). During studies on the control of disease in gamebirds, the sheep tick was found to be associated with areas of bracken (Hudson 1986c), the removal of which, through both chemical and physical means, leads to a fall in the tick population. In reality such approaches are effective although not always commercially viable without an integrated control programme involving a number of other techniques.

This is far from a comprehensive list of possible control methods for parasitic infections, and there are currently a wide range of exciting possibilities being developed to tackle the diversity of parasitic agents. The object of any control programme is to reduce the value of the parasite's basic reproductive rate, R. Success depends on the initial value of R, the greater this is, the greater the difficulty in controlling the parasite.

5.8 Conclusion

Parasites can be divided into two convenient categories: the microparasites (viruses and bacteria) and the macroparasites (worms and ticks). Although the population ecology of each type is fundamentally different, they are both capable of reducing the growth rate of the host population in a density-dependent manner and thus regulating its size. Observations supported by experimental work show that parasites can directly reduce the condition, survival and reproductive output of game species while indirect effects can lead to reduced competitive ability of the host and vulnerability to predators.

The development of a broad theoretical framework for the dynamics of parasitic agents and their host population has allowed a clearer understanding of how parasites act and how effective control measures should operate. Parasites which are moderately pathogenic and spread randomly through the host population suppress the size of the host population more than relatively harmless or highly pathogenic species. In the management of a game species, it is these moderately pathogenic species that often require efficient control programmes. Even so, in many systems there is a lack of information on certain parameters, in particular the factors influencing transmission between hosts. Transmission is a critical part of the life-history of all parasites. Many show elaborate adaptations to increase the efficiency of transmission, while effective control often requires a reduction in transmission rate.

Traditionally, parasite control includes sanitation, chemotherapy or vaccination; such direct techniques are often impractical in the management of a wild species, and alternative methods need to be developed. Overall, it would seem that the management techniques used in game management often reduce the effects of predation but, by increasing host density, increase the significance of parasites; as such, parasite control should be considered an important aspect of management.

6 Habitat Quality and Gamebird Population Ecology

Michael R. W. Rands

6.1 Introduction

An animal's habitat may be defined as the set of environmental characteristics or resources upon which it depends for its survival. These include the food supplies of both adults and young, a suitable site for breeding, and some form of protection against predators and inclement weather. Variation in the quantity of these specific resources determines the quality of the habitat.

To understand how resource variation affects the population size of any animal, it is necessary to examine the relationships between habitat quality and the processes which alter survival and reproductive output of individuals within that population. The objective of this chapter is to illustrate how habitat quality can influence population processes in gamebirds, and then to show how an understanding of these interactions can be used in the management of gamebird populations.

I have chosen to concentrate on the two most intensively studied gamebird species in Britain, namely the red grouse and the grey partridge (which represent upland and lowland gamebirds respectively). The approach adopted in the study of each species has been quite different. The early observation that red grouse populations showed large fluctuations in numbers (Lovat, 1911) eventually led to investigations of the behavioural and other mechanisms which limit populations and can cause changes in numbers (see Moss and Watson, 1985; Hudson, 1986a). By contrast, the study of the grey partridge stemmed from the concern over its decline as a major quarry species; this prompted a long-term investigation of the effects of modern agriculture, predation and game management on the species' population ecology (see Potts, 1986). Thus ecological studies of the red grouse were designed to answer theoretical questions relating to population regulation, whereas our knowledge of the ecology of the grey partridge has its origins in the practical problem of how to halt the species' decline.

Ultimately, the information collected on both species can be used as a basis upon which management practices can be built for the conservation of game. The examples discussed below will not only demonstrate this, but will also show that a scientific basis for the management of animal populations has much to offer the wider field of wildlife conservation.

6.2 Habitat quality and population processess

Birth and death are ultimately the only processes responsible for limiting population size in birds (Lack, 1954, 1966). However, significant changes in the size of local populations may be brought about by changes in the rates of immigration, emigration, recruitment (entering a breeding population, whether by remaining in the natal area or by immigration from elsewhere), and by variation in spacing behaviour (Begon *et al.*, 1986). The roles and relative importance of these various population processes in the regulation of bird populations have been widely discussed and argued (see Taylor and Taylor, 1977; Lomnicki, 1982; Moss and Watson, 1985), but it is now generally accepted that they all play some part in determining the abundance of a species within a given area. At the most basic level, variation in any one of these population processes is often caused by variation in habitat quality. For example, birth rates may be lower where food supplies are of a lower quality, and adult mortality is often higher (whether through increased starvation, predation or parasitism) where environmental resources are less suitable. Similarly, emigration behaviour may be linked to resource availability, the 'choice' to emigrate or not being in this case based on the quality of the surrounding habitat at the time.

The resources required by a bird from its environment include food, nesting cover and a safe refuge. There is much evidence to support the supposition that the population processes of birth, death, immigration and emigration are largely determined in predatory and insectivorous birds by variation in food availability (the quality of the feeding habitat) (e.g. for raptors see Newton, 1979). Much of this evidence has come from close correlations between bird densities and food supplies, based on long-term field studies (see Newton, 1980), which provide a strong indication that food may be locally limiting. More definitive evidence comes from the experimental manipulation of food quality, which has been shown to change reproductive output, emigration rates and spacing behaviour in red grouse (see Section 6.3).

Food is not, however, the only resource for which birds have been shown to compete: safe refuges and nesting cover can also be limiting. A shortage of nest sites has been shown, for instance, to limit local breeding densities in several hole-nesting species (e.g. Perrins, 1979) and seabirds (e.g. Potts *et al.*, 1980). With species that have less easily recognisable nesting requirements, the shortage of suitable nest sites is more difficult to establish and has often been assumed to be unimportant. For example, it was not realised until recently that variation in nesting cover quality significantly affects grey partridge recruitment rates, breeding densities and levels of nest predation (see Section 6.3).

The remainder of this chapter comprises two major sections. The first examines the ecological relationships between habitat quality and population processes in gamebirds by considering how the production of young, breeding density and nest predation are influenced by variation in the quality of food and nesting cover. The second section illustrates how, by understanding the ecological interactions, feeding habitat and nesting habitat can be managed in order to increase gamebird numbers.

6.3 Effects of habitat quality on gamebird numbers

6.3.1 Production of young

The number of offspring that an individual female, once mated, can produce in a breeding season is determined by three parameters: the number of eggs laid (clutch size), the number of those eggs that hatch (hatching success), and the number of chicks that survive to maturity (chick survival). In turn, each of these parameters depends on a number of ecological and/or environmental factors. For example, clutch size may be related to maternal condition and age; hatching success may vary with egg fertility, embryo survival through incubation, and clutch survival (i.e. avoiding predation); and chick survival may depend on food availability, parental care, weather and predation. These parameters can be further influenced by particular nesting strategies such as multiple brooding, egg dumping and repeat nesting (after the first nest is lost). Many of these factors are directly related to characteristics of the available habitat, while others, such as a bird's age, are not necessarily related and therefore cannot be easily manipulated. The special case of nest predation, which can affect the mortality of both adults and young, is discussed in Section 6.3.

RED GROUSE

Evidence of the relationship between productivity and habitat quality, via the effects of food quality, comes from a long-term study of the red grouse in Scotland. This bird feeds mainly on heather, and selects preferentially those heather shoots that are rich in nitrogen and phosphorus (Moss, 1972; Lance, 1983) by choosing particular heights, ages and parts of the plant (Moss *et al.*, 1972; Savory, 1978; Hewson, 1976). Correlative evidence suggested that grouse populations on moorland overlying basic rocks (i.e. rocks such as limestone, that readily break down to provide nutrient-rich soils) tend to produce consistently more young birds than populations on moorland overlying acid bedrock or peat (Jenkins *et al.*, 1967; Picozzi, 1968; Moss, 1969). In a study of the breeding success of red grouse, Miller *et al.* (1966) found that the number of young raised was positively correlated with the amount of new heather growth in the summer of the previous year. This prompted a series of experiments comparing brood sizes on fertilised and control (unfertilised) plots of heather moorland in Scotland (Miller *et al.*, 1970; Watson *et al.*, 1977; Watson *et al.*, 1984) and Ireland (Watson and O'Hare, 1979).

For the first of these experiments, an area of 32 ha of uniform heather moorland was divided into two roughly equal sized plots. Since grouse remain territorial for most of the winter and spring (Watson and Jenkins, 1968), movement between plots was expected to be minimal. Ammonium nitrate fertiliser was applied to the experimental plot in spring; and over the summer, grouse were removed from both experimental and control plots to eliminate the possibility of previous experience influencing the results. Grouse then colonised both plots. Subsequently, heather shoots from the fertilised plot contained significantly more nitrogen than shoots from the control (unfertilised) plot and the heather growth (shoot length) on the fertilised plot was also significantly greater. Breeding density in the year after treatment was equal on both plots, suggesting that the territory size chosen by immigrants was unrelated to heather growth. However, the number of young birds produced per adult by August of that year was much greater on the fertilised area (1.8:1) than on the control plot (0.6:1). Furthermore, grouse chicks hatched later on the unfertilised plots (Miller *et al.*, 1970). Thus, by temporarily increasing the growth and nutrient quality of the heather, the production of young grouse was significantly increased. This result supports the correlation between breeding success and the amount of heather growth in the summer of the previous year (Miller *et al.*, 1966) and is consistent with the 'indirect nutrition hypothesis' (Watson and Moss,

1972). This hypothesis suggests that the nutritional condition of a female grouse determines the quality of her eggs and the viability of her chicks. Thus, in the experiment described above, it was concluded that the fertilisation of the heather increased food quality for laying hens on the experimental plot and they consequently produced larger broods than hens that fed on the unfertilised plots during egg laying.

To test further the indirect nutrition hypothesis, a series of additional experiments (Watson *et al.*, 1977, 1984) were carried out, in which plots were fertilised after egg laying. This failed to increase brood size later that summer, indicating that the improvement in food quality came too late to improve the nutrition of laying hens. In later years, and during a similar experiment conducted in Ireland (Watson and O'Hare, 1979), brood sizes again increased on fertilised plots. This provides further evidence that while fertilisation does not improve chick survival *per se* in the first year, it does increase the production of young in subsequent years by improving maternal nutrition.

As an alternative to the indirect nutrition hypothesis, the 'direct nutrition hypothesis' predicts that autumn densities are determined by adult nutrition in summer, so that well fed birds take small autumn territories and poorly fed birds take large ones (Watson and Moss, 1972). Since the latter hypothesis does not require habitat quality to affect the production of young red grouse, but implies that variation in food resources directly determines adult densities, evidence to support it is discussed in Section 6.3.2.

While the results of the moorland experiments are informative, and further reference to them will be made throughout this chapter, they must be interpreted with caution. For example, the plots were of practical necessity too small to entirely exclude the possibility that grouse moved into them following the treatment. In their most recent account summarising all their food enrichment experiments, Watson *et al.* (1984) state that more immigration occurred on fertilised plots than on controls, suggesting that movement into treated plots does indeed occur; this could potentially explain the observed differences in brood size. A further problem is that fertilising heather moorland does change factors other than the quality of adult food supplies. For instance, in two of the experiments carried out in Scotland, heather shoot length was increased by the addition of nitrates, leading to increased cover and shelter for the birds and a greater build-up of litter (Watson *et al.*, 1984). In the long term, the enrichment may also have increased insect abundance and hence the survival of grouse chicks (which, like many other gamebird chicks, feed on insects during their first 1–2 weeks of life: Savory, 1977), although this was clearly not a direct effect in the year of fertilisation. Finally, several attempts to repeat this type of experiment have not brought about the changes predicted. Such failures can almost always be explained by differences in the timing of treatment, exceptional field conditions or unexpected changes in other population or habitat variables, but the actual reasons for these failures are rarely fully understood. Thus, while the experimental manipulation of heather moorland provides invaluable insights into the ecology of red grouse, it cannot yet yield guaranteed prescriptions for grouse management.

Another gamebird in which food selection by breeding females has been investigated in Scotland is the ptarmigan. Gardarsson and Moss (1970) showed that this species, like the red grouse, grazes selectively for the most nutritious foods. Furthermore, Moss (1968) found that birds eating better foods laid larger clutches: again suggesting that one of the factors responsible for productivity is related to the quality of the feeding habitat of the female.

PARTRIDGES

In contrast to the red grouse and the ptarmigan, the factors affecting the productivity of lowland gamebirds (the grey partridge, red-legged partridge and pheasant) appear to operate mainly after the eggs have hatched. Southwood (1967), for instance, concluded that pre-hatching conditions did not materially affect subsequent chick mortality in the grey partridge. However, there is now a wealth of evidence that chick mortality during the first three weeks of life is the major cause of fluctuations in the production of young grey partridges (Potts, 1986), and this may also be true of the pheasant (Hill, 1985).

Studies of the diet, movement and survival of grey partridge chicks and correlations between grey partridge chick survival and a wide range of habitat characteristics have led ecologists to conclude that the chick survival of grey partridges, pheasants and, to a lesser extent, red-legged partridges depends upon the quality of the chicks' foraging habitat (i.e. the abundance of their preferred insect foods).

In an intensive investigation of grey partridges, Green (1984) located females and their chicks (which remain with the hen throughout early life) by attaching a small radio transmitter to the females' backs just before their eggs hatched. Using this technique, Green showed that partridge broods preferred to forage for insects in the outer edges of cereal fields, where arthropods and weeds were most abundant. By locating and marking the roosts of broods at night, he also obtained (on the following day) droppings from both adults and chicks. Analysis of these enabled him to confirm that the chicks fed almost exclusively on insects (which are rich in protein) for the first 1–2 weeks, before gradually turning to a herbivorous diet. Once the chicks were able to fly (at about three weeks of age), repeated flushing of the known broods revealed how many chicks had survived. Furthermore, using these techniques both Green (1984) and Rands (1986a) were able to show that broods with the highest chick mortality were those that had moved farthest in order to obtain food, suggesting that the quality of the chicks' foraging habitat determined their survival.

Surveys of chick survival and arthropod abundance on different farms in East Anglia (Green, 1984) and Sussex (Potts, 1980, 1986) revealed that the survival of grey partridge chicks increased with increasing densities of certain preferred insects, and in a multiple regression analysis Potts (1986) was able to explain 58% of the observed variation in grey partridge chick mortality by two factors:

(1) The density of preferred insects per m^2 of cereals during the week of peak partridge hatch (which accounted for 48%).
(2) The mean daily temperature during the chicks' first three weeks of life (which accounted for the remaining 10%).

These correlative studies further support the hypothesis that variations in chick mortality are caused by variations in the chicks' food resources.

In order to test experimentally the relationship between the survival of chicks and the quality of their foraging habitat, a series of field trials were carried out on 11 km^2 of an arable farm in north-east Hampshire (Rands, 1985, 1986a). On extensive areas of arable land, densities of preferred prey for partridge chicks were reduced by the use in cereals of various pesticides (see Section 1.4.1), both by direct killing and by the removal of the insects' host plants or fungal food supplies (Potts and Vickerman, 1974; Vickerman, 1974; Sotherton, 1982; Potts, 1986). For the purposes of the experiment, 37 of the farm's cereal fields were divided up into six trial plots in 1983, each of three gamekeepers' beats having two plots. Around the edge of every field in one plot of each beat, a six-metre strip was left unsprayed with pesticides from 1 January while the remainder of each field was fully sprayed. In the other plot of each beat, the entire area of each field was sprayed in accordance with normal farming practice. The boundaries between sprayed and unsprayed treatments were chosen to coincide with natural barriers to grey partridge movement, such as woods and shelter-belts, so as to minimise the likelihood of broods moving between plots. In 1984, the treatment of each plot was reversed so that fields with unsprayed edges in 1983 were fully sprayed in 1984 and vice versa (see Rands, 1985, 1986a, for further details of the experimental design).

This experiment significantly increased chick food supplies (Table 6.1). The mean brood size of grey partridges on unsprayed experimental plots was significantly higher (6.4) than that on the fully sprayed control plots (2.1) in 1983 (Fig. 6.1). A similar result was obtained when the treatments were reversed in the following year: mean brood size was 10.0 on unsprayed plots and 7.5 on sprayed plots (Fig. 6.1). During the experiments in 1984, a small number of grey partridge broods were radio-tracked on both experimental and control plots: their survival, movements and home range characteristics are shown in Table 6.2. It is clear that broods with access to unsprayed field edges moved less far, tended to have smaller home ranges, and survived better, than broods in fully sprayed plots of fields.

Additional experimental manipulation of chick food supplies on over 20 farms throughout Britain in 1984, 1985 and 1986 have shown that the conclusions of the above study are widely applicable, i.e. that

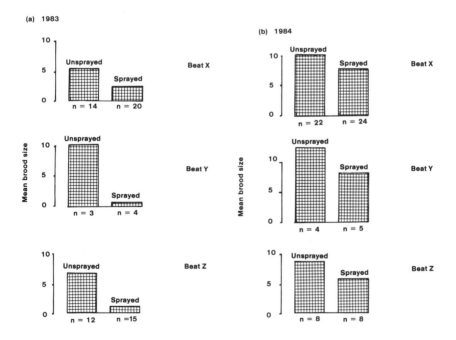

Fig. 6.1 Grey partridge brood sizes on sprayed and unsprayed treatments in (a) 1983 and (b) 1984.

Table 6.1   A comparison of the abundance of grey partridge chick foods in sprayed and unsprayed field edges, as sampled with a sweep net (after Rands, 1985).

Prey species	Mean number per 50 sweeps		
	Sprayed area	*Unsprayed area*	*Statistical significance (P)*
Plant bugs	53.9	163.2	<0.02
Sawfly and lepidoptera larvae	3.4	5.0	<0.09
Leaf beetles and weevils	4.2	12.3	<0.05
Total prey	62.2	180.0	<0.001

the productivity of grey partridge populations can be increased by increasing the amount of food available to chicks (Rands and Sotherton, 1987). This has also been demonstrated for the pheasant (Rands, 1986a).

Variation in reproductive output from one year to the next is strikingly large in gamebirds (see, for example, Chapter 2). The evidence presented so far suggests that significant variation in the productivity of red grouse occurs in response to variation in the quality of food available to the females that will produce the young. Thus in this species, and perhaps the ptarmigan, maternal nutrition may limit productivity through its influence on egg quality or clutch size. While adult condition may determine these parameters in all gamebirds, there is as yet no evidence that maternal nutrition limits the productivity of lowland gamebirds in the wild. Rather, the number of young that survive in these species is largely a function of the quality of

Table 6.2   A comparison of the survival, movement and home range size of radio-tagged grey partridge broods in fields with sprayed or unsprayed areas (after Rands, 1986a).

	Sprayed	*Unsprayed*	*Statistical significance (P)*
Survival to 21 days (%)	59.7	97.7	<0.05
Distance between successive roost sites (m)	102.3	43.5	<0.05
Home range size (ha)	2.1	0.8	<0.10

their feeding habitat immediately after hatching: the availability of insects seems to be the principal limiting factor in the lowland arable environment.

6.3.2 Breeding density

Gamebirds exhibit a wide range of social systems (see Chapter 7). The nature of these systems affects the spacing behaviour of individuals, which is itself often related to the quality of resources available. Spacing behaviour and the factors influencing breeding density have been studied in a number of gamebirds, most notably the red grouse.

RED GROUSE

Male red grouse take up their territories in autumn and it was initially postulated (Jenkins et al., 1963) that changes in breeding populations from one year to the next on a given area were related to heather growth during the summer. This became known as the 'direct nutrition hypothesis' (Watson and Moss, 1972). Since red grouse are selective feeders, it has been argued that their breeding density is limited by the amount of good quality food readily available to them (Moss, 1969). This is supported by the work of Lovat (1911) and Miller et al. (1966), who found that by burning old heather to bring about regeneration, red grouse numbers could be increased. The latter workers obtained high correlations between red grouse densities in the spring and the amount of heather cover and age of heather on 15 study areas. In a very different habitat of mountain vegetation in Norway, dominated by *Betula nana* and *Vaccinium myrtillus*, Phillips et al. (1984) also recorded a significant increase (when compared to controls) in willow grouse density between 1979 and 1983 on plots where 15% of the area was burnt, although the data are insufficient to suggest any causal mechanism for this increase.

To investigate these relationships experimentally, Miller et al. (1970) burnt patches of heather on one plot of moorland between 1961 and 1965. Changes in grouse numbers were recorded and compared with changes on a control (unburnt) plot of similar moorland 2.5 km away. Grouse densities on the unburnt plot remained roughly constant at 44–57 birds per km^2 throughout the experimental period (1962–1968). On the burnt plot densities were 49–51 birds per km^2 from 1962 to 1964, but then rose to 78 in 1965 and remained at this level until 1968 when they dropped back to 51 birds per km^2. There were no differences in breeding success on burnt and unburnt treatments, and the increase in density on the experimental area was not preceded by a large increase in the production of young birds. Burning does not alter the productivity of heather plants, but young shoots are more nutritious than old ones. Thus, the observed increase in breeding density after burning appeared in this case to have been due to an improvement in food quality for adults, which resulted in increased immigration or survival of breeding birds. This conclusion is supported by the association between high average grouse densities and a fine-grained patchwork of burnt areas, reported by Picozzi (1968), and by one fertiliser experiment (Watson *et al.*, 1977) in which grouse breeding densities increased directly after improvement of their heather food. However, heather burning, like the addition of fertiliser, does alter the moorland habitat for grouse in many other ways, and may improve the

Plate 6.1 Habitat management can influence habitat quantity and quality. Grouse feed on heather and the quality of the growing shoots varies with age. By burning areas (a) in a patchwork pattern feeding and nesting areas can be produced. Both grey and red-legged partridges nest in hedgerows (b) but the frequency of hedge trimming affects the likelihood of a hedge being chosen as a nest site and the chances of avoiding predation.

Plate 6.1 (b)

vegetation structure (e.g. by increasing the amount of 'edge' between burnt and unburnt heather swards) for nesting hens, foraging young or territorial defence by cocks. These possibilities have yet to be examined in detail.

Leaving aside the direct within-year effect of feeding habitat quality on breeding density, there is also an indirect effect: improved maternal nutrition leads (as we have seen) to greater production of young, which results in higher breeding densities in subsequent years. This is demonstrated by the increased number of territories in the experimental plots of the moorland fertilisation experiments as compared with the control plots (Fig. 6.2).

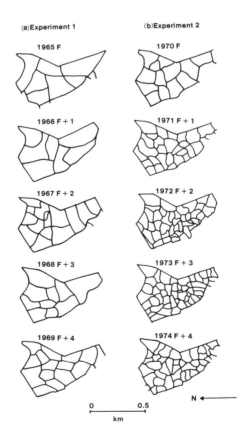

Fig. 6.2 Changes in the number of red grouse territories following experimental fertilisation of plots of heather moorland. For (a), the left half of the plot was fertilised; for (b), the right half of the plot was fertilised. (*After* Watson *et al.*, 1984.)

Quality of feeding habitat may therefore affect red grouse in two ways: firstly by improving the summer diet of adults who consequently take smaller autumn territories, allowing more birds to inhabit an area of moorland (the direct nutrition hypothesis); and secondly, by increasing the production of young that subsequently enter the breeding population of that area and so raise the density (the indirect nutrition hypothesis).

PARTRIDGES

For partridges and pheasants, farm modernisation, including increased mechanisation and pesticide use, have resulted in dramatic habitat changes. One such change is the reduction in the amount of grain and weed seed available to adults. Surprisingly, Potts (1980, 1986) could find no evidence that these changes in food supply have affected either the weight of adult grey partridges in autumn or their mortality rates.

Studies of grey and red-legged partridges have suggested that both species prefer to feed on arable farmland, and that high breeding densities are associated with more cover in early spring (Jenkins, 1961; Blank et al., 1967; Green, 1984). To examine how variation in arable cropping, and hence feeding habitat, affect the breeding density and recruitment of young partridges into subsequent breeding populations, Rands (1982, 1987a) compared variation in cropping with partridge breeding density on 10 farms and with recruitment on 17 farms. No significant correlations were found between breeding density or recruitment and any of the variables chosen to describe feeding habitat, suggesting that adult food supply did not influence the number of grey or red-legged partridges breeding within an area.

Although there are no data to show that partridge breeding density will increase in direct response to an improvement in adult feeding habitat, breeding densities can be raised by increasing the production of young. In the red grouse, high productivity led to higher subsequent breeding density; similarly, in the grey partridge, Rands and Sotherton (1987) found that by experimentally improving the habitat quality for chicks on cereal farmland, the resulting greater productivity led to higher breeding densities. The breeding density before and after the improvement of chick habitat is shown in Fig. 6.3.

Food, whether it be for adults or young, is only one of the aspects of habitat that may vary in quality. Another is nesting cover. For the red grouse there is no evidence that variation in the quality of nesting habitat influences breeding density; for the partridges the situation is rather different.

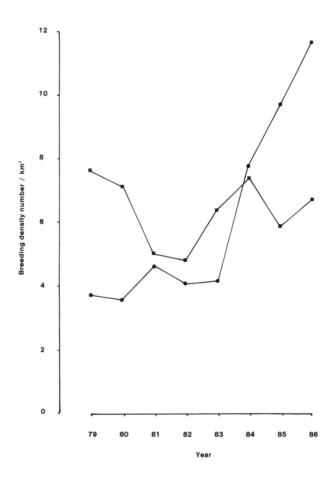

Fig. 6.3   Grey partridge spring breeding densities on a study farm where field edges were left unsprayed from January 1983 onwards (●), and on 27 kms² of fully sprayed arable farmland in the region (■).

Both species of partridge in Britain nest predominantly at the bottom of hedges and in other types of permanent field boundary; Blank *et al.* (1967) suggested that certain types of hedgerow provided better nesting habitat than others for grey partridges. A number of studies have found close correlations between partridge breeding densities, or rates of recruitment, and the amount of nesting habitat available (see Rands, 1982, or Potts, 1986, for a review). Furthermore, Green (1983) was able to show, with an individually marked population of birds, that the proportion of male red-legged partridges remaining to breed within an area reflected the abundance of suitable nesting habitat.

To examine the relationship between partridge densities and nesting habitat quality in some detail, Rands (1986b, 1987a) carried out a survey of the structure and vegetation characteristics of all permanent nesting cover on 10 farms in Britain (1266 field boundaries in all). The variation in habitat characteristics was then related to within-farm variation in spring breeding densities of grey and red-legged partridges. Using multiple regression analysis it was possible to show which aspects of habitat quality were correlated with breeding density, once variation in the total amount of nesting cover had been accounted for. It was found that the amount of dead grass in the hedge bottom was closely correlated with grey partridge breeding density and, together with length of nesting cover, explained between 47% and 94% of the variation observed in density (Rands, 1986b). A similar relationship was found for the red-legged partridge except that the amount of nettle (and not dead grass) present in the hedge bottom was correlated with breeding density; this explained between 48% and 99% of the variation when combined with length of nesting habitat. Dead grass and nettle are the preferred nesting vegetation for grey and red-legged partridges respectively (Rands, 1982, 1988; Blank, 1969), and the correlations strongly suggest that these aspects of nesting habitat quality determine, in part, the breeding densities of partridges.

Further support for this comes from a study of the factors affecting the recruitment of young grey and red-legged partridges into future breeding populations (Rands, 1987b). An analysis of long-term population data showed that the density of first-year birds recruited into a farm's partridge breeding stock increased with the density of young birds available for recruitment, but decreased with the density of adult birds. However, the relationship between recruitment and adult density differed significantly between farms and was used as an index of the attractiveness of a particular area to settlers, termed 'recruitment efficiency'. Differences in recruitment efficiency were found to be related to variation in the quantity and quality of nesting habitat. For the red-legged partridge, as in the case of breeding density, the amount of nettle present at the base of the nesting cover was the habitat quality characteristic found to explain the most variation in recruitment efficiency. Grey partridge recruitment efficiency was related to two aspects of habitat quality: the amount of dead grass in the hedge bottom and the height of the earth bank at the base of the hedge – both characteristics known to be selected by nesting birds.

In conclusion, habitat quality clearly plays an important, if complex, role in determining the breeding densities of gamebirds. For some species, the quality of adult food supply probably has a direct influence on breeding density. In addition, improving productivity in both the red grouse and the grey partridge (by improving food quality for pre-breeding adults or for chicks) can result in increased densities in the following year. For species such as grey and red-legged partridges, nesting habitat quality also clearly has an effect on breeding density.

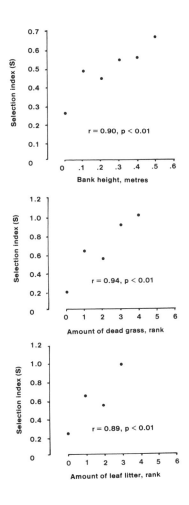

Fig. 6.4   Grey partridge nest site selection in relation to bank height, amount of dead grass and leaf litter available.

6.3.3 Nest predation

The importance of predation in the population dynamics of verte-brates is controversial, but is probably more significant in ground-nesting birds than other bird species. Predation is considered in detail in Chapter 4 but in this section I will briefly review the evidence that nest site quality may influence the level of predation directly.

During a detailed study of the breeding ecology of red-legged and grey partridges in north-west Norfolk, nests were located and visited at roughly seven-day intervals until they hatched or were lost through predation or desertion (Green, 1981). Using these data, Green calculated the daily nest losses due to predation for both species of partridge and found that red-legged partridge nests were three times more likely to be taken by predators than grey partridge nests prior to incubation. This was thought to be because grey partridge conceal their eggs with vegetation during this period, and because the onset of incubation is often delayed in red-legged partridges due to double nesting (Green, 1981).

In 1981, a study of the habitat characteristics of some of these partridge nests, plus others found in Norfolk and Wiltshire, was carried out to identify the criteria used by partridges when selecting nest sites and to examine the effects of this nest site selection on nest predation (Rands, 1982, 1988). By comparing partridge nests with randomly chosen control sites, it was established that grey partridges were choosing to nest where the amounts of residual dead grass in the nesting cover were greatest (Fig. 6.4). Furthermore, it was shown that the rate of nest predation was lower for nests where there was more residual dead grass (Fig. 6.5). This suggests that the habitat quality of the nest site determines nesting success and that the birds choose to nest where their eggs are less likely to be lost to predators.

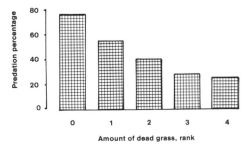

Fig. 6.5 Grey partridge nest predation in relation to the ranked estimate of dead grass around the nest site.

The same study showed that red-legged partridges nested where amounts of dead grass, nettle, bramble and leaf litter were greater than in surrounding nesting cover; but these aspects of habitat quality, although apparently selected, did not influence the rate of nest predation (Rands, 1982, 1988). Red-legged partridge nests were, however, less likely to be lost to predators as the ground vegetation height around the nest increased (Fig. 6.6).

The structure of habitat used by capercaillie for nesting was studied by Jones (1984) in Scotland and by Storaas and Wegge (1985) in Norway. By comparing nest sites with randomly chosen control sites, Jones concluded that nesting capercaillie selected certain habitat characteristics: they chose to nest amongst less dense stands of trees, closer to tree trunks, in more concealed sites with dead branches as cover, and amongst dwarf shrub vegetation, especially heather. However, he did not investigate the relationships, if any, between this choice and nest predation. Storaas and Wegge (1985) also found that capercaillie (and black grouse) preferred to nest in certain habitat types, although they were unable to identify particular site characteristics that were selected. In this study, nest losses in both species were

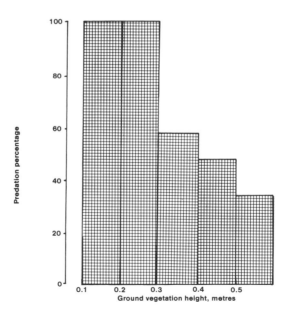

Fig. 6.6 Red-legged partridge nest predation in relation to the ground vegetation height at the nest site.

not correlated with habitat type, density of forest around the nest or nesting cover.

Red grouse have been shown to prefer mature, as opposed to pioneer or recently burnt heather as a nesting habitat (Jenkins *et al.*, 1963; Hudson, *in litt.*) and nesting success has been found to be very high where predators were controlled (Jenkins *et al.*, 1963; Hudson, 1986a). Nesting success has not been examined in relation to habitat quality.

The relationships between predation and habitat quality so far described have been concerned with the quality of nesting habitat and the consequences of this for predation. An indirect way in which habitat quality may reduce nest losses is through increased vigilance on the part of an incubating bird. For example, Watson *et al.* (1984) postulate that adults feeding on high quality food spend more time being vigilant and are better able to avoid predation of their eggs and chicks than adults with access to relatively poor food (unfertilised areas). While further studies are required, it is not unreasonable to suggest that well-fed birds will be more attentive to their eggs and chicks, and better able to defend them from predators.

Ground-nesting birds are particularly vulnerable to predation during egg laying and incubation, and the choice of where to nest may affect both the adults' chances of survival and their breeding success. The evidence reviewed above suggests that variation in the quality of nesting habitat can and will influence the likelihood of nest predation in some species of gamebird. The impact of nesting habitat quality on rates of nest predation may vary between species and areas, depending on the overall amount of nesting habitat available and on the diversity and abundance of predators. Thus for partridges, the loss of potential nest sites resulting from hedgerow removal may have increased the value of nest site quality, whereas for the red grouse nesting cover is still plentiful and there is no evidence to suggest that nest site selection is based on habitat quality or that habitat quality influences nest predation. However, with the current increases in many predator populations, in both upland and lowland environments (Tapper *in prep.*), good quality nesting habitat may in the future become more important for the survival of gamebird populations.

6.4 The management of habitat quality for gamebirds

In British gamebirds, the relationships between habitat quality and population processes – especially the production of young, recruitment into breeding populations and mortality during nesting – suggest that habitat may be manipulated to increase local populations. Some of the potential management options are obviously not feasible at present. Nevertheless, it is interesting to consider, from the ecological studies discussed in the previous section, how habitat management might benefit gamebirds and what the consequences of this might be for other species of wildlife.

6.4.1 Food supplies

The abundance and quality of food supplies can clearly sometimes limit gamebird numbers. For example, the experimental improvement of foraging habitat for lowland gamebird chicks not only increased insect abundance and chick survival, but also raised subsequent grey partridge breeding densities. These experiments provide the basis for a management technique that could significantly increase grey partridge populations and potentially benefit a wide range of other farmland wildlife.

The experiments show that by improving the quality of chick foraging habitat, by leaving the outer six metres (about 6% of the total cropped area) of cereal fields unsprayed with pesticides (herbicides, fungicides and insecticides), grey partridge and pheasant chick survival can be significantly increased. The technique is effective because the reduced use of pesticides increases the density of broad-leaved weeds that act as host plants (food supplies) for a range of cereal-dwelling arthropods; the increased abundance of these arthropods provides more food for gamebird chicks and consequently more chicks survive.

The feasibility of leaving such unsprayed edges around fields, from a farming point of view, is still being investigated. Preliminary results suggest that overall cereal yields are not substantially reduced (Rands *et al.*, 1985; Boatman, 1986). Weed seed contamination of the grain, weed ingress from adjacent field boundaries, and the 'inconvenience factor' (mainly harvesting difficulties and the need to store contaminated grain separately) may all be more of a problem. But continuing research aims to refine the design and management of unsprayed (conservation) headlands, for example by allowing limited pesticide use, in order to maximise the benefits to game and other farmland wildlife while minimising the inconvenience to the farmer.

These experiments, and the principles underlying them, also show how habitat management for game can benefit other, non-game, species. For example, a significantly greater number of adult butterflies were observed over unsprayed field margins compared to sprayed ones during the original experiments (Rands and Sotherton, 1986). Similar differences in butterfly abundance have now been reported in 1985 and 1986 (J. Dover, pers. comm.), as well as a difference in the behaviour of butterflies when encountering the two habitat types. In addition, the plants found within unsprayed areas are known not only to be host plants to cereal-dwelling arthropods, but are also used by some species of butterflies as egg-laying sites. The effects of this on butterfly populations are still being studied.

The benefits of this form of management to the arable flora in Britain have also yet to be fully assessed, but a recent survey of unsprayed headlands has already recorded 15 out of the 25 rare arable weeds considered by the Botanical Society of the British Isles to be threatened by modern farming (N. Sotherton, pers. comm.). A similar technique is widely practised on arable farmland in the Federal Republic of Germany for the benefit of rare arable flowers (Schumacher, 1980, 1981): here, 3-metre field margins are left unsprayed with herbicides in spring, a practice for which farmers are financially compensated by the government (see Potts, 1986, for further details).

Although much emphasis has been placed on the possible advantages of improving adult feeding habitat for the benefit of red grouse, work on the diet of red grouse chicks has shown that they too feed on insects during the first ten days of life (Savory, 1977) and cannot survive on a diet of heather shoots alone (Hudson, 1986a). While pesticides are rarely used on heather moorland, insect abundance there is far from uniform. Hudson (1986a) showed that within a few days of hatching red grouse broods had often moved long distances from their nest sites, apparently in search of 'bog flushes' (damp areas rich in insect life). Such habitat can be in short supply, especially on freely drained heather moorland in the north of England. Artificial bog flushes are currently being experimented with in the North Yorkshire Moors, where spring water is run into man-made ponds filled with limestone chippings to provide nutrients (Hudson, 1986a). The benefits of this are currently being assessed, and initial results indicate a three-fold increase in insect production (D. Newborn, *in litt.*). Drainage is a traditional aspect of moorland management, used to improve heather growth; but since it reduces tipulid abundance in May and June on blanket bog (Coulson and Butterfield, 1982), extensive use in some areas could reduce the survival of grouse chicks.

The management of habitat quality for red grouse may also affect productivity by affecting adult condition just prior to egg laying. The experimental manipulation of heather moorland carried out to demonstrate the ecological relationships between habitat and population processes yields some possible habitat management recommendations. The application of ammonium nitrate fertiliser to heather moorland increased the production of young red grouse in the two years following its application, by improving maternal nutrition and consequently brood sizes. This increased productivity led to subsequent increases in breeding density. Clearly, the fertilisation of heather moorland, especially where it overlies base poor rocks such as granite, is a management technique that could be adopted for grouse moors, although it is not currently very practical or financially viable (Watson *et al.*, 1977). Hudson (1986a) also suggests that heather burning may improve red grouse feeding habitat on the richer and freely drained moorlands of northern England. However, it must be remembered that improvement of food quality will not always prevent a decline in grouse stocks because there are other factors, such as predators (Chapter 4) and parasites (Chapter 5), which may also influence changes in population density.

6.4.2 Nesting habitat

For those bird species with very specific nest site requirements, like hole-nesters or even cliff-nesting seabirds, there is evidence that the quality of particular sites can affect both breeding densities and nesting success. Studies of partridge, capercaillie and black grouse nesting requirements (Section 6.3) have shown that these ground-nesting species are also quite specific nest site selectors and that this selection may have, at least for some species, consequences for their survival.

For the grey partridge, it was shown that the recruitment of young grey partridges was greatest, breeding densities were highest and that hens chose to nest in areas where amounts of residual dead grass at the base of the hedgerow were greatest. Nest sites where there was more dead grass were less likely to be lost to predators. Given this information, the question that must be answered by the game manager is: how is it possible to improve the nesting habitat quality? In this particular case, how can the amounts of residual dead grass at the base of the field boundaries be increased? To answer this question, Rands (1987a) compared the management of field boundaries with their habitat characteristics. The study showed that the amounts of dead grass, and other characteristics preferred by grey partridges, were greatest in hedges trimmed every other year. Furthermore, it was found that, of the 1266 field boundaries measured, only 12.4% were managed in this way – compared to 24.6% cut annually and 37.2% not cut at all. Thus, a relatively simple change in the frequency of hedgerow management might dramatically improve the quality of nesting habitat for the grey partridge, by reducing predation of both nesting hens and eggs.

While emphasis has been placed on the two lowland species, for which the total amount of nesting cover has been dramatically reduced by the removal of many hedgerows, some upland gamebirds have also been shown to select good quality nest sites. Both capercaillie and black grouse have been found to nest where certain habitat characteristics were most abundant, and Jones (1984) and Storaas and Wegge (1985) put forward tentative recommendations for the improvement of nesting habitat quality to encourage these species.

Unfortunately, these nesting habitat management techniques require further testing before managers can apply the recommended criteria to increase gamebird populations. An experimental approach is required to test whether the hedgerow management practices suggested by Rands (1987a) for grey partridges would be effective. Detailed studies of the relationship between habitat quality and predator behaviour and prey selection are also needed. Such studies should attempt to evaluate habitat management in relation to the requirements of predator control (see Section 4.7).

To sum up, it is now possible to suggest how the quality of both nesting habitat and feeding habitat can be manipulated in such a way as to enhance the attractiveness of an area to a particular species of gamebird and further increase its breeding success. However, there are always limits to such management. Habitat improvement will only be beneficial where habitat quality is limiting; and once improvement has taken place, numbers will only rise to the point at which some other (possibly unknown or unmanageable) factor limits the population.

6.5 Conclusion

This chapter has explored the relationships between habitat quality and some of the major processes governing gamebird population dynamics. For some species the production of young, emigration, recruitment, and certain types of mortality are all influenced to varying degrees by changes in habitat quality.

Unlike many ecological factors, habitat quality is one that can be manipulated by man. For this reason ecologists have conducted experiments to test the effects of altering the supply of resources upon gamebird populations. For both red grouse and grey partridge, this has been exceptionally valuable not only in furthering our understanding of ecological principles but also in suggesting methods of habitat management for the conservation of these species, even though it may not yet be feasible to apply these methods on a large scale.

Most resource manipulation experiments have involved the food supply of either adults or young, and have led to an increase in the productivity of the population and a subsequent increase in population density. The long-term consequences of these changes in food supply have yet to be fully investigated, but there is no doubt that the techniques are available, in principle, to increase populations in a particular place and at a particular time.

The evidence that aspects of habitat other than food supply are important comes less from experimental manipulation and more from correlative studies. Nonetheless, there are good reasons for believing that gamebird populations are affected by variation in the quality of nesting habitat, and possibly by other even more subtle characteristics of habitat.

I hope that this chapter has demonstrated the value of gathering insights into the relationships between habitat and population processes – both so as to increase our ecological understanding of the environment in which we live, and in order to manage and conserve populations of organisms upon which we may depend.

7 Gamebird Mating Systems

Mark I. Avery and Matt W. Ridley

7.1 Introduction

Gamebird mating and social systems take a variety of forms. Our aim in this chapter is to describe that range and give some outline explanations for these behaviours. In attempting to explain why different species behave in different ways we need evolutionary explanations; why have different species evolved different mating systems? The appropriate level for explaining why birds behave in the way they do is in terms of the advantage to the individual (Darwin, 1859; Dawkins, 1976) since it is individuals that succeed or fail to pass on their genes to the next generation. This creates a problem for us in relating this chapter to management since the methods and perspectives of evolutionary biologists are not those of the game manager. Whereas a keeper will be interested in the productivity of the population, the evolutionary biologist will seek to determine factors influencing the reproductive success of individuals. The evolutionary biologist is interested in the natural situation while the keeper's job is to tip the natural balance towards the interests of his game and away from predators and disease. We therefore feel that the link between the subject of this chapter and management is more tenuous than that for predator control (Chapter 4), parasite control (Chapter 5) or habitat improvement (Chapter 6) and so have avoided making any extravagant claims in that direction. The social system determines the constraints inside which management can operate but the underlying system is not usually a feature which can be manipulated.

In this chapter we describe the broad determinants of avian mating systems and how these apply to gamebirds, and conclude with a brief discussion of how social behaviour and management may interact.

7.2. The ecology of mating systems

7.2.1 The evolution of mating systems

Internal fertilisation in birds creates an asymmetry in the relationship between the sexes. Females are committed to parental care until at least the point in time when they finish laying their clutch. For males, once insemination has occurred, there is no immediate commitment; males can leave their mates 'holding the baby' while they seek other mating opportunities. There are few examples of avian species where sole responsibility for parental care is handed over to the male after the completion of the clutch; this does not occur in any of the gamebirds (Lack, 1968) although red-legged partridges have an unusual system in which each parent may incubate a separate clutch of eggs.

The factors which determine whether or not male parental care will evolve are those which affect the reproductive success of males who do provide paternal care compared with those who do not. Most birds produce helpless young which require feeding for the first few weeks of their life (nidicolous young). Under these circumstances a male maximises his reproductive success by pairing monogamously and helping to feed his offspring rather than by seeking to form multiple pair bonds. However, it is becoming clear that in many monogamous species, copulations outside of the pair bond do occur (McKinney *et al.*, 1984; Ford, 1983; Mock, 1983). Where males are territorial and resources are distributed unevenly then some males may control sufficient resources to support two or more families and polygamy can evolve (Orians, 1969). However, the scope for multiple mating by males is greatest where the young leave the nest soon after hatching and feed themselves (nidifugous young). Under these circumstances parental care is limited to brooding, guiding the young to feeding sites, vigilance and defence from predators, so the presence of two parents need not be twice as effective as a single parent but on the other hand could be much greater than twice as effective. This allows males to pursue polygamous strategies by reducing the length of the pair bond and becoming sequential polygamists or simultaneously pairing with many females. Although all gamebirds have nidifugous young there is still a broad range of mating systems, varying from almost no male investment and extreme sequential polygamy (black grouse), through simultaneous polygamy (pheasant), to monogamy involving each partner incubating a separate nest (red-legged partridge). This range of mating systems is reflected in the different territorial systems exhibited by different species.

7.2.2 Territoriality

One way in which dominance can be expressed is in the occupation and defence of a territory. Territoriality is a special form of dominance in which rank depends on the convention of local ownership. The effect is to space out populations of animals. However, the resource held by successful dominant birds (e.g. food, breeding habitat, mating sites etc.) varies considerably between species and this variation is reflected in the many different forms that territories can take. They vary in size from not much larger than the occupying animal to the whole of the animal's home range; the vigour with which they are defended varies from mutual avoidance to fierce exclusion; and the season of occupation can vary from a matter of days to the whole year.

Most species of gamebird show some form of territoriality at some times of the year, but there are as many forms as there are species and this diversity is instructive; it reveals some of the factors affecting reproductive success in the various species. Black grouse territories are extremely small (and smaller in dominant than in subordinate birds) and occupied only during the breeding season, while red grouse territories are much larger and occupied throughout most of the winter as well as the beginning of the breeding season. Grey partridge territories are loosely defined, overlapping extensively and based not on defence but on mutual avoidance between pairs (Jenkins, 1961). Male pheasants vigorously exclude other males from their territories, though only during the breeding season, while females are not territorial among themselves and for much of the season ignore male territories.

Under a narrow definition of territoriality, ('defended areas'), most partridges do not qualify as territorial birds at all. Under wider definitions ('spacing out', see Davies, 1978), though, they are territorial and their behaviour during the breeding season undoubtedly results in a spacing out of breeding pairs that probably has some function. Only the two species found in Britain, the grey partridge and the red-legged partridge, have been studied in any detail, but both appear to have similar patterns of territoriality (Jenkins, 1961; Green, 1983), and it is likely that many of the other species of partridge (*Perdicinae*) and new-world quail (*Odontophorinae*) adopt a similar pattern (Ridley, 1983). The more solitary and colourful forest-dwelling partridges of South-east Asia, such as the roulroul may be exceptions.

In grey and red-legged partridges in Britain, the winter coveys (flocks based around the previous year's broods) break up during early February and new pairs are formed by young birds from different coveys. The resulting pairs settle down in a home range smaller than that of the covey, but nonetheless larger than the average pheasant territory: red-legged partridge breeding home ranges in East Anglia averaged about 10 hectares in the study by Green (1983). The pairs avoid each other, but their ranges may nonetheless overlap substantially. More overlap was tolerated when the two males in question had been in the same covey in the previous winter.

From what is known it is not clear that partridges even weakly defend their food supply from the attention of neighbours. Green (1983) found that there was proportionately more aggression between

Plate 7.1   Gamebirds display a wide variety of mating systems and social behaviours. Male pheasants vigorously advertise that they are territory holders during the breeding season.

male red-legged partridges in areas with poor nesting habitat, although the partridges may not have been defending any absolute quantity of nesting habitat. Jenkins (1961) found that grey partridges sometimes nest outside the area they occupied during the early breeding season. It would seem that spacing itself is advantageous: behaviour that spreads nests evenly over the landscape probably reduces the chances of nests being taken by foxes and other predators (Potts, 1980, 1986).

Pheasant territories are very different. The following description is based on Taber (1949), Burger (1966), Lachlan and Bray (1976), Goransson (1980) and Ridley (1983). Territories are established at the beginning of the breeding season, usually in March, though a few yearling males may start to defend areas as late as April. Unlike partridge and red grouse territories, they are entirely the concerns of males until the formation of harems in April and May. Feeding flocks of females move through male territories ignoring boundaries. The great majority of pheasant territories consist of a patch of open ground (i.e. with vegetation too short to conceal a pheasant) adjacent to cover. Most are on woodland-field boundaries, though woodland clearings and hedgerows can also provide suitable sites. At the cover edge, the boundary between two territories is sharply defined; away from the edge it is not. Territory size varies with population density, but two hectares is typical for dense British and American populations. Many yearling males remain non-territorial throughout the breeding season.

During April, territory-owning males acquire harems of females, which they guard against harassment by neighbouring and non-territorial males. When in the open, harem members generally confine their activities to their mate's territory, but when in cover they may move outside his territory. Their nest sites are not only outside his territory, they are also outside the females' normal home ranges. This rules out the premise that pheasant territories are defended areas of suitable nesting habitat. Since females are not mutually intolerant – indeed they remain gregarious throughout the early breeding season – it seems unlikely that territories are areas where males defend food supplies for groups of breeding females. One important clue to the function of pheasant territories is that the age of the male is a better predictor of his harem size than the extent of his territory (Goransson, 1980; Ridley, 1983). Thus the pheasant territory seems to be a device by which a dominant male, in exchange for mating access, guarantees a group of females vigilant protection on a suitable feeding area, where they are dangerously conspicuous both to predators and to other males. It is a protection racket.

Red grouse territories are different again. As a result of extensive studies in north-east Scotland, red grouse territorial behaviour and its influence on population dynamics is among the best known features of bird behaviour (Jenkins *et al.*, 1963; Watson, 1967, Watson and Moss, 1970; Watson *et al.*, 1984; Moss and Watson, 1985). In autumn, males compete for territories on heather moorland. Successful males pair with females, while old males that lose their territories and young males that fail to win territories stay in packs and suffer a high mortality rate. Each territory is usually between 1 and 12 hectares in size (Bergerud *et al.*, 1985), occupied by a single pair of birds and defended throughout most of the winter when snow cover is sparse and during mating and incubation. Territories are evenly distributed over heather moorland and usually fill the available habitat. High grouse density both compresses territory size and excludes surplus birds from territories altogether.

Although red grouse eat less than 10% of the food available in their territories (Savory, 1978), they selectively eat the shoots rich in nitrogen and phosphorous (Moss, 1972; Savory, 1983). It seems likely that food quality is a limiting factor (see Section 6.3) and the function of territory defence might be to protect a good food supply for the female to obtain sufficient nutrients for egg production. Other functions, such as the spacing out of nests to reduce predation pressure may also be important, and the territory is often not used to rear the brood (Hudson, 1986a).

The red grouse is a subspecies of the widespread willow ptarmigan. Other races of the willow ptarmigan live in areas that are usually snow-covered throughout winter and do not depend, as red grouse do, on a single species of plant for food. These two factors are associated with a different pattern of territoriality. Willow ptarmigan may defend territories briefly in the autumn but the main period of territory defence does not begin until spring: there is no defence during winter, at which time the birds live in flocks that are partly segregated by sex (Weeden, 1964). Not only does the snow protect their food from drying winds but it also requires territory owners to abandon their snow covered territories in search of food. This pattern is very similar to that shown by rock ptarmigan. Male ptarmigan in the Cairngorms begin to defend their territories in late February or later if snow cover persists (Watson, 1965).

The habit of defending a territory during the autumn and then returning to it in the spring is characteristic of those species of grouse that lek, most notably the black grouse. Territoriality in black grouse is complicated. Kruijt *et al.* (1972) concluded that the whole range of black grouse on their study area near Fochteloo in Holland was divided up by male black grouse into territories, but that there was a very uneven distribution of males. Some males held large territories and displayed in them alone, but most were clustered around traditional arenas (leks), where a few central males held small 'courts' entirely surrounded by other larger territories held by marginal males. However, unlike red grouse and pheasants, male black grouse do not remain within their territories, but visit them each day for varying lengths of time. An intruding male is tolerated on a territory unless the intruder displays (de Vos, 1983). This suggests that the function of territory defence in black grouse is to monopolise display sites rather than to defend a food supply or nesting habitat. This is supported by the discovery that after a male has managed to display to a female on another male's territory for some time he often makes a successful challenge for that area of territory. Experiments in which wild males were exposed to either caged females or caged males clearly demonstrated that non-territorial males established territories where they had previously courted females and where they found groups of other males (de Vos, 1983). In lekking species, central males with their small territories (about 100 m^2 in Holland) perform the most matings. They often co-ordinate their activities so as to be on the arena at the same time: a fully occupied arena seems to attract more females (de Vos, 1979). The function of black grouse territories seems to be purely ceremonial, in the sense that no resource is defended within them. Instead they seem to be badges of rank: a senior male will have a central court on the lek and will attract more females.

In capercaillie and other forest-dwelling grouse, and probably also in many of the forest-dwelling pheasants (see Davison, 1981a; Ridley, 1983), males also defend courts in the breeding season, though these tend to be more spread out and larger. In blue grouse, males display in groups (like black grouse) when in open habitats and solitarily (like some capercaillie) when in dense cover (Hoffmann, 1956; Blackford, 1958, 1963). This seems to imply that territory size is compressed in such promiscuous species in open habitats.

7.2.3 Polygamy

Polygamy has been defined in a number of ways but is considered here simply as any mating relationship which is not monogamous. Most birds are monogamous while most mammals are polygamous. The reason for this difference probably lies in the fact that most mammals rear their young inside the female's body and on her milk, a process that a male cannot directly assist. There is consequently less evolutionary pressure on males to remain with one mate and on females to choose attentive mates. Most birds rear their young in nests on animal food; a male can make as great a contribution to brooding eggs and feeding young as a female. Male birds are required to assist females in the care of offspring, reducing the opportunities for males in particular to be polygynous.

But there are exceptions, and a disproportionate number of them are gamebirds. Of 63 genera in the family *Phasianidae* (which includes grouse), 19 probably include regular polygamists (Ridley, 1983). In part, these are exceptions that prove the rule. Since gamebirds do not feed their young, there is less that males can do to help their mates rear their young than in other birds, so one would expect polygamy to be more common. But this cannot be the whole explanation: most monogamous gamebirds do not feed their young either.

The gamebirds provide an interesting test case of theories to explain the circumstances under which polygamy is adaptive. For example, polygamous mating systems have been linked with particular habitat structures (Verner and Willson, 1966; Haartman, 1969), maturation patterns (Wiley, 1974) or food supplies (Crook, 1964; Lack, 1968; Jarman, 1974; Wittenberger, 1978). There are two ways in which birds can be polygamous: simultaneously or sequentially (Emlen and Oring, 1977). In simultaneous polygamy, a female chooses a male as a mate that already has one or more mates. This pattern is most common among polygamous passerine birds (Oring, 1982). In sequential polygamy, the duration of each pair bond is short and males can therefore mate with several females during one breeding season. This pattern is more common among gamebirds.

Most partridges are monogamous, including grey partridge and red-legged partridge. So are the tundra-dwelling ptarmigan including red grouse, although the rock ptarmigan and occasionally the red grouse attract two or more females to breed in their territories, especially at high densities and in Arctic populations. Hannon (1983) recorded that 6% of male willow ptarmigan had two females; Martin and Cooke (1987) studied bi-parental care in willow ptarmigan and found no overall difference in breeding or survival between widowed and paired birds. Most pheasants and other species of grouse are polygamous. This is reflected in the greater sexual dimorphism in size and colour that such species show.

Only the pheasant is simultaneously polygamous. Each male consorts with a harem of females that lives within his territory. The females in the harem generally feed together as a group and there is almost no evidence of mutual aggression amongst them. Harem size usually averages 2–3, with harems greater than 5 being rare. Selective shooting of males can artificially increase harem size but even so some territorial males do not attract harems during the season, implying that polygamy is the natural state.

The pheasant mating system seems to be based on mate guarding, in that males provide protection from harassment in exchange for mating. It is thus similar to the partridge system except that female partridges are in harems of one. There are several possible explanations for the difference; for example, because pheasants live on woodland edges, females are concentrated in particular spots, enabling males to guard groups as easily as single birds. Only one other species of gamebird, red junglefowl, has a similar mating system; reports that peafowl are harem guarders are based on poor evidence (Rands *et al.*, 1984). Among mammals, however, it is quite common for males to guard harems of females, especially in species where females congregate, such as seals, or remain in groups, such as deer. In some antelopes such as pronghorn, harem defence is also combined with territory defence (Kitchen, 1974), as it is in pheasants. It is tempting to conclude that it is the fact that pheasants appear more reluctant to fly compared to other birds that makes them susceptible to mate guarding in groups (Ridley and Hill, 1987).

The other form of avian polygamy is sequential, an extreme example of which is the black grouse. A successful male, with a central territory, has no parental duties after courtship and copulation. After mating he immediately resumes his attempts to mate with other females. In such lekking species, mating opportunities are very unevenly distributed among males. For instance, in a population of a North American species, the sage grouse population, it was estimated that over 90% of the matings in any one year were performed by less than 10% of the males (Wiley, 1973).

Grouse and pheasants that live in forests tend to have mating systems based on brief pair bonds which consequently provide the opportunity for sequential polygamy (de Vos, 1979; Ridley, 1983). For example, male capercaillies (Lumsden, 1961) and male great argus pheasants from south-east Asia (Davidson, 1981a) display and call loudly throughout the breeding season to attract solitary females to their display sites. The pair bond lasts only long enough to ensure mating.

There have been several attempts to explain why such species have this mating system. Wiley (1974) argued that polygamy in grouse was associated with large size, according to the following chain of cause and effect: large size results in greater sexual dimorphism, which leads to deferred male maturity, which alters the sex ratio of breeding birds in favour of females, which allows male polygamy. Wittenberger (1978) criticised Wiley's hypothesis as supported by no good evidence and instead suggested that the chain of logic led the other way: in polygamous species, young males have insufficient mating opportunities with which to offset the cost of obtaining full adult size or plumage in the first year.

Wittenberger's own explanation of the origin of polygamy in grouse is based on food. He suggested that in species feeding on an abundant food supply for which there is little competition (e.g. capercaillie and pine needles), females do not select mates on their ability to defend an exclusive feeding range, but on other characteristics such as size or appearance (Wittenberger, 1978). There are, however, two problems with this idea. First, there is evidence that, even in grouse species that feed on leaves, competition between breeding females for food is important. Second, the correlation between vegetarian diet and sequential polygamy does not apply to pheasants. Davison (1981b) has concluded the opposite to Wittenberger: that competition for scarce animal food has led to solitary habits and hence a shorter pair bond in forest pheasants such as great argus. An additional factor in the tropics is the greater length of the breeding season, which gives males more time for second pair bonds.

Explanations based on habitat structure are at least as plausible as these (de Vos, 1979; Ridley, 1983). In forest species the need for mate guarding is largely absent, because females are not conspicuous at a distance either to predators or to conspecifics. Indeed, living in larger groups probably decreases rather than enhances vigilance in forests, since larger groups make more noise and can listen less carefully for approaching predators. In other words, the same pressures that encourage solitary habits in forests outside the breeding season can act within the breeding season to encourage shorter pair bonds and so more opportunities for sequential polygamy.

This does not explain why lekking species also have extreme polygamy and brief pair bonds. Gamebirds that lek inhabit open or patchy habitats – sage grouse in sagebrush, prairie chickens in prairies, black grouse on heathland and peafowl in broken bush country. It is thought that lekking grouse and lekking pheasants are descended from forest-living species (de Vos, 1979; Rands et al., 1984) and that such species therefore already had brief pair ponds when they colonised open habitats. The only change was that clustering of displaying males brought advantages in vigilance and the exploitation of patchy food supplies.

7.2.4 Mate guarding and sperm competition

The obvious manifestations of competition between males for mates includes bright plumage, bizarre displays, loud calls and legs armed with spurs. Such adaptations tend to distract attention from a more covert competition which occurs after copulation. Whenever females mate with more than one male there is a possibility of sperm competition. Just as males have evolved strategies which tend to maximise their mating opportunities, we would expect that adaptations would also exist which maximise the chance that insemination would lead to fertilisation. The battlefield for sperm competition is the female reproductive tract so the ground rules are set by female anatomy, physiology and behaviour.

Much of the research into sperm storage has been carried out on domestic fowl so it is quite likely that many of the findings will apply generally to gamebirds although it is also likely that interspecific differences will occur. Female chickens can store viable sperm for periods of up to five weeks in a special organ called the utero-vaginal sperm host gland. The sperm host gland is basically a storage sac which leads off the main reproductive tract. However, studies have shown that sperm viability drops during the storage period (McKinney *et al.*, 1984), so the most successful male is the one that inseminates the female last. Compton *et al.* (1978) showed that, when competing inseminations were four hours apart, the second insemination was responsible for 80% of the progeny. This proportion is too high to be due to loss of viability through storage and indicates that the sperm storage mechanism operates on a first in/last out basis. New sperm to be stored in the host gland probably are deposited on top of those already there and are therefore nearest to the gland's exit when sperm release occurs. This strongly suggests that sperm from different males do not mix in the sperm host gland. Each insemination remains separate.

The scope for females to mate with more than one male in a season differs with the mating system. In monogamous territorial species such as ptarmigan, red grouse and partridges, intruding males are vigorously driven out of the territory when detected by the territory owner. Jenkins (1961) describes unpaired male grey partridges entering the territories of pairs in the spring and displaying to females. Sometimes this leads to the initial owner being displaced and the intruder taking over the territory. In such cases it is possible that the female will already have been inseminated by her first mate and so the scope for sperm competition exists. In red-legged partridges, females sometimes associate with two males (Jenkins, 1957) which suggests that sperm competition occurs. We do not know of any cases of extra-pair copulations being observed in monogamous gamebirds but the evidence is building up for other species that the incidence of this behaviour has certainly been overlooked in the past (McKinney *et al.*, 1984). For most species of gamebirds the frequency and time of copulation within the pair bond is not known, let alone the frequency of extra-pair copulation. The existence of non-territorial or unpaired males in some basically monogamous species (red grouse, ptarmigan) suggests that there may be a constant possibility of intrusion onto the territory for the purpose of extra-pair copulation. Non-territorial pheasants sometimes attempt to force copulations with females (Taber, 1949; Ridley, 1983). It is likely that much of the behaviour of paired males during the period leading up to, and including, egg-laying can be interpreted as mate-guarding behaviour. Males tend to be alert and stay close to their mate, especially when other conspecifics are nearby (Jenkins, 1961): behaviours which aid detection of other males.

At the other extreme in the range of possibilities for copulations with many different males is the lek systems. Here females can wander from one territory to the next and choose their mates. This choice is not totally accepted by males since in many species males will violently try to prevent their neighbours from mating (black grouse – Lack, 1946; Selous, 1909–10; sage grouse – Simon, 1940; Scott, 1942; Wiley, 1973; prairie chickens – Breckenridge, 1929; Schwartz, 1945; Ballard and Robel, 1974; Robel and Ballard, 1974) but it is likely that females could choose to mate with many different males if they liked. We have found a surprising lack of evidence for multiple insemination in lekking species. Kruijt and Hogan (1967) observed one female who mated with more than one male on the same morning but this seems to be the only unambiguous case. Watts and Stokes (1974) suggested that subordinate groups of turkeys which were unlikely to have been successful in obtaining copulations on the mating grounds sometimes gain copulations later in the season on the nesting grounds but it is not clear whether these copulations occur too late in the season to be of any reproductive importance.

We find the lack of evidence for multiple insemination surprising. It is not possible to say to what extent this is due to multiple matings being rare and to what extent it is not observed or recorded. Much more attention has been directed to male behaviour than to female behaviour in lekking species so multiple copulations by the same female on the same day could easily have been overlooked. Another possibility is that since few studies have involved marked birds, females may return to the lek and mate on several days with different males. One interesting example raises more questions than it answers. Robel (1969) radio-tracked a female black grouse during and after incubation. The female was caught immediately after mating at a lek and the observed copulation occurred 17 days before she laid her last egg but information on her movements up to and including laying is not given. This female either provides field data on successful long term sperm storage or there were other copulations which went unrecorded. Radio-tracking provides an excellent technique which could improve our understanding of these problems.

The mating behaviour of females remains a large gap in our knowledge of gamebird mating systems. For practical reasons the emphasis has been on counting the numbers of copulations that different males achieve but if females mate several times with different males then the realities of reproductive physiology mean that there will not be a simple relationship between mating frequency and fertilisation frequency of males. Paternity exclusion studies using genetic techniques provide useful ways of studying the incidence of successful extra-pair copulation in supposedly monogamous species but would be more difficult to apply to lek species where the number of potential fathers is much higher.

Reproductive constraints may also provide an explanation for why most lekking activity occurs in the early morning. Ovulation usually occurs within 75 minutes of the laying of the previous egg and fertilisation must occur soon after ovulation (within about 15 minutes) (Sturkie, 1976). Since most birds (though not partridges and pheasants: Ridley, 1983) are thought to lay early in the morning this provides an explanation for why the vast majority of mating occurs at leks in the very early morning; two-thirds of black grouse copulations occur within half an hour of sunrise (Kruijt and Hogan, 1967).

7.2.5 Lifetime reproductive success

As discussed in Chapter 3, with sufficient knowledge it would be possible to measure the lifetime reproductive success of different individuals of different species to give an ultimate measure of an individual's success at passing on his/her genes to the next generation. Regardless of the mating system, but assuming an equal sex ratio at birth, the lifetime reproductive success of all males will be equal to that of all females simply because all offspring have a mother and a father. However, the variance in reproductive success probably differs greatly between the sexes and between different mating systems. In monogamous species where the care of offspring is shared equally, the same factors (e.g. the acquisition of a good territory and avoiding predation) a're likely to act with equal force on both sexes. This means that the variances in lifetime reproductive success of males and females are likely to be very similar, although the actual size of these variances is not known.

In lekking systems it is clear that the variance in annual reproductive success between males is very high, but the variance in lifetime reproductive success is not known. In a system such as that of the sage grouse, where success seems to depend on waiting one's turn for a central position at the lek (Wiley, 1974), it is possible that everyone's turn comes eventually, hence the very big differences in seasonal reproductive success which exist between birds of different ages is much less when success over a lifetime is considered. In lekking species, the variance in male reproductive success need not be greater than for females because the differences in female quality may be similar to differences in males. If some females are consistently successful mothers yet many males eventually have a single year of high success it is quite possible that the variance in reproductive success for females is greater than that for males. At present the true picture is not clear, although measures of annual reproductive success may give a very misleading picture of the differences between individuals over their lifetimes.

If lifetime measures existed then it would be possible to examine in detail what factors lead to high reproductive success for each sex in different mating systems and answer some of the fascinating questions facing evolutionary biologists: Is large body size a better predictor of high success for males of the monogamous red grouse or the lekking black grouse? We would guess the latter, but this remains to be demonstrated. Is longevity a better predictor of high success for males or females? And in monogamous or polygamous mating systems? What are the relative roles of territory quality and avoiding predation in determining lifetime reproductive success?

7.3 Mating systems and management

7.3.1 Dominance and providing supplementary feed

The social system of a game species can influence aspects of management. Where supplementary feed is provided then whether the species is territorial or not will determine the best way to provide food. For territorial species central feeding is not appropriate but the potential exists to provide food selectivity to territories which are poor in food. Thus the effort which is needed for provisioning territorial species may be greater than for non-territorial ones but with territorial species the food can be supplied to the individuals with the greatest needs.

In non-territorial species the form of the dominance hierarchy within the species may also affect the efficiency of feeding. We present a simple arithmetic model to illustrate this. Consider two species, each of which comprises dominant birds and subordinate birds. In both species the dominants are 1.2 times more efficient competitors for food than the subordinates. The two species differ in the proportion of birds who are dominant and subordinate: in species A, 80% of birds are subordinates whereas in species B, 50% are subordinates. Assume that dominants and subordinates appropriate food in proportion to their competitive abilities.

The first finding from this model is that, given similar amounts of food the weight gains of both dominants and subordinates are greater in species A than in species B. This at first sight seems paradoxical: how can both groups be better off in species A if the same amount of food is provided for each species? In species B, there are more dominants so they take more of the food and the subordinates do less well. But because there are also more dominants, then each of them does less well. The greater the proportion of dominants the less well the subordinates fare, but this also applies to the dominants. As a result of this, if a keeper wished to make sure that each bird (regardless of status) gained at least 10 units of food from his feeding (so as to reduce mortality or dispersal) he would have to feed about 6% more in species B than in species A.

The model can also be applied to discover the consequences of culling different classes of bird. A 10% harvest of birds before feeding would result in different feed bills for the winter if birds are still to gain 10 food units from feeding under different harvesting regimes. With a 10% harvest which does not discriminate between dominants and subordinates, feed bills are obviously reduced by 10%. If subordinates are selectively harvested then feed bills are only reduced by about 9% in both species but if the harvest is selectively of dominants then the savings are 11.5% in species A and 11% in species B.

This example is hypothetical and illustrative. It does show that social systems can influence the effectiveness of management practice. However, we recognise that since the social system of the species, will not normally be susceptible to manipulation there is little that a game manager can do about this. Similarly, although it may be in his interests to be able to select birds of particular status to harvest it will often not be possible to do this. However, in some species, particularly polygamous ones, a bird's sex may be a good predictor of dominance so that with some modification similar considerations could apply to sex-selective harvesting.

7.3.2 Sexual selection and sex-selective harvesting

In polygynous species, most males are sexually redundant and can therefore be harvested without affecting the stock. For this reason, there is a long tradition among hunters of preferentially shooting male pheasants and black grouse, which are polygamous, but making relatively less selection when shooting red grouse or partridges, which are monogamous. It would be an almost impossible task to shoot only male partridges (although inadvertent selection for males does occur: Potts, 1986; see also Section 8.3.1) for they are very hard to distinguish from females either by size or by plumage in the field, whereas it is quite easy to select male pheasants and black grouse.

This is no coincidence. It reflects a basic biological truism, well known to Darwin (1871), that polygamy goes with large size and conspicuous plumage in the sex that has multiple mates (usually the male). Indeed, so well known is the connection that sexual dimorphism has often been used (by circular argument) as a clue to polygamy, for example among peafowl, where a mating system of harem polygamy was assumed long before anything was known about the species' habits in the wild. Peafowl do not guard harems but attract females to arena display sites (Rands et al., 1984). This could also have been predicted from the male's appearance since harem guarding generally goes with large male body size and ornaments that are of use in battle. Alternatively a mating system based on competitive display for the attention of females goes with splendid but often 'useless' ornaments such as the peacock's tail (Ridley et al., 1985).

Fisher's (1930) explanation of how such ornaments evolve has basically stood up to subsequent testing (Andersson, 1982; Halliday, 1983). He argued that it could become fashionable for females to select decorated males. Suppose, in the peacock's ancestor, females chose males with bright plumage because that indicated health. In doing so, they not only got the benefits of the male's genetic quality, but they also produced sons that were attractive to other females. Therefore selection would penalise any female that went against the trend and produced an 'unfashionable' son. The modern theory of sexual selection holds that females choose mates on the basis of genetic quality in the absence of more utilitarian criteria. For example, a female red-legged partridge probably chooses a male that will be a good parent, since both birds incubate eggs; a female red grouse probably chooses a male that holds a good territory and defends it well; a female pheasant probably chooses a male that is good at protecting her from harassment by other males. But a female black grouse chooses a male that displays good genetic quality in the vigour of his courtship and the central position of his court on the lek. An interesting refinement to this theory has been put forward by Hamilton and Zuk (1983) who suggest that colourful plumage may be used by females to distinguish males with small parasite loads. This idea is being tested on pheasants (N. Hillgarth, pers. comm.).

To return to the idea of sex-selective harvesting. There is evidence from pheasants that the selective killing of males does not reduce the fecundity of females. For example, Twining *et al.* (1948) found that, in captivity, male pheasants could be kept with up to 50 females each without much reduction in the fertility of the eggs laid by the females. Ball (1950) reported that, on Pelee Island in Lake Erie, Ontario, where there was exceptionally heavy shooting of males in 1947, only 500 male pheasants survived to fertilise 5000 females; yet, there was no reduction in breeding success. However, it is possible that, if many males are killed on one area but not on others nearby, females will emigrate during the breeding season to find better mates or smaller harems than are available locally – but this has not been shown by experiment.

On the contrary, it has been argued that leaving too many males, especially in a dense population of pheasants, results in a large floating population of non-territorial males, which attempt to harass and break up harems; it is to prevent harassment by non-territorial males that females join harems with senior males (Ridley, 1983). Such surplus males would, from the points of view of the dominant males, the females and the game manager, be better shot.

7.4 Conclusion

Gamebirds exhibit a wide range of mating systems. Ptarmigan and partridges are monogamous while the black grouse is a sequential polygamist (many females, one after another) and the pheasant is a simultaneous polygamist (many females at once). The different strategies have evolved to maximise an individual's reproductive success. While the large variation in mating systems is of great interest to the evolutionary biologist it provides certain constraints inside which management practices must act. Nevertheless, an understanding of these constraints can assist the development of management practices, for example the pattern of providing supplementary feed to territorial versus non-territorial species and the importance of selectively harvesting males.

8 Harvesting Gamebirds

Peter A. Robertson and Andrew A. Rosenberg

8.1 Introduction

The hunting of game has a history as long as that of man himself; from the earliest times man has developed and used a wide range of techniques in his pursuit of game for food and sport. More than 3400 years ago the Egyptian aristocracy coursed game with dogs and killed wildfowl with boomerangs. Falconry was a popular sport in medieval Europe while blowpipes, bola, traps and various types of bows and arrows have been, and are still used to hunt game in various parts of the world (Mannix, 1968).

In modern times firearms have become the most frequently used method for harvesting game. The first firearms date from 1338 and by the 1480s those firing single lead projectiles were being used to kill deer. Initially gamebirds were shot on the ground but during the 1560s a practice evolved in Europe of shooting birds in flight. This reached Britain in the 1680s and subsequently became accepted as the main sporting practice. By the early part of the 19th century a conventional day's shooting consisted of three sportsmen with accompanying keepers who would use pointing dogs to locate birds which were then flushed and shot. The single-barrelled muzzle-loaded weapons in use around this time were slow to load and detonated by unreliable flint-locks.

With the development of a prototype percussion lock and the advent of breech loaders in 1847, the scene was set for the basic design of the modern shotgun. Sportsmen now had a reliable, light firearm capable of rapid loading. Walked-up shooting with dogs gave way to 'battue' or driven shooting in which game was driven towards a line of standing guns. Walked-up shooting remains the norm in many countries such as the United States and Canada but in Britain, driven shooting is considered a more challenging sport and is used extensively.

As with the development of hunting techniques, the methods and legislation used for game conservation have a long history. Genghis

Kahn restricted hunting in Mongolia to the winter months (Lamb, 1927); Charlemagne limited bag sizes and introduced legislation to protect habitats in France during the 8th century (Graham, 1973) while predator control to protect domestic livestock is described by Homer. On the other hand, there are numerous examples of man's over-exploitation of a natural resource. At the turn of the century the passenger pigeon in America became extinct as a result of excessive harvesting at the birds' nesting colonies. The population of American bison almost suffered the same plight at the end of the last century (Roe, 1951) when bison were eliminated from the plains; the remnant population that survives is a result of semi-domestication. Most harvesting is nowadays controlled through game laws and voluntary restrictions to conserve the resource.

Early game laws in Europe restricted the right to hunt to the nobility. Charles II only allowed the richest 5% of landowners to hunt, even on their own property; these rights were jealously guarded and the penalties were severe. Nowadays, British law allows anyone to hunt

Plate 8.1 The hunting of game animals has a long tradition in many cultures. Driven shooting is now the most extensive harvesting technique in Britain.

game but only with the permission of whoever owns the shooting rights to the land, one exception being certain areas of the foreshore which are accessible to all. In North America, the situation is rather different. Settlers to the New World in the 18th century saw hunting as free to all and game is now considered to be the property of the people rather than the landowner. The American sportsman expects to have free access to enormous tracts of land and any game that it may contain.

The contrasting private property rights of Britain and North America have led to differences in the methods of game management. As American landowners do not own the game living on their land they have little incentive for management and it is left to the state to subsidise schemes for planting cover, hedges and food plants. The shooting seasons tend to be shorter in America but are more intense; season length and bag limits are assessed annually on the basis of surveys of each quarry species. In Britain the laws regarding hunting seasons tend to be liberal and most of the restrictions on bag sizes are left to the individual landowners. These differences tend to favour the intensive management of individual estates for game in Britain while the American system lends itself to large-scale but very general management techniques.

It is against this background of a variety of shooting methods and opportunities for management that the harvesting of gamebirds must be considered.

8.2 The theory of harvesting

Determining the best strategy for harvesting a game population, depends on the objectives of management. These are usually centred on obtaining the maximum long-term yield, although this yield may be defined in a number of different ways:

(1) The economic revenue generated by the sale of the harvest or sporting rights.
(2) The number of individuals or the biomass harvested.
(3) The aesthetic benefits arising from the conservation of the resource.

Further to this there may be other constraints such as producing a constant yield with little short-term variability, or in some instances the opposite – large spectacular bags in one season and then nothing for a period of years. Each of these options will require a slightly different management strategy.

In general terms, harvesting theory seeks to determine the harvesting rate and yield in accordance with the objectives of management. Since biological resources are renewable the object is to determine the long-term level of harvesting which produces a yield that remains stable over a period of years – the sustainable yield (SY).

Harvesting theory attempts to derive simple mathematical models which describe the growth and reproductive processes of the population. Such models are usually a gross oversimplification of the population processes and are inevitably subject to a wide range of criticisms. Nevertheless, it is necessary to keep sight of the objective of the exercise and ensure the model's validity (see Section 9.3.5). For example: does the model incorporate the essential features which relate to the level of harvesting? By introducing 'more realistic' complexity in the model does it gain accuracy, predictive power or insight concerning the response of the population to harvesting? Does the model produce the quantities we require for management? In many cases a simple model may reveal general features regarding harvesting and yields which a more detailed model would obscure.

The simplest model of harvesting describes the change in the size of the population, X, over time, dX/dt, which will be equal to the growth rate of the population minus the harvesting rate. The growth of the population can be considered a function of its size, $G(X)$, and the harvest a function of the effort of harvesting $H(E)$, thus:

$$dX/dt = G(X)X - H(E)X \tag{8.1}$$

For a gamebird population the harvest can be considered as the proportion of the population shot over an interval of time (dt). Since the growth and harvesting functions can be of virtually any degree of complexity this is quite a general model. While there are other possibilities than making population growth a function of population size and harvest rate a function of effort, these are quite reasonable suppositions to make.

When the population is stable, i.e. when $dX/dt = 0$, then an equilibrium has been reached at which point the yield is:

$$G(X) = H(E) \tag{8.2}$$

In other words, when the harvest rate equals the growth rate of the population the sustainable yield will be that harvest rate times the average equilibrium population size during the hunting season. Obviously, there are many harvesting rates which will obtain a sustainable yield. The task for the manager is to aim for a harvest rate whose sustainable yield can be considered optimal, according to some predetermined criteria.

This basic model can be expanded by incorporating the logistic

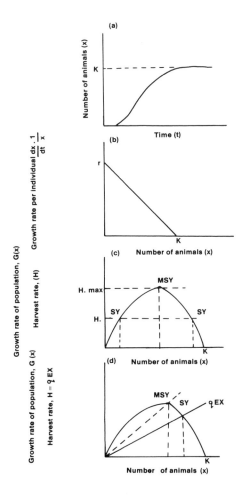

Fig. 8.1 The logistic growth curve and a summary of the maximum sustainable yield (MSY): (a) the increase in the number of animals (X) to carrying capacity (K) over time (t); (b) the logistic curve describes a decreasing rate of increase per individual with increased population size, falling from the maximum (r) to zero at the carrying capacity; (c) the rate of population increase (the slope of the curve in (a)) reaches its maximum when $X = 1/2K$ and this is the point of the MSY; (d) when harvesting rate increases with population size the sustainable yield (SY) is the point where this line crosses the curve; increases in harvesting effort can increase the SY towards the MSY although further effort or changes in the shape of the harvesting curve can lead to over-exploitation.

model of population growth, a model described in detail in many ecological texts (e.g. Begon *et al.*, 1986) and historically reviewed by Hutchinson (1978). The sigmoid curve produced by the model is a simple yet adequate description of density-dependent population growth, where the growth rate of the population falls with an increase in population size (Fig. 8.1). This growth rate falls to zero when the population size reaches carrying capacity, *K*, and is at its greatest, *r* (known as the intrinsic rate of increase), when the population is very small. From the logistic model:

$$G(X) = r(1 - X/K) \tag{8.3}$$

and

$$H(E) = qE \tag{8.4}$$

The complex birth, death and growth processes for the population are included in this simple function *G(X)*. One example of a population exhibiting a logistic growth curve is presented by Einarsen (1942) as an increase in a pheasant population introduced onto a previously unoccupied island in America (Fig. 8.2). It can be seen from this example that the simple form of the logistic model adequately describes the growth rate of a population in relation to its density.

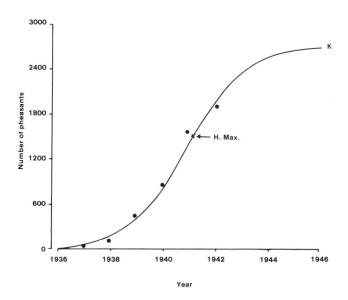

Fig. 8.2 An example of a population showing logistic growth. The number of pheasants on an island after introduction. (Einarsen, 1942.)

Returning to the implications of this model, the harvest rate is simply proportional to harvesting effort, E, by a constant of q, often called the catchability coefficient in fisheries. For game hunting we can think of q as the efficiency in shooting the birds over a unit area, which can be influenced by such factors as firearm restrictions or bag limits. Shooting mortality can simply be described as the percentage of the population shot, in other words $qE = H$, the proportional rate of harvesting. Substituting into the original equation produces:

$$dX/dt = rX(1 - X/K) - HX \tag{8.5}$$

and at equilibrium, when $dX/dt = 0$:

$$rX(1 - X/K) = HX \tag{8.6}$$

Given a harvest rate H*, the population size at equilibrium, X^*, is:

$$X^*, = K(1 - H^*/r) \tag{8.7}$$

and the sustainable yield for that harvest rate is given by:

$$Y^* = H^* \, X^* = H^* \, K(1 - H^*/r) \tag{8.8}$$

In this equation if H^* is greater than r then this produces an unsustainable yield. In other words, if the harvesting rate is greater than the intrinsic rate of natural increase of the population then the yield from the resource and the population size will fall to zero. Given that we can accept that the population we are managing can be described by the simple logistic model and that the shooting mortality results in a harvesting rate which is directly proportional to the shooting effort (e.g. number of days shot), the sustainable yield can be determined for any level of harvesting, H^*. As yet, variations in any of the processes are ignored and for simplicity the model operates in a perfect, deterministic world. An obvious question to ask at this juncture is: what is the equilibrium harvest rate that produces the maximum yield from the population? According to the model this is the maximum point on the parabola described by the equilibrium yield relationship, equation (8.3), and is at the point when $dY^*/dH^* = 0$:

$$dY^*/dH^* = HK - (2KH/r) = 0 \tag{8.9}$$

Solving this we obtain that at the maximum sustainable yield (MSY) the harvest rate is $H^* = r/2$ and the MSY will be $Kr/4$.

There are important lessons here. Although many managers of game are concerned with keeping their breeding stock at as high a level as possible this is clearly a poor strategy for many harvested populations since the best sustainable harvest will be obtained when the growth rate of the population is maximised and this is not when the population size is at carrying capacity. This will be the case in any model where there is density-dependence in population growth, i.e. when the growth rate of the population decreases with increasing population size.

There are also many possible levels of sustainable yield. It is feasible for the population to be held at a low but sustained level by a harvest smaller than the MSY. This could lead to serious problems since the real world is far from deterministic and a series of poor breeding seasons with a relatively high harvest rate could result in a population collapse.

The model as presented is a static one. Extensions to a dynamic solution are presented by Clark (1976) but for the purposes of this appraisal the static solution illustrates the rationale of these harvesting models. While the logistic model is closely linked to the concept of MSY the idea can be applied to virtually any model of the form of equation (8.1) which has an equilibrium solution. In fact, the $G(X)$ function could be given by a quite complicated set of equations for population growth, fecundity, breeding success and mortality. Even so it may not be possible for many models to find a simple analytical solution for MSY and harvesting rate, H^*, although a numerical solution using a computer is in many cases easy to obtain. For these sorts of analyses, electronic spreadsheet microcomputer program packages are often very useful as yield can be examined in relation to effort or population size. Exploration of the model equations in this way can provide insight into the sensibility of the model and the effects of various harvesting policies.

There are two important complications to the simple theory of harvesting as presented here. First, the models are completely deterministic. If variability is included in population size, reproduction or growth in general, or economic factors, the models become far more complex. The variability produces uncertainties in the predictions of the model and this could lead to erroneous harvesting strategies. If the prediction of MSY is considered uncertain, it may be unwise for the manager of a resource to harvest at the MSY. To some extent this uncertainty can be provided for by harvesting a population at a lower rate and maintaining the population size at a size greater than that producing the MSY. In fisheries management, several rather arbitrary criteria have been developed to try to compensate for the risks inherent in MSY prediction (Gulland, 1983). These criteria seek to choose a point below MSY which will maintain the population within the region of high growth without the high risk of passing the maximum and causing a decline in population size. This point can be called the optimum sustainable yield, or OSY. Balancing short-term variability and long-term yield is a difficult task. Models such as the logistic have little predictive power in the short-term. To gain some measure of prediction of short-term yields it is necessary to resort to statistical forecasting models (e.g. see Wonnacott and Wonnacott, 1979).

The second complication arises when we consider that game are not distributed evenly within an area but tend to be clumped in favourable habitat and in groups, e.g. grouse in packs, partridge in coveys and deer in herds. Harvesting techniques, both walking-up and driven shooting, tend to concentrate effort on the groups and in areas where the game is concentrated. This type of harvesting leads to a decrease either in the size of the groups or the number of groups left. In species where there is an advantage in being in a group (for example individuals in groups may be less vulnerable to predation) any reduction in average group size can lead to reduced survival amongst the remaining individuals. This is known as a depensatory relationship between population size and growth rate and is the opposite of the density-dependent compensatory response described within the logistic model (see Section 8.3.3). If group size is not reduced then harvesting will result in a decrease in the number of groups. The presence of large groups may lead the manager to assume that the population is in fact larger than it actually is and inadvertently result in over-harvesting. Further problems and alternative models are reviewed by Cooke and Beddington (1984).

8.3 Harvesting gamebirds

8.3.1 Selective harvesting

The harvesting models described in the previous section assume that individuals are removed from the population at random. The probability of a particular individual being harvested is independent of its sex, age or social position. Such an assumption may not be valid since it is possible that certain cohorts within a population are more vulnerable to harvesting than others. Selective harvesting of any one cohort can affect the response of that population to harvesting and the yields obtained. Selective harvesting can arise either as a conscious decision by the resource manager or inadvertently when one cohort is more vulnerable than another.

The models required to assess the effects of selective harvesting on a population can incorporate age and sex structure in both the *G(X)* and *H(E)* functions. The mathematical description of these models can be found in Usher (1972), Beddington and Taylor (1973), and Beddington (1974). Basically these use a set of simultaneous equations for the age groups in matrix form and use matrix algebra to determine the properties of the population. These are described by a form of the so-called Leslie population projection matrix (Leslie, 1945, and see Section 9.2.3) and can be used to investigate harvest output in relation to population growth and age structure.

Using the Leslie matrix as a tool it is possible to examine the effects of different patterns of harvesting by age or sex. Beddington and Taylor (1973) show that when conscious selective harvesting of specific age groups can be controlled it is best to harvest partially the youngest age and completely remove one of the older age groups. With regard to sex-selective harvesting the constraint on harvesting of males is that the fecundity (potential breeding success) of the females must not be reduced by over-harvesting of their mates (Section 7.3.2). However, the optimal strategy for the sex ratio is more difficult to assess (see Beddington, 1974, for details). Caughley (1977) discusses some of the implications of sex- and age-specific harvesting of game and points out that selective harvesting of males, given the above constraint, can substantially increase MSY if the growth rate of the population is unaffected by reducing males, provided all females can still be fertilised.

Increasing yields by managing the proportions of each sex or age group harvested obviously depends on the ability of the sportsman to identify members of that group. This generally rules out the selective shooting of gamebirds by age; most attain adult plumages prior to their first winter and can rarely be separated by age when in flight. With regard to selection by sex, only those species with conspicuous sexual plumages can be distinguished easily – usually the polygamous species such as the pheasant and black grouse, or those with sex-specific behaviour such as the roding of woodcock – a behaviour performed only by the males.

The behaviours of the different sex and age groups within the population and the methods of harvesting can also result in the unintentional selection of particular cohorts. For instance, mature male red grouse are inadvertently shot on driven shoots (Hudson, 1985). On driven days, grouse pass over the line of guns as single birds or in large packs of 100 or more birds. The proportion of birds shot from large packs is lower than that from small groups: 60% of grouse flying over the guns as singletons are shot as compared to only 12% of those in groups of ten. This is principally as a result of relatively fewer shots being fired at large groups rather than a decrease in accuracy. The mature males tend to be relatively solitary during the shooting season since they have left the family coveys and commenced territorial behaviour; as such they tend to be flushed as singletons and are more vulnerable than the birds which remain in packs (Fig. 8.3).

Mature male grey partridges are more vulnerable than females and young males to both driven and rough shooting (Potts, 1986). When disturbed the males tend to flush as singletons and consequently suffer higher losses. The greater vulnerability of single birds appears to be a general feature of shooting, and has also been reported for wood pigeons (Murton *et al.*, 1974). Any feature of the social organisation of a species which leads to one cohort being found as singletons during the hunting season could conceivably lead to a heavier shooting mortality amongst that part of the population.

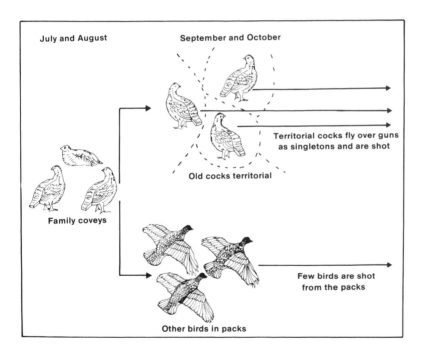

Fig. 8.3 The behaviour and vulnerability of red grouse during the shooting season. When old cocks commence territorial behaviour they leave the family coveys; on a shooting day they then pass over the guns as singletons and are more vulnerable than the grouse in packs. (*After* Hudson, 1985.)

8.3.2 The extent of shooting mortality

Within the harvesting models discussed the sustainable yield must be calculated from the size of the population, once it has reached an equilibrium with that level of harvesting. The question: what percentage of the population can be harvested each year? is meaningless. It must be rephrased as: if the population has been reduced below its unharvested size, what fraction of the reduced population must be harvested to keep it at that level? (Caughley, 1977).

This question can be asked for a population reduced to any fraction of its original unharvested size; at each reduced density there is an appropriate sustainable yield. The question most relevant to game managers should then read: to what size must the population be reduced and what fraction must be harvested from it each year thereafter to provide the MSY? Unfortunately this question is rarely asked and even more rarely answered with regard to game populations.

To illustrate the way in which harvesting theory has been interpreted by game scientists we reviewed a total of 67 scientific papers dealing with the harvesting of gamebirds. These were obtained from a general literature review carried out by Braun (1975) and by a search of the *Journal of Wildlife Management* for the years 1975–1985. Of these papers, 43% ($n = 29$) restricted themselves to giving details of the proportions of the populations shot, without reference to the effects of shooting on total annual mortality or the size and productivity of the breeding population. A further 37% ($n = 25$) also gave the proportion shot but stated that there was no apparent effect on the size of the breeding population. These may reflect low levels of shooting mortality or populations at equilibrium with the observed level of hunting. Either way the papers in question did not consider a reduction in the size of the breeding population to be a natural consequence of harvesting. However, 18% ($n = 12$) did conclude that hunting resulted in a reduction of the size of the breeding population. Despite the fact that this is the expected result, 9 of the 12 concluded that this was a result of over-shooting and represented an unacceptable level of harvesting, only 4% ($n = 3$) saw a reduction in breeding population size as a natural consequence of hunting. Only one study actually modelled the population to estimate the MSY. In summary, 94% of the studies reviewed did not consider a reduction in breeding stocks to be a normal or acceptable result of hunting, demonstrating that the dynamics of harvesting are poorly understood by many game scientists and managers.

Maximum sustainable yields have been estimated for gamebird populations in a number of instances. For bobwhite quail, the predicted MSY (Roseberry, 1979) can be obtained by shooting 55% of the autumn population. Such a level of harvesting should reduce the population to 72% of its unharvested size. For the grey partridge, the MSY was estimated to be between 30 and 45% (Potts, 1986) depending on the rate of chick survival. In mallard, the MSY has been estimated as 29% in Britain (Hill, 1984a) and in pheasants as 20% of the females (Chapter 9). Red grouse populations fluctuate in a cyclic manner (Chapter 2) and this large variation makes any assessment of MSY difficult.

8.3.3 Is shooting mortality additive or compensatory?

Hunting mortality can be additive to natural mortality where each bird shot does not affect the survival chances of other birds. Alternatively, the shooting of some proportion of the population may be compensated for by the enhanced survival chances of other birds. This may come about by a variety of mechanisms such as decreased competition for cover, nesting sites or food.

The extent of any compensatory response essentially concerns the degree of density-dependence in mortality rates. In the logistic model the growth of the population was described as:

$$dX/dt = rX (1 - X/K) = rX - rX^2/K \tag{8.10}$$

where the growth rate of the population falls with an increase in population size. If the intrinsic rate of increase, r, is defined as births minus deaths, $r = B - D$, the logistic model can be rewritten as:

$$dX/dt = (B - D)X - (B - D)X^2/K \tag{8.11}$$

This contains two mortality components, one linear ($-DX$) and the second non-linear ($-DX^2$). The linear part expresses additive (density-independent) mortality and the non-linear the compensatory (density-dependent) effect.

In natural populations the observed relationship between hunting mortality and annual rates of survival has been established as usually occurring somewhere between the two extremes of totally additive or totally compensatory mortality, although opinions on this topic vary. For instance, Stoddard (1951) regarded hunting losses as purely additive to other causes of mortality in populations of bobwhite quail. The opposite condition was proposed by Errington (1934) who suggested that quail annually produce a surplus of birds by virtue of their high reproductive rate which cannot all survive the winter due to limited resources. These excess birds could, he proposed, be considered as a doomed surplus which could be shot without producing any measurable decreases in the size of subsequent breeding populations. A subsequent examination of field data (Roseberry, 1979) collected in Illinois over a 24-year period concluded that both the natural mortality and reproductive success of bobwhite quails operate in a density-dependent fashion and that this could compensate for some, but not all, of the losses caused by hunting.

In North America, an analysis of mallard harvest rates (Anderson and Burnham, 1976) compared the results of their investigations with the two alternative hypotheses of totally additive or totally compensatory mortality in response to shooting. The relationship they observed between hunting and non-hunting mortality rates fell between those predicted by the two hypotheses suggesting partial compensation (Fig. 8.4). These examples appear to be typical of the effect of hunting losses on the total mortality of a population (Nichols *et al.*, 1984), such losses

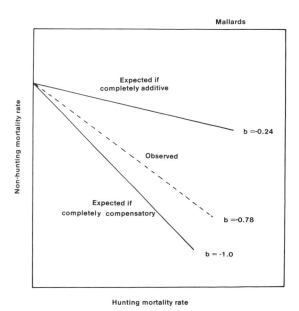

Fig. 8.4 Calculated mortalities of mallard assuming either compensatory or additive mortality compared to observed mortality. The observed line falls between the two extremes indicating that mallard populations partially compensate for hunting mortality. (*After* Anderson and Burnham, 1976.)

being partially compensated for by changes in other population parameters.

There are a number of mechanisms by which compensation for shooting mortality may occur. Compensation acts by removing competition within the population for certain limiting resources such as food supplies or potential breeding sites, or by decreasing the effect of density-dependent causes of mortality such as predation or disease. For instance, mature male red grouse are vulnerable to shooting and defend exclusive territories during the winter. The ownership of such territories confers distinct survival advantages and is an essential prerequisite for breeding (Watson, 1985). Territories left vacant by the removal of the owner are quickly filled by non-territorial males who would otherwise disperse off the moor and be unlikely to survive the winter (Watson and Jenkins, 1968). In this way the loss of one individual through shooting is compensated for by the increased probability of another surviving.

Two further mechanisms for compensation for hunting mortality have been described for the grey partridge (Potts, 1986). In areas where nesting mortality is reduced by predator control the size of the population increases and the individuals surplus to those which obtained nesting sites emigrate. On two such areas, one of which was left unshot and the other where an average of 24% of the population was shot per year, there were no significant differences in the total annual losses (51% and 55% respectively). This was brought about by a density-dependent decrease in the rate of emigration on the shot area which compensated for hunting losses.

On areas where nest predators are not controlled the rate of grey partridge nest loss acts in a density-dependent way. The removal of a proportion of the population through shooting reduces nest density and hence the rate of nest predation which in turn compensates for the original loss.

One further example can be drawn from American research on mallard. An analysis of a large sample of ringed birds whose body condition had been measured (Hepp et al., 1986) showed that birds in poor condition were more likely to be shot than their healthier counterparts. They speculate that this may be due to differences in behaviour: the weaker, subordinate individuals are forced to be more mobile and hence are more likely to come into contact with hunters. As the ducks in poor condition are also more likely to die from natural causes than their healthier counterparts the heavier losses of these birds through shooting will tend to replace natural mortality rather than add to it.

The mechanisms outlined here of density-dependent over-wintering loss and breeding success in their many forms are neither complete nor unlimited in their ability to compensate for losses caused by shooting. For instance, in the example of density-dependent nest predation in the grey partridge the increase in nest success can only compensate for 84% of the losses incurred by shooting; the compensation is only partial. Furthermore, the level of hunting that can be compensated for is limited, for example by the number of non-territorial red grouse available to fill vacated territories, or the number of potentially emigrant grey partridges. Once these surplus birds have been depleted further hunting is likely to become additive in its effects on total annual mortality.

Even taking such partial compensation into consideration, the harvesting models still predict that shooting will reduce the size of the breeding population (Roseberry, 1977; Potts, 1986). A stable and unshot population will have birth and death rates that are, by definition, equal. When they are harvested for the first time the rate of mortality will temporarily exceed the rate of reproduction and the population will decrease in size. This reduction in density will usually be accompanied by an increase in breeding success which is often the strongest density dependent factor acting to compensate hunting losses. When the increased rate of reproduction and lower rate of natural mortality are again sufficient to balance the higher, total rate of mortality, including shooting, the population will stabilise but at a lower density and with a higher population growth rate than before harvesting started. The strength of the density dependence in breeding success and natural mortality, and their ability to compensate for hunting losses, will determine how greatly the population is reduced by given levels of harvesting.

8.4 Management implications

8.4.1 Determining a maximum sustainable yield

The determination of a maximum sustainable yield requires accurate estimates of the parameters for the chosen model of the population. For the logistic model the parameters r and K can be estimated using various types of data (see Ricker, 1975, or Caughley, 1977). The most straightforward data are records of population size, harvest rate and yield. Unfortunately it is unusual to find such data for more than a few years. A simple approach is to plot yield versus both harvest rate and population size and fit the chosen model to the plotted points. For instance the logistic curve fitted to the pheasant data (Fig. 8.2) can be used to estimate the sustainable yield at each population size (Fig. 8.5). This can be done using statistical procedures or, for many purposes, initial estimates can be made by eye to obtain values which follow the observed data as closely as possible.

It is often the case that the observed data are clumped tightly together since population size and harvest rate have remained relatively constant for a long period. This can make the curve fitting of dubious value. Alternatively, there may be so much variation in the catch that no pattern can be identified (e.g. with red grouse). If the data are tightly clumped this implies population stability but the sustainable yield obtained may be far from optimal. MSY is not easily determined from such data unless we have independent information on r or K (e.g. life table studies, see Deevey, 1947; Emlen, 1973).

Highly variable data may be a more common situation, reflecting the influence of environmental factors on reproduction or survival. This need not imply that there is no level of sustainable yield. The simple concept of MSY may be inadequate for the management of a highly variable population such as a cyclic population of red grouse. In such instances it may be just as important to manage the population to

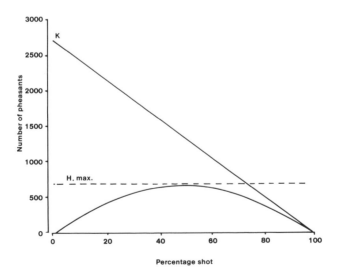

Fig. 8.5 Estimating the maximum sustainable yield for the pheasant population described in Fig. 8.2.

minimise variation in the yield as to maximise the average yield. More detailed statistical models of the population, given sufficient data, are needed in such a situation. Some simple methods of assessing yield may still be applicable, however; there are several *ad hoc* rules for fitting yield curves to variable data (Shepherd, 1982).

Variability in population production also means that targeting harvest mortality to the MSY level can lead to over-exploitation of the birds because the MSY harvest rate can be excessive in any one or a series of years. It is important to be cautious in the application of MSY and Sissenwine (1978) discusses the shortcomings of the most common methods of determining MSY and some of the possible alternatives. For this reason harvesting should really be aimed at shooting slightly lower levels than those which produce the MSY. This is usually called the optimum sustainable yield or OSY.

There are two very different definitions of over-shooting in use by game managers: either a reduction in the breeding population or a reduction in the size of the harvest. If maximum sustainable yields are the aim then a reduction in the size of the breeding population is an acceptable result, as it is typically associated with increased productivity. Over-shooting actually occurs in two instances, first when the harvest rate exceeds the rate for MSY so that the population level and total productivity are depressed, and second, when a population is harvested at the rate necessary to achieve the MSY but the population has already been depressed below that point. In the extreme this can lead to extinction, particularly in species with a large variation in reproductive output. However, the popular view is that any reduction in the size of the breeding population reflects over-shooting. Nevertheless, in the absence of the data necessary for the calculation of MSY, a situation all too common amongst gamebirds, setting hunting regulations on the basis of no significant reductions in subsequent breeding populations is a safe and conservative strategy even if it does not exploit the population resource to the full.

The number of birds shot is not the only criterion used when establishing optimum levels of harvesting. Game managers in America also included the number of days' recreation created by hunting and the various types of benefits obtained from the sport. Considerations of the size of the bag and the number of days' recreation provided can easily be incorporated into models while the open seasons and game laws can be manipulated to maximise these aims. Hunter satisfaction is a more elusive aim, although a number of studies have examined how it can be affected by game laws and hunting regulations (Hendee, 1972; Beattie, 1981). Although the maximisation of hunter satisfaction is an admirable aim it is subjective in the extreme, a situation that does not lend itself to incorporation into harvesting models. It is probably of more use in identifying specific laws or regulations that are unpopular with hunters.

Hunter satisfaction is probably of greater importance on driven shoots in Britain as it can have consequences for the value of let days. Sportsmen will pay more for a day of shooting truly wild birds such as red grouse compared to hand-reared pheasants, while an estate specialising in high fast birds can charge more per bird shot than one providing easier shots.

Naturally, the yield models presented above can, and have, been applied to economic revenue as opposed to biological yield. The principles are the same but in incorporating the economics of the shoot, the models can become quite complicated, as with age-structured population (see Clark, 1976, for details).

Decisions on hunting seasons and bag limits are generally made by committees which seldom include a practising biologist and research findings contribute little towards their formulation. The regulations may be arbitrary but they are usually also cautious; although unscientific they take a common-sense approach and ensure that over-shooting does not occur. For instance, a number of workers (George *et al.*, 1980; Whiteside and Guthery, 1983) have reviewed the effect of pheasant season length on hunter bags and subsequent population size in three American states. Although longer seasons result in larger bags there was no evidence of any reductions in the sizes of subsequent populations. Clearly pheasants were being harvested at a rate well below the maximum sustainable yield as breeding populations were not being affected, yet both studies were reluctant to recommend further relaxation of hunting seasons; such reluctance being due to opposition from sportsmen and concern for decreasing the size of the breeding stocks. While this approach may waste some resources it seldom results in catastrophic declines and as such is politically more acceptable than attempting to control the activities of a multitude of individual sportsmen in such a way as to obtain an MSY (Caughley, 1985).

8.4.2 Controlling the harvest

In Britain the control of the harvest is left to the individual landowner, open seasons are fixed by law and not subject to annual changes. Under these circumstances the harvest is usually adjusted to what the manager, owner or gamekeeper thinks is reasonable. However, in most other countries attempts are made to control the harvest by altering the length of the season, the number of licences issued, or by imposing bag restrictions.

In America the open seasons are varied from year to year in response to perceived fluctuations in the size of the prey populations in an attempt to control the harvest. Many states institute some form of monitoring scheme to obtain an index of population density to be used in determining season lengths. For instance, there is a simple linear relationship between the density of calling male scaled quail in the spring and hunter success in the following autumn (Brown *et al.*, 1978). Such relationships can be used to estimate the length of the shooting season. However, there is some evidence that annual bags are not always directly influenced by changes in season length or bag limits. For instance, in blue grouse populations in Colorado there was no relationship between the size of the harvest and season length over a period of nine years even though season length varied between 23 and 67 days (Hoffman, 1985). The number of hunters and production of young in the previous summer together accounted for 85% of the variation in the harvest and neither of these factors was related to season length. Similarly, no relationship between season length and bag have been recorded for wild turkeys (Weaver and Mosby, 1978) and sage grouse (Braun and Beck, 1985). In fact in sage grouse hunters took between 7 and 11% regardless of legislative restrictions. One possible explanation for this is that the majority of the harvest occurs during the first few days of the season (Harper *et al.*, 1951) and subsequent changes in the season have relatively little effect. Even so, hunting restrictions can directly influence the size of the bag (George *et al.*, 1980; Whiteside and Guthery, 1983) and, even where they do not, it is possible that they result in a more even spread of game amongst participating sportsmen.

One feature of game laws that can successfully reduce bags is the restriction of hunting to certain cohorts within the population. After restricting hunters to shoot only male turkeys in Virginia there was a two-thirds reduction in the bag (Weaver and Mosby, 1978). Many American states limit pheasant shooting to the males and an average of 74% of these are shot each year (range from 45% to 93%). Despite the restrictions on shooting hen pheasants, hens are still shot as a result of error, frustration or a blatant disregard for the law. Estimates of the extent of this illegal kill average 17% of the pre-hunting hen population (range from 15 to 20%; Edwards, 1962, 1963; Wagner *et al.*, 1965). It is interesting to note that by banning hen pheasant shooting many

American states may only be restricting the harvest to a level approaching that necessary to achieve MSY. The bans may be correct, but for entirely the wrong reasons.

Many other restrictions to harvesting are contained, not in written laws but in sporting traditions. For instance, the use of guns firing more than two cartridges without reloading is considered 'unsporting' on most British estates, as is the killing of low flying or sitting birds.

8.4.3 Game management to increase yields

The aim of game management is primarily to increase the harvestable population of an area. There are three principal methods used to achieve this: increasing a population's size and rate of production; decreasing non-hunting losses; and supplementing the population through the release of new individuals.

INCREASING THE SIZE OR PRODUCTIVITY OF A POPULATION

As discussed in Chapter 6, habitat management to increase the quality or quantity of the habitat can lead to a direct increase in population size. Reducing the effects of predators or parasites can improve productivity and potential harvest from a population. The control of nest predators has been shown to increase nest survival in the grey partridge (Frank, 1970; Potts, 1986) while the bags of this species (Middleton, 1967) and of red grouse (Hudson, 1986a) are higher where gamekeepers are more active. Improving the quality and quantity of nesting cover can decrease nest predation and increase productivity as demonstrated by Rands (1982) for grey partridges and Hill (1984b) for mallard and tufted duck. The latter author also demonstrates the higher survival of wildfowl nests on artificial islands which provide some protection from ground predators. Reducing nematode infections of red grouse by treatment with an anthelmintic drug (Chapter 5) can also increase clutch size, total productivity and the harvest of grouse (Hudson, 1986b).

Chick survival is typically the key factor influencing the size of autumn gamebird populations (Hill, 1985; Hudson, 1986a; Potts, 1986) and in pheasants, red grouse, grey and red-legged partridges, is strongly influenced by insect prey abundance within brood feeding ranges (Green, 1984; Rands, 1985; Hill, 1985; Hudson, 1986a). This appears to be a common feature of most gamebird populations. Modified pesticide use on cereal fields can increase insect abundance without appreciably decreasing crop yields, with consequences for increased chick survival (Rands, 1985; Sotherton *et al.*, 1985; and see Section 6.3.1).

DECREASING NON-HUNTING LOSSES OF ADULT GAMEBIRDS

Methods of decreasing non-hunting losses typically are aimed at emigration rather than direct mortality and are usually secondary to the effects of fecundity and survival with regard to determining harvests (Roseberry, 1979; Hill, 1985; Bergerud *et al.*, 1985). Decreasing emigration or, alternatively, increasing immigration typically involves increasing the amount of food or suitable habitat within an area such as planting game crops to hold or attract pheasants.

THE RELEASE OF HAND-REARED GAMEBIRDS

Released birds provide an artificial supplement to natural productivity and permit the shooting of large numbers of birds, virtually on demand. Although hand-rearing can provide large numbers of birds for shooting it can also be detrimental to the wild population. For example, Potts (1985) discusses the effects of releasing hand-reared partridges on the wild population in Italy. At present approximately 275 000 hand-reared birds are released annually and around 65% of the population are shot each year. In a situation such as this the level of shooting is too high for the wild population to survive yet, because of the continual release of hand-reared birds, this level of harvesting can be maintained indefinitely (Fig. 8.6). The rearing of birds for release can also divert the attention of gamekeepers away from the

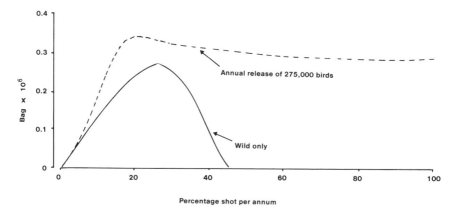

Fig. 8.6 A simulation of the effects of releasing partridges on the number shot in Italy. Shooting above 15% does not affect the size of the bag although it can lead to the loss of the wild population. (*After* Potts, 1986.)

traditional management techniques of habitat management and predator control. Furthermore, hand-reared birds tend to display higher rates of natural mortality, typically from being particularly vulnerable to predation, while they are also less successful breeders and produce fewer chicks than their wild counterparts (Robertson, 1986; Hill and Robertson, 1986). As such, hand-rearing can increase subsequent bags but can be associated with decreased management and heavier shooting of wild stocks, to their detriment.

These forms of management are used both to increase the yield at MSY and to raise the proportion of the population that can be harvested on a sustainable basis. Potts (1986) models the effects of two particular management techniques on the harvesting dynamics of the grey partridge (Fig. 8.7): firstly the effect of increasing nest survival through predator control, and secondly the implications of increasing

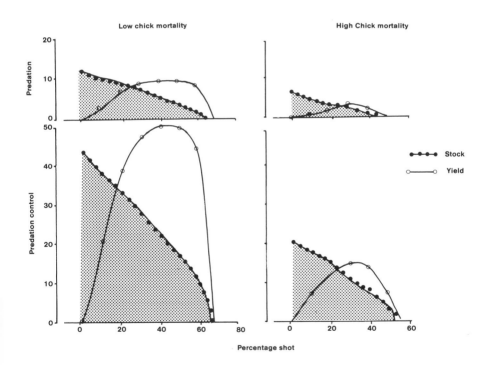

Fig. 8.7 Predictions from a simulated partridge model of stocking levels much reduced by shooting and yield in relation to management procedures (after Potts, 1986). Predator control led to a five-fold increase in the bag when chick mortality was low and a three-fold increase when mortality was high. Note that the MSY fell from 45% to 30% with an increase in chick mortality.

chick survival by modifying pesticide applications to cereal fields. Comparisons with observed populations are given in Potts (1980). The removal of nest predators results in a five-fold increase in the bag at MSY where chick mortality is low and a three-fold increase where it is high. Nevertheless, predator control does not have any great effect on the rate of shooting which gives the MSY. Increasing chick survival does however shift the MSY from 30% to 45% of the unshot population. These examples demonstrate the dramatic effects that gamebird management can have on the productivity of populations. Although, in each of the scenarios described above, shooting depresses the number of breeding birds, management raises the stocks to levels beyond those encountered in unmanaged populations. Whilst appearing to be something of a paradox, shooting can be said to benefit many game populations as it provides the motive and financial incentive for their management.

8.5 Conclusions

Most gamebird populations exhibit some degree of density-dependence in their intrinsic rates of growth. The reduction in the density of a population through harvesting can result in increased growth rate of the remaining population and an increased harvest on a sustainable basis.

Models of harvesting can be used to simulate the response of a population to shooting and predict how many birds can be harvested year after year to maintain a stable population. This is termed a sustainable yield. The aim of game management is to determine which level of shooting can give the largest sustained harvest, known as the maximum sustainable yield (MSY), or in the light of conflicting aims or a highly variable population, the optimum sustainable yield (OSY). The size of these yields can be increased through the selective shooting of certain cohorts within the population, most typically the males.

One consequence of harvesting is that it will reduce the density of a population although this is rarely recognised by game managers. However, in most gamebird populations the relationship between natural and hunting mortality is such that there is partial compensation. This implies that increasing hunting mortality results in a partial decrease in the extent of natural mortality.

The extent of the harvest is controlled by individual landowners in Britain and by legislation in most other countries. In America the potential harvest is assessed on an annual basis and the activity of sportsmen controlled by bag and season limits. These restrictions rarely aim to achieve MSY, partly due to the reluctance of sportsmen and managers to reduce breeding populations, a situation often wrongly referred to as over-shooting.

The size of the harvest can be increased by a variety of different forms of management, habitat manipulation, predator control and increasing the foods available to chicks. Although harvesting reduces the density of the prey these techniques can raise the density beyond that encountered in unmanaged populations

9 Population Simulation Models as an Aid to Gamebird Management

David A. Hill and Nick Carter

9.1 Introduction

Models which describe either an ecological system or an animal population are gaining popularity in ecology; particularly as computer knowledge amongst biologists increases. Indeed, the application of models in ecology has been considered 'almost compulsory if we want to understand the function of such a complex system' (Jorgensen, 1986).

Ecological models have been used to design surveys of complex systems as well as to reveal weaknesses in current knowledge so that future research might be better directed. Furthermore, they have been used to investigate scientific hypotheses by producing, through simulation, an expected distribution of animal numbers to compare with observed distributions in nature. However, models have sometimes been used with little regard for the complexities of the system and it is necessary to state that models can only be as accurate and useful as is permitted by the quality of the information from which they are built.

Most models developed for game populations have concentrated on the factors influencing the potential harvest but considerable effort has also been given to constructing models which incorporate the habitat requirements of game populations. If a model predicts the effects of different management techniques, then much time and money can be saved. Also the predictions can be used to influence directly the way in which experiments are conducted.

This chapter describes the types of models that can be used in the management of a wild gamebird, the techniques and principles used to construct a model and the application of such models to game management.

9.2 Types of mathematical models

There are many different approaches to mathematical modelling. No single one can be said to be appropriate for all gamebird management investigations, as each has its advantages and disadvantages. The personal preference of the modeller also plays an important part in the choice of mathematical model. We describe a number of approaches which have either been used or may prove useful for modelling gamebird and wildfowl populations and discuss, using examples, their relative merits. The list is incomplete as this section is intended only as a guide to the ways in which models can be used to assist the objectives of management.

Mathematical models can be classified in several ways: static-dynamic, deterministic-stochastic, analytical-statistical-simulation, discrete-continuous, or deductive-empirical. Some models are hybrids of different approaches and these are discussed in the examples below, whereas Jeffers (1978) presents a fuller account of the modelling process in relation to general applications for ecological problems. In gamebird management, models are generally used to:

(1) Describe and explain the population dynamics of a species and to identify the potentially important causes of change in population density or equilibria density levels.
(2) Investigate specific management problems and options.
(3) To propose meaningful field experiments which test hypotheses.

Nearly all the models which would be of interest to the gamebird manager are dynamic, dealing with changes in density over time, either seasonally or annually. The origin of a model determines whether it is deductive, i.e. based on conclusions derived from reasoning and logic, or empirical, when it is based on observations or experiences. Most management models are empirical since they are developed from relationships between sets of data. These relationships are not necessarily causal. In the following examples we shall include, where appropriate, original equations to show relationships between variables used in modelling. They are not essential to the understanding of the value of modelling but can be used if required.

9.2.1 Example of a deductive model

An example of a deductive gamebird model is that of Page and

Bergerud (1984). They developed a simulation model based on Chitty's Polymorphic Behavioural Hypothesis (Chitty, 1967) in which populations of animals are self-regulatory through different behavioural traits due to changes in their genetical composition. They assumed that at high densities aggressive individuals with low reproductive rates are selected for. Thus an increase in the proportion of these individuals in a population leads to a population decline. In contrast, at low densities less aggressive and more productive individuals are favoured, leading to a population increase. This results in periodic fluctuations or cycles which are common features of some grouse populations (see Section 2.3). Whilst Page and Bergerud's main investigations concerned the 10-year cycles in willow ptarmigan (a close relative of the red grouse) in Newfoundland, their conclusions were generalised to other grouse species.

The model was based on three main assumptions:

(1) The level of aggression was genetically determined according to the simple laws of Mendelian selection.
(2) Recruitment was inversely related to the level of aggression of the female parents.
(3) Aggressive individuals were completely successful in breeding competition.

The predictions from the model were close to observations of grouse populations which, although not confirming the original hypothesis, do lend support to it. To obtain further support for the theory the authors suggested eight tests. For example, one stated that population cycling was not dependent on predation, thus the removal of predators from an area should not interfere with the population fluctuations.

9.2.2   Examples of empirical models

GROUSE

Several grouse models have been developed on observations. Potts *et al.* (1984) used time-series analysis to describe the fluctuations in the number of red grouse shot in northern England. They found that although the bag records showed cyclical behaviour, auto-correlation analysis indicated that year-to-year relationships broke down if periods longer than several years were used. As described in Chapter 2 (Section 2.3), this is termed quasi-cycling. Auto-regression equations were fitted to data from moors to calculate the average cycle length of

4.8 years. Thus, the auto-regression equation provided a model which described some data well.

To describe the population dynamics of red grouse and to discover the cause of the quasi-cyclic fluctuations Potts *et al.* (1984) developed a dynamic statistical model based on census data. The model had four main components:

(1) Breeding production was a function of the level of infection with the parasitic nematode *Trichostrongylus tenuis.*
(2) The rate of infection with the worms was a function of grouse density and time.
(3) Shooting losses increased with density to an asymptote, described by a logistic equation.
(4) Winter losses were density-dependent to reflect territorial behaviour.

The relationship between breeding production and worm burdens does not prove that an increasing worm burden causes a decline in breeding success – only that there is an association between them. A third, as yet unknown factor, may be the cause of the association. A study of captive birds (Wilson, 1979) does however support this hypothesis and experiments conducted in the field by Hudson (1986a,b) have demonstrated that breeding success can be significantly increased when the worm burden of hen grouse is reduced by treatment with anthelmintic drugs (for details see Section 5.3.2).

When simulations were run with the model in its deterministic form no quasi-cycles in the numbers shot were produced regardless of how much the initial conditions of the model were changed. As the model was deterministic no allowance for random variation in values taken by variables was included. Thus for a given set of circumstances there was only one possible outcome. This may not be important if the amount of variation is relatively small but it becomes more unrealistic as variability increases.

A model which allows for the effects of random factors (such as that caused by weather) in one or more variables is termed stochastic. The actual value for a particular calculation is dependent on a probability distribution about the value mean chosen to mimic the observed variation. Thus if the frequency distribution is a normal curve, values will tend to be relatively close to the mean and will be symmetrically arranged around it. Details of modelling stochastic variation are given in Nisbet and Gurney (1982).

In the grouse model stochastic variation, representing the effects of weather, was included on:

(1) The breeding production of the grouse; this represented the effects of weather on food quality in early spring (Moss *et al.*, 1975) which influenced hen condition and production.
(2) The worm burden of young birds; this represented the effects of weather on the rate of infection.

The model produced bag records that fluctuated in a quasi-cyclic manner similar to those observed in the north of England. Removal of the worm effects from the model resulted in no quasi-cycling, indicating that the relationship between grouse density and worm uptake was the factor responsible.

Thus we have already seen two models which reach two different conclusions of the cause of population fluctuations in grouse populations, one for red grouse, the other for the closely related willow ptarmigan. Another set of red grouse models (Watson *et al.*, 1984) based on statistical relationships with neither a genetical basis nor taking the effects of parasitic worms into account has indicated a third possible mechanism. Correlation analysis between population variables was carried out, treating the males and females together and separately, to determine significant interactions. This procedure can provide interesting insights into the mechanisms involved in the workings of a population but must be used with caution as some significant relationships can arise by chance. Various models were produced using either one or two independent variables with different time delays. In general the results from the models indicated that emigration was the most important intrinsic factor while predation on eggs, probably by crows, was the only observed extrinsic one.

Whilst the hypotheses in these models are not mutually exclusive (they are summarised in Table 9.1), there are four possible causes for the apparent discrepancies between the models:

(1) Each model applies only to its particular data set.
(2) One of the explanations is correct and the other two are incorrect.
(3) All these explanations play a part in influencing the population cycles but their relative importance varies with data sets.
(4) None of the explanations is correct and the population fluctuations are caused by an undiscovered factor.

Although the differences proposed have caused controversy (e.g. Bergerud *et al.*, 1985; Watson and Moss, 1987) there are explanations which can account for certain parts of the disparity (see Moss and Watson, 1979; Hudson *et al.*, 1985). Even so, testing the models on

Table 9.1 Summary table of the three grouse models discussed in the text.

Source	Model type	Factor investigated	Conclusions
Potts, *et al.* (1984) (red grouse)	Empirical – dynamic statistical (used time series analysis) with stochasticity	Cyclical fluctuations in autumn numbers	Parasitic worm burdens in breeding hens in association with random effects responsible for cycling behaviour
Page and Bergerud (1984) (willow ptarmigan with inferences about red grouse)	Deductive simulation deterministic	Cyclical fluctuations and effects of genetically determined aggression based on Chitty's polymorphic behaviour hypothesis (C.P.B.H.). Recruitment assumed inversely related to female aggression and aggressive birds were completely successful in competing for breeding sites	Aggression important determinant of cyclical fluctuations, cycling not dependent on predation
Watson, Moss and Rothery and Parr (1984) (red grouse)	Dynamic statistical	Cyclical fluctuations in autumn numbers, also determinants of breeding population size. Used a series of between variable correlations. Worm burdens not taken into account. Incorporated different time delays	Emigration considered the most important intrinsic factor. Predation of eggs the most important extrinsic factor

other data sets, together with experiments, will help to clarify their relative importance.

PARTRIDGES

Another dynamic statistical model is that for the grey partridge developed by Potts (1980, 1986) and summarised in Fig. 9.1. The model is initiated by a density of breeding pairs. From this the potential egg density and hatching density are calculated. After discounting the numbers of chicks dying, the remainder are added to the number of adults present after breeding to give the post-breeding

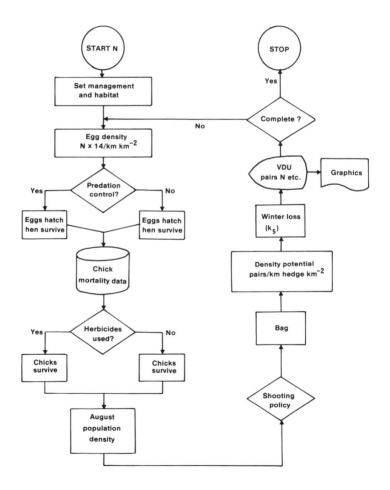

Fig. 9.1 Computer simulation model of the Sussex partridge population (after Potts, 1986) illustrating the sequence of steps.

population. This is further reduced by shooting losses, by winter losses, and the difference between immigration and emigration, to give the number of breeding pairs the following spring.

The number of chicks hatching per successful nest varies little and in the model is set at 14. Chick mortality rates could not be predicted and so observed annual data were used, with a suitable adjustment according to whether herbicides were applied; these effectively reduced food abundance and chick survival as described in Chapter 6. The mortality rates of both hens and eggs were dependent on nest density and predator control. Simple linear regressions were used to describe these relationships; shooting losses were also density-dependent but the relationship was logistic, with a maximum harvesting rate of 55% of the autumn population. However, this relationship did not hold in areas where red-legged partridges were released since in these areas grey partridges were still shot even when their densities were very low. Also more males were shot than would be expected from their proportion in the population and this was also incorporated into the model.

The effects of controlling nest predation on partridge numbers were examined by running the model with and without the effects of predation. With ideal nesting cover and in the absence of shooting and pesticides, the respective equilibrium pair densities with and without predation control were 64 and 16 km^2. For reasons explained in Chapter 6, this latter equilibrium density was strongly dependent on the amount of nesting cover – the more cover in a square kilometre, the greater the number of partridges. Thus, the model was used to estimate the likely change in population with a given change in certain management practices.

The model was also used to estimate the relative importance of the three factors which could have caused the dramatic decline in the grey partridge population (described in Chapter 2) on a study area in the Sussex Downs:

(1) The application of herbicides on cereal fields which removes weeds and their associated invertebrates, on which the chicks feed.
(2) Increased nest predation due to a reduction in gamekeeping.
(3) Reduced nesting cover as a result of hedge removal.

Several runs of the model were carried out using different values for the above factors and as a result Potts (1986) concluded that the introduction of herbicides was the primary factor causing the decline on the main study area in West Sussex, although the lack of predator control also caused a reduction in population levels. The latter factor was the primary cause at another location. Thus practices which offset the adverse effects of herbicides, such as reduced spraying in cereal crop margins (Rands, 1985; details in Section 6.3.1), should have a beneficial effect on partridge population levels, especially if coupled with some form of predator control. An increase in the length of hedgerow per unit area also results in an increase in breeding numbers if chick survival is improved in the previous year. It must be stressed that, in such models, the logical outcome of, say, improving the abundance of chick food items would be an increase in population level. However, the value of modelling is more subtle in that it allows the researcher to deal with successive mortalities, each differently related to pre-mortality density. The levels of density-dependent mortality determine the long-term model outcomes.

WILDFOWL

A number of mallard population models have been produced to rationalise management and hunting practices. One (Hill, 1982) is described later as an example of how a model is constructed but at least five models exist describing the population dynamics of mallard in North America.

Three of the models are dynamic and statistical. In the first, Walters *et al.* (1974), the number of breeding pairs is dependent on the availability of suitable breeding ponds, the number of which varies around an observed mean value in relation to rainfall. Breeding production is inversely dependent on the density of breeding females while shooting is directly dependent on the size of the autumn population. An increase in shooting pressure led to a population decline due to the reduction in young birds entering the breeding population.

In the second model, that of Anderson (1975), a positive relationship between rainfall and the number of ponds in the early summer is incorporated to influence breeding density. Age and sex-specific survival rates, along with the number of young fledged, were dependent on breeding density. Sensitivity analysis (see Section 9.3.6) indicated that population fluctuations are more closely related to annual changes in recruitment rather than changes in survival rates, in contrast to the predictions from the model of Walters *et al.* (1974).

The third model, produced by Hochbaum and Caswell (1978), incorporated a density-dependent harvest rate and inversely density-dependent survival, which was sex-specific. The model found that as the percentage of hens that successfully raised young decreased, so a lower harvesting rate on all ages and both sexes was required to maintain equilibrium densities. Habitat improvement was recommended to increase breeding density and hen productivity.

The remaining two mallard models are analytical. The dynamics of the population are summarised in one or two equations which can be solved mathematically without resorting to simulation procedures. Their simplistic nature is both an advantage and a drawback in that it is assumed that variables remain unchanged over long periods which makes analysis easy but is unlikely to occur in nature. Land managers may, however, find such models relatively useful tools since they are easy to apply.

In the fourth model, that of Cowardin and Johnson (1979), the proportional annual change in mallard numbers (C) is related to annual adult female survival (S), the ratio of young survival to that of adults (D), the probability of eggs hatching in a nest (P), the average size of fledged broods (B), survival of broods from hatch to census (Z), and summer survival rate (S_b).

$$C = S (1 + 0.5\ D\ P \exp (1 - P)^2\ ZB/S_b) \qquad (9.1)$$

When $C = 1$ the population remains stable from one year to the next and the value of any parameter can be found given values for all the others. Likewise, the effect of any slight change in the value of one parameter on the annual change in the population can be easily calculated, so long as all the other parameters remain constant. Cowardin and Johnson (1979) used the model to study the effect of planting dense nesting cover and introducing predator control on population change. They found that the former factor alone had little effect on population change but in combination with predator control caused a rapid increase in population density, a finding supported by key-factor analysis (Hill, 1984a).

The model of Brown et al. (1976) is a modification of the fish population models developed by Beverton and Holt (1957). The number of immatures surviving to the autumn, I_t, is dependent on the number of adult birds in May, W_t, and the amount of wetland suitable for mallard production, P_t:

$$I_t = (c/W_t + (aP_t^b)^{-1})^{-1} \qquad (9.2)$$

where a, b and c are constants greater than zero. The number of immatures surviving decreases at a rate approaching aP_t^b (a limit which can be varied according to changes in wetland habitat) when the population of ducks is large. The number alive the following year, W_{t+1}, depends on the number of adults surviving to the autumn, S_3, the number killed by hunting, K_t, and the number surviving the winter, S_2:

$$W_{t+1} = S_2 (S_3 W_t + I_t - K_t) \qquad (9.3)$$

Thus if the area of wetland remains constant year-to-year and the number of adult birds remains the same:

$$P_t = P_{t+1} = P* \qquad (9.4)$$

and $$W_t = W_{t+1} = W* \qquad (9.5)$$

$$W* = S_2 (S_3 W* + I* - K*) \qquad (9.6)$$

The number of mallard which can be shot to maintain a constant stock can be calculated for any combination of $W*$ and $I*$, given values for the natural survival rates:

$$K* = I* - W* ((1/S_2) - S_3) \qquad (9.7)$$

Data for the two survival parameters were determined from censuses and steady state values for the number of immatures and the number killed by hunting at various densities.

The maximum sustainable yield, defined in Chapter 8, can also be found using the equation in combination with the modified Beverton and Holt (1957) equation. Surprisingly, perhaps, the number which could be killed for the maximum sustainable yield hardly changed with an increase in breeding density while the number of ponds remained constant, but when the number of ponds decreased, even with constant density, the maximum sustainable yield was reduced. Introducing stochastic elements to the numbers of breeding pairs and immatures hardly affected the maximum sustainable yields.

9.2.3 Matrix models

The final modelling approach is rather specialised and seems to have been little used in the study of gamebird populations, although it has been applied to mammals, e.g. the blue whale (Usher, 1972), various species of seals and deer, and a modified version for insects (Lefkovitch, 1965, 1966, 1967). Matrix models, describing the population dynamics of animals, were first proposed by Lewis (1942) but received little attention until Leslie (1945, 1948) advanced the principles further.

A matrix is a table of numbers (elements) which can be one-dimensional (row or column vector) or composed of x rows and y columns ($x . y$ matrix). The reproductive and survival rates of different age classes of animal are stored as elements in a Leslie matrix while their densities are stored in a column vector. The numbers of animals are updated by multiplying the Leslie matrix with the column vector:

$$
\begin{bmatrix}
F_0 & F_1 & \ldots & F_m \\
P_0 & O & \ldots & O \\
O & P_1 & \ldots & O \\
& & & \\
& & & \\
O & O & p_{m-1} & O
\end{bmatrix}
\times
\begin{bmatrix}
N_{t,0} \\
N_{t,1} \\
N_{t,2} \\
. \\
. \\
. \\
. \\
. \\
. \\
N_{t,m}
\end{bmatrix}
=
\begin{bmatrix}
N_{t+1,0} \\
N_{t+1,1} \\
N_{t+1,2} \\
. \\
. \\
. \\
. \\
. \\
. \\
N_{t+1,m}
\end{bmatrix}
$$

where F and P are the reproductive and survival rates respectively of the $m + 1$ age classes and N is the number at a specified time, t, in a particular age class. Matrix multiplication is such that the first number in the updated column vector is found by summing the products of the individual elements in the first row of the Leslie matrix with their corresponding elements in the column vector. The second number is found by summing the products of the individual elements in the second row by the elements in the column vector, and so on. Thus the number in the first age class is the sum of the products of the reproductive rates and the number of adults. The number in each succeeding age class is the product of the number in the next youngest age class of the previous time interval and its respective survival rate.

Repeated multiplication of the Leslie matrix with the population column vector eventually leads to a column vector with a stable age distribution (called the dominant eigenvector) which increases at a constant rate (called the dominant eigenvalue, λ). The natural logarithm of λ is the intrinsic rate of natural increase. Eigenvectors and values can be determined mathematically as well as numerically and the effects of harvesting rates can also be estimated; for example the percentage of the population (H) which can be removed to bring it back to its initial population size:

$$H = 100 \, \frac{\lambda - 1}{\lambda}$$

The Leslie matrix can be modified to allow for density-dependent survival and reproductive rates and for different harvesting rates for each age class.

Tipton *et al.* (1980) used a matrix approach to simulate the effects of methyl parathion (an organophosphate pesticide) on a bobwhite quail population. The model was used to study the consequences of two dosages of pesticides, applied at weekly intervals. Halving the dosage from 1.13 to 0.57 kg ha^{-1} significantly reduced mortality such that extinction of the population became less likely. However, these simulation results were not supported by any direct observations of effects in the field.

9.2.4 Summary

The aim of this section was to introduce the reader to several modelling approaches using examples drawn from game management. Models do not provide irrefutable proof for hypotheses, as borne out by the controversies surrounding grouse population cycling behaviour and mallard management programmes. Models are useful, however, in formulating ideas in a framework which can then be studied and tested.

9.3 Constructing a population model

Most gamebird and wildfowl population models are dynamic and statistical. To illustrate this, an example, describing the population dynamics of mallard, is constructed and used in this section. The mallard is a common duck, distributed throughout the temperate northern hemisphere, with subspecies inhabiting parts of Australasia. It breeds around the edges of permanent and semi-permanent lakes, river systems, marshlands and small ponds. In the United States, a controlled system of bag limits has operated to prevent over-exploitation, although in recent years evidence has been found to suggest that shooting and natural mortalities are not additive (which gave rise to the bag limit system) but, at equilibrium, are largely compensatory (Anderson and Burnham, 1976). Management objectives for mallard in the States require modifications to those adopted for other more sedentary species because of the migratory habits of mallard.

In Britain, approximately 600 000 mallard are released for shooting purposes per annum in addition to wild bred mallard, many of which are Scandinavian, Icelandic and continental populations.

In the past 30 years in particular, gravel has been extracted from lowland river floods to supply the building and motorway construction industries; this has resulted in the formation of new, ecologically immature wetlands (gravel pits), and increased available nesting habitat for mallard. Partly as a consequence the British mallard population has been increasing at approximately 2% per annum since the early 1960s (Atkinson-Willes and Frith, 1964) though in recent years the increase has been less apparent (Owen et al., 1986). These gravel pits often have a low productivity for ducklings for several years after flooding. A number of other factors are involved, for example high silt levels reduce light penetration and therefore the growth of macrophytic plants, a major factor with wet dug pits (N.Giles, in litt).

One consequence of the initially sparse growth of vegetation around gravel pits is that mallard nests have little cover and eggs are more often eaten by predators than those on mature lakes where the vegetation is well developed and provides greater concealment (Hill, 1984b). In addition, the low numbers of insects which are a crucial part of the ducklings' diet can increase duckling mortality (Hill et al., 1987). Overall, duckling survival is much lower on gravel pits than on more natural habitats such as chalk streams.

The model is based on mallard population data collected at the Sevenoaks gravel pit reserve in Kent, England. The reserve consists of four closely adjoining lakes in the Upper Darent valley which cover 35 hectares of open water. Maximum water depth varies from 30 metres in the two larger lakes to 2 metres in the smallest. Extraction of gravel ceased for the most part in 1960, after which plant development accelerated. The number of pairs of mallard breeding on the site together with the number of newly hatched broods and the number of fledged young have been counted since 1962 (Harrison, 1974).

9.3.1 Definition of objectives

Before constructing a model it is necessary to establish whether a modelling approach is the most suitable method of achieving the objectives and aims of a project. It would seem obvious that these considerations are crucial but they are often undervalued (Caswell et al., 1972; Overton, 1977). As we have seen, modelling is useful since it allows the manipulation of certain relationships which can have implications for the development or improvement of management practices. To carry out many of the possible manipulations experimentally in the field would be prohibitively expensive in time and effort.

The objectives determine the type of model to be constructed, the data required and what level of accuracy is needed in the output (Ruesink, 1976). Conversely, the complexity of the model might depend on the data already available and the effort required to collect more, i.e. a model might have to be simplified if only limited information can be obtained with the available resources. Ideally a model should have generality, realism and precision but reconciling all these is often difficult (Levins, 1966).

The objective of the mallard population model is to establish, on ecologically immature wetlands, how the breeding population and size of the harvestable population can be increased. In this respect three possible management options which could be instigated are:

(1) Improving nesting habitat to reduce nest losses; by providing more islands and taller vegetation nest concealment will be improved.
(2) Duckling survival could be improved by increasing the production of insects, in particular the emergent *chironomid diptera*; grading shorelines, planting macrophytic plants in the shallow water of the lake's fringe and increasing organic levels should increase insect abundance.
(3) Improving breeding habitat (nest site habitat plus female areas) could reduce winter losses, caused largely by dispersal.

Having defined the objectives of the modelling approach the next step is to describe the system.

9.3.2 Description of the system

A useful starting point in the construction of any model is to represent the annual cycle diagrammatically (Fig. 9.2). In this example three density-dependent mortality factors are thought to be important:

(1) Predation of eggs and incubating females.
(2) The loss of ducklings up to the time of fledging.
(3) The loss of individuals during winter due to mortality and emigration.

Management practices which would reduce all or any of these losses might result in significant increases in the population available for shooting.

9.3.3 Data collection and collation

Counts of breeding adults in March, mean clutch size, the number of broods observed to hatch, the number of broods and young fledged and hence September population, were conducted on the Sevenoaks reserve from 1962 to 1977. These data were used to calculate (in $\log_{10}$) the number of clutches destroyed by predators (the difference between the number of breeding females and the number of clutches which

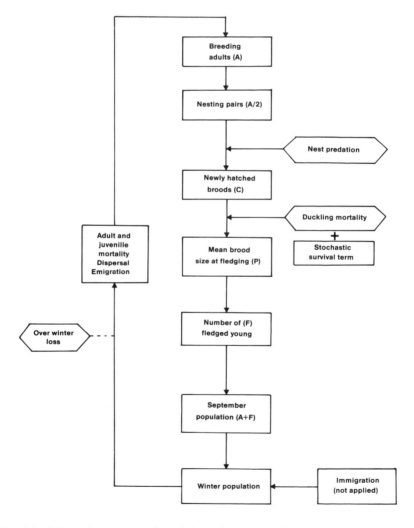

Fig. 9.2   Schematic representation of the mallard population model.

hatch), duckling mortality (the difference between the number of newly hatched young and the number which fledge) and over-winter losses (the difference between the size of the autumn population and the population in the following spring).

9.3.4 Formulation

For species such as the mallard with discrete breeding seasons, a series of linear regression equations has been used to describe the different parts of the life-cycle. It is commonplace to express the variables in the system as logarithms so that the strengths of density-dependence can be determined. This is done by expressing the mortalities as k-values; the difference in log densities before and after the mortality operated:

$$k_i = \log N_i - \log N_{i+1} \tag{9.8}$$

where N_i and N_{i+1} are the numbers of individuals in successive stages (Podoler and Rogers, 1975; Hill, 1984a).

The three mortalities can now be expressed in more formal terms:

(1) Clutch predation (k_1) was found to be dependent on the density of clutches (Fig. 9.3a):

$$k_1 = -0.176 + (b_1.\log_{10}\text{Eggs}) \qquad r = 0.81 \tag{9.9}$$

where b_1 (0.15 ± 0.01) is the slope of the density-dependent relationship.

(2) Duckling mortality (k_2) was weakly dependent on the density of hatched ducklings (Fig. 9.3b):

$$k_2 = -0.436 + (b_2.\log_{10}\text{ Hatched ducklings}) \; r = 0.41 \tag{9.10}$$

where b_2 (0.32 ± 0.05) is the slope of the density-dependent relationship.

(3) Over-winter loss (k_3) was dependent on the density of the September population (Fig. 9.3c):

$$k_3 = -0.781 + (b_3.\log_{10}\text{ Sept. popn.}) \qquad r = 0.82 \tag{9.11}$$

where b_3 (0.46 ± 0.03) is the slope of the density-dependent relationship. This relationship includes both natural mortality and dispersal occurring between autumn and spring.

Density-dependence in clutch predation and over-winter loss was confirmed by the two-way regression test (Varley and Gradwell, 1968) by plotting $\log N_t$ on $\log N_{t+1}$ and then $\log N_{t+1}$ on $\log N_t$. Density-dependence is taken as valid if the slopes are both significantly different from unity and lie on the same side of a slope of $b = 1$.

These three relationships, clutch predation, duckling mortality and over-winter loss, operate sequentially in the natural situation, the survivor output from each forming the independent axis for the next relationship. In this instance there are four outputs:

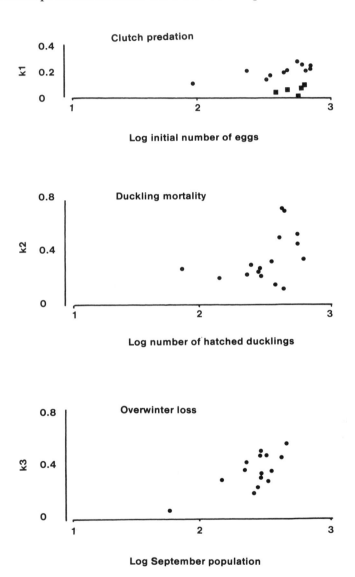

Fig. 9.3 Density-dependence plots for the three mortalities investigated in the mallard model. The black squares in (a) represent years when predators were controlled more heavily.

(1) Size of breeding population.
(2) Number of fledged young produced at each generation.
(3) Duckling survival rate.
(4) Size of the September population.

For the most part it is changes in the breeding population which are used to investigate the importance of management options, but at a later stage we will consider the breeding population after shooting.

9.3.5 Model verification and validation

Before a model can be used to provide advice or to investigate the effects of management options it has to be verified and validated. These two terms are often used interchangeably for model testing but it is useful to differentiate between them. Validation is the quantitative comparison of output from the model with independent observed results (Jeffers, 1978; Carter *et al.*, 1982). Verification comprises the comparison of the structure and general behaviour of a model with the real system (Jeffers, 1978) and ensuring that the model is operating on the data in the intended way. A model which fails either validation or verification may have errors in its structure or its formulation or both.

One aspect of validation is calibration (or tuning) which involves changing parameter values to improve the fit of a model to observations. This may result in the lowering of a model's explanatory role and degenerate into sophisticated curve fitting (Loomis *et al.*, 1979). In certain circumstances the value of a parameter may be impossible to estimate independently and calibration may be the only way of determining it. This estimate should always be considered with caution.

The most common way of validating a simulation model is by visual comparison of the model output with independent sets of data. This is usually represented graphically with associated confidence limits. Independence of data is an important consideration which is frequently ignored, especially in regression models where predictions are compared with the data used to calculate the equations. It is useful to make the comparisons with several state variables, e.g. number of breeding pairs, number of ducklings hatched, etc., over as wide a range of conditions as possible (Gilbert *et al.*, 1976). Two criteria are important – the general shape of the curve and the degree of quantitative agreement. Sometimes a poor fit results from inaccuracies in the field data.

This subjective assessment of the accuracy of a model is not entirely satisfactory and the development of statistical tests for validation is a major priority in simulation modelling.

Linear regression analysis (see Draper and Smith, 1966) of observations against the results predicted from a model should yield a slope not significantly different from 1 and an intercept of zero. These can be tested separately using t-tests or in combination with an F-test (Teng et al., 1980). Unfortunately violations of the assumptions of regression analysis are likely to occur in such tests, particularly in a time series where there is interdependence of points from one year to the next (Barlow and Dixon, 1980). Non-parametric methods have also been suggested, such as the Kolmogorov-Smirnov test, which measures the significance of the greatest vertical distance between two curves, but its disadvantage is that it is unlikely to show significant discrepancies when numbers are low (Teng et al., 1980), although this may be relatively unimportant. Cross-validation and predictive jack-knifing are useful techniques in the assessment of models (Stone, 1974). Basically they involve splitting a sample (size N) into two, developing a hypothesis using one part and testing it on the other. Usually the hypothesis-construction sample is of size $N - 1$ and the validation sample 1.

Validation of our model only involved checking a few equations to ensure they were correctly represented and occurred in the right order. The input and output procedures were also checked to make sure no errors were present. Linear regression was used to test the significance of the slope from unity and the plot of observed data against modelled data showed that the deterministic version over-predicted the observed population of breeding adults (slope $= 1.16 \pm 0.004$, $r = 0.98$, $df = 13$) because the slope was greater than unity ($P < 0.05$). This can be considered a reasonable error since the model is deterministic and lacks the reality of random variation.

Validation using independent data has not been possible because no further data were collected in a similar way. Collection of new data to test the model is time-consuming given that only one point for the graph can be assimilated each year. This is one of the main reasons why vertebrate models have been slow to emerge in comparison to their counterparts involving invertebrates with higher reproductive rates and shorter generation times.

The validation of a model can never be absolute since it needs to be verified; however, when the modeller is confident that the model is sufficiently accurate for its objectives, sensitivity analysis can be started.

9.3.6 Sensitivity analysis

Sensitivity analysis is a process of experimenting with models and involves changing their structure and parameter values. It can also be useful during model formulation to determine the relative importance of processes and hence concentrate attention on the most critical parts.

Two forms of sensitivity analysis are recognised (Carter *et al.*, 1982):

(1) A coarse form where processes are omitted from the model to test their overall effect. This can also involve changes in the structure of relationships such as the replacement of a density-dependent mechanism with a constant.
(2) A fine form where small positive and negative changes are made to parameter values to study the consequences for model output.

Table 9.2 The effect of holding density-dependent mortality factors constant but above zero on equilibrium densities of the Sevenoaks deterministic mallard population.

	No. breeding adults
Normal density-dependence	143
Constant clutch predation $k_1 = 0.155$	153
Constant duckling mortality $k_2 = 0.354$	146
Constant over-winter loss $k_3 = 0.315$	114

Usually only one parameter is changed at a time to examine its effect on model output, as complications of interpretation arise if several changes are carried out simultaneously. During fine sensitivity analysis, if a small change in a parameter leads to a large change in

Table 9.3 Equilibrium densities of breeding mallard in the deterministic model under varying density-dependence.

	No. breeding adults
Normal parameters	143
50% *decrease* in density-dependent clutch predation	170
50% *increase* in density-dependent clutch predation	123
50% *decrease* in density-dependent duckling mortality	254
50% *increase* in density-dependent duckling mortality	98
50% *decrease* in density-dependent over-winter loss	6500
50% *increase* in density-dependent over-winter loss	27

model output then its value must be known accurately, whereas if the effect is small then less precision is needed.

In the mallard example coarse grained sensitivity analysis involved the individual replacement of the three density-dependent losses with mean k-values ($k_1 = 0.155$, $k_2 = 0.354$, $k_3 = 0.315$). Output was constrained to the number of breeding adults. This change to duckling mortality had very little effect on outputs whilst the greatest difference was obtained with changes to over-winter loss. This is to be expected since this is the strongest density-dependent term (Table 9.2).

Fine-grained sensitivity analysis involved successive changes of the strength of the density-dependent relationships, by increasing and decreasing the slope of the logarithmic regression equations by a standard deviation or a set proportion. Because these relationships are logarithmic, change of the slope without any change to the intercept will give rise to greater effects at high densities. This resulted in greater disparity in duckling mortality than clutch predation, and large differences were caused by changes in over-winter loss (Table 9.3).

We conclude from these preliminary sensitivity analyses of the deterministic model that, for mallard:

(1) Changes in the dynamics and extent of clutch predation have little effect on breeding numbers.
(2) Changes in the dynamics and extent of duckling mortality give rise to larger effects on breeding populations.
(3) The most important term for the dynamics of the model is over-winter loss.

The next step in the development of the model was to identify the stage or stages in which stochastic variation might be important.

Mallard ducklings are susceptible to starvation on gravel pits because of the scarcity of invertebrate foods, and as such are directly and indirectly vulnerable to poor weather conditions during their first three weeks of age. This is because insect activity and hence availability is suppressed under poor conditions (Hill *et al.*, 1987). Mean (± 1 se) survival of mallard ducklings to fledgling on the Sevenoaks reserve was $53.3 \pm 2.5\%$, and so a stochastic function with a normal distribution is used in the model to simulate this variation between years. For each run when the model reaches the section dealing with duckling mortality, the computer calculates the value and then adds or subtracts it from the mean value.

If this stochastic variation improves the realistic nature of the duckling survival term then the fit of the model predictions with observed results should be improved. Indeed the slope of the regression of observed data on model prediction is decreased from 1.16 to 1.01 – providing an acceptable fit and validation of this step. This is reflected in the predictions from the stochastic model of breeding population size over time being very close to the observed data (Fig. 9.4).

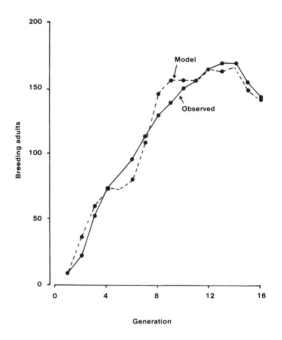

Fig. 9.4   Stochastic model prediction of population size (_ _ _) compared to observed data (___).

9.3.7 *Implications of the model for management*

CLUTCH PREDATION

The major predators of mallard eggs at Sevenoaks were carrion crows and magpies; for many years these have been controlled on British estates as part of game management. Whether predators of clutches are controlled or whether habitat features are managed to mimic predation control, the net effect is to improve the success of clutches. For example, previous field experiments have suggested that:

(1) Increasing the heterogeneity or 'patchiness' of nesting habitat can reduce the efficiency of some predators of ground nesting birds (Bowman and Harris, 1980; Chapter 4).

(2) Destruction of some corvids, particularly nesting pairs, can have the short-term effect of reducing the loss of clutches (Parker, 1984).

Before such management practices are carried out, however, our mallard model will allow us to establish their effects on the size of the breeding population.

Fine sensitivity analysis of the stochastic model was also carried out. Firstly, the intercept of the density-dependent relationship between the density of clutches and clutches destroyed was increased by 30% from an average clutch predation of 39.5% to 46%, and then decreased by 30% to 32%, keeping the same level of density-dependence. This gave the approximate range of clutch predation recorded in this species.

These changes produced little effect on the number of breeding adults (Fig. 9.5), largely because of the compensatory effects of density-dependent relationships (duckling mortality, over-winter loss) acting later. Consequently the management of nesting vegetation and the creation of islands so as to increase nest success (Hill, 1982) will only be of benefit to the following year's breeding population if other factors which reduce duckling mortality and over-winter loss are

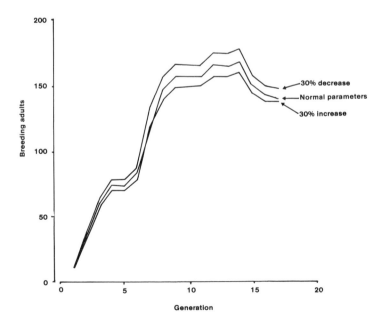

Fig. 9.5 Effect of a 30% increase and decrease of the intercept of density-dependent clutch predation on the number of breeding adult mallard at Sevenoaks, as predicted by the stochastic simulation model.

implemented. The model has proved useful in revealing this interdependence between the mortalities which otherwise might not have been found.

DUCKLING MORTALITY

A method designed to improve insect abundance by providing an input of organic material to the lake system would increase duckling survival. One technique would be to enrich the sterile lake bed with deposits of untreated barley straw. Another would be to grade the shoreline to produce a rich feeding shelf, planted with various species of submerged macrophytic vegetation.

The model allows us to investigate the effect of such management practices on future breeding populations by changing the intercept in the duckling survival relationship. Increases and decreases of 30% to the intercept of this relationship had a greater effect on breeding adults than did the changes in clutch predation (Fig. 9.6). The increase in the intercept reduced the average duckling mortality rate from 53.3% to 40.8%. Consequently, for the Sevenoaks mallard population at least,

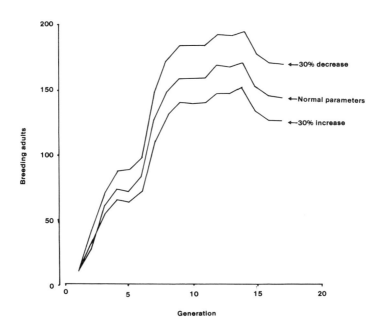

Fig. 9.6 Effect of a 30% increase and decrease of the intercept of density-dependent duckling mortality on the number of breeding adult mallard at Sevenoaks, as predicted by the stochastic simulation model.

there would be greater benefit in improving conditions for feeding ducklings during their early lives than in reducing clutch predation.

OVER-WINTER LOSS

Mallard begin to pair up after September and the males start to guard specific feeding territories or home ranges in March. Mallard populations on man-made wetlands often suffer density-dependent over-winter losses (Hill, 1984a), since there are only a limited number of nesting sites and feeding territories. Hence birds which survive the winter but are not able to establish breeding sites are likely to disperse to other areas or die (Hill, 1984a). As a consequence, increasing the number of nest-sites per unit area by constructing well vegetated islands with gradually sloping banks, and increasing shallow feeding areas, free from disturbance, should increase densities of breeding pairs by reducing density-dependent emigration.

There is a continuing argument as to whether mallard can compensate for shooting losses in subsequent breeding populations (Anderson and Burnham, 1976; Rogers *et al.*, 1979; Nichols *et al.*,

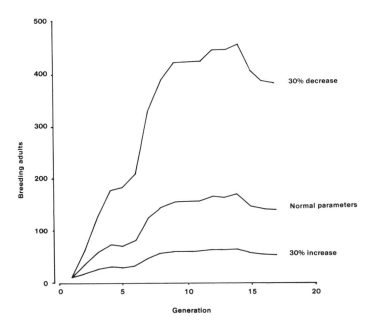

Fig. 9.7 Effect of a 30% increase and decrease of the intercept of density-dependent over-winter loss on the number of breeding adult mallard at Sevenoaks, as predicted by the stochastic simulation model.

1984). Modelling provides one way in which this problem can be investigated. Consider what occurs when density-dependent over-winter losses are altered by a 30% increase and a 30% decrease in the intercept. These changes resulted in large differences, supporting the argument that the population is particularly susceptible to over-winter losses (Fig. 9.7).

9.3.8 Implications of the model for harvesting

In Chapter 8 the term maximum sustainable yield (MSY) was discussed in detail; the MSY being the level of harvesting which produces the highest annual yield which can be sustained over a long time period. We can use the mallard model to investigate the effects on harvest, if management practices are aimed at improving nest success and duckling survival. The survival of birds from shooting is inversely related to the autumn population density (see Hill, 1982, for further details). Increasing the slope of this relationship effectively increases density-dependent shooting mortality. In an initial run, using all density-dependent parameters, we observed an anomaly caused by duckling mortality which tended to take unrealistically low mortality values when harvesting pressure was high owing to its density dependent nature. However, Hill (1984a) has shown duckling mortality is only weakly density-dependent ($p < 0.1$), and is the key factor affecting the autumn mallard population at Sevenoaks. Consequently it is highly variable and, because of the sensitivity analyses conducted, we replaced the density-dependent term with a mean of 53.3% duckling survival.

Altering clutch predation, by changing the intercept of the density-dependent term but keeping duckling survival constant, had a significant effect on the harvest, but changes to duckling survival had an even greater influence (Fig. 9.8a,b). The dynamics of the model were such that as shooting pressure increased, the point at which maximum sustainable yield (MSY) was obtained shifted; in other words higher shooting pressures were possible, but were attained at lower equili-brium densities.

9.3.9 Model summary

The last section has shown the important steps in the modelling process using data for a mallard population as an example. Three density-

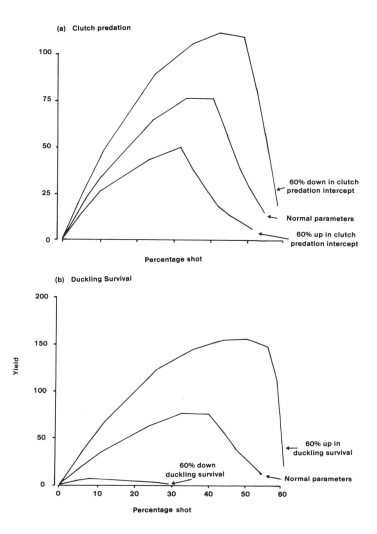

Fig. 9.8 Effect on yield of increasing and decreasing (a) clutch predation and (b) duckling survival by 60% as predicted by the stochastic simulation model.

dependent terms were identified: clutch predation, duckling mortality (weak), and over-winter loss. Duckling mortality was least sensitive to changes in levels of density-dependence, and was therefore replaced in the harvesting section by a constant with standard errors. Changes in clutch predation had little effect on the size of subsequent breeding populations, changes in duckling mortality had more effect, and changes in over-winter loss had the most effect. The model was used to determine levels of harvesting under different management regimes whose objectives were to improve nest success and duckling survival.

A similar approach to that presented here can be used to develop models for gamebirds in general. Hill and Robertson (1987) have developed a generalised model on pheasants which investigates the role of releasing hand-reared pheasants on the productivity of pheasants breeding in the wild.

9.4 Conclusion

Models are important tools to the ecologist. Those constructed for gamebird populations are generally of the dynamic statistical kind, empirically constructed from relationships between real data sets. The predictions they give, based on the objectives set and the questions asked by the modeller, are only as valuable as the quality of the data from which they are constructed. Formulation, validation, verification, sensitivity analyses and experimental testing are essential parts of the modelling process.

Models designed to answer management-related questions are useful for two reasons. First, they can be used to isolate the most important components in the biological system. Second, they can point to specific areas requiring further research. Using such models, a series of management practices can be investigated at little cost, whereas the field implementation of combinations of such practices would be an impossible task. Field experiments can then be designed to test specific predictions of the model.

This chapter has shown that different models for the same species can point to different factors being responsible for changes in a population, such as those constructed for grouse and mallard. Models do not provide proof of hypotheses, nor, in many circumstances, can their conclusions be applied uncritically from one locality to another. These cautions accepted, models do have an important role to play in the study and management of animal populations.

References

Anderson, D.R. (1975) Population ecology of the mallard v. temporal and geographical estimates of survival, recovery and harvest. *U.S. Fish and Wildlife Service Resource Publication* **123**, 110 pp.

Anderson, D.R. and Burnham, K.P. (1976) Population ecology of the mallard VI. The effect of exploitation on survival. *U.S. Fish and Wildlife Service Resource Publication* **128**, 66 pp.

Anderson, R.M. (1978) The regulation of host population growth by parasitic species. *Parasitology* **76**, 119–158.

Anderson, R.M. (1979) The influence of parasitic infection on the dynamics of host population growth. In *Population Dynamics* (eds R.M. Anderson, B.D. Turner and L.R. Taylor), 245–281, Blackwell Scientific Publications, Oxford.

Anderson, R.M. (1981) Population ecology of infectious disease agents. In: *Theoretical Ecology* (ed R.M. May) 318–355, Blackwell Scientific Publications, Oxford.

Anderson, R.M. (1982a) The population dynamics and control of hookworm and roundworm infections. In: *Population Dynamics of Infectious Diseases: Theory and Application.* (ed R.M. Anderson) 67–108. Chapman and Hall, London.

Anderson, R.M. (1982b) Epidemiology. In: *Modern Parasitology. A textbook of parasitology.* (ed F.E.G. Cox). Blackwell Scientific Publications, Oxford.

Anderson, R.M. (1982c) Fox rabies. In: *Population dynamics of infectious diseases: Theory and application.* (ed R.M. Anderson). Chapman and Hall, London.

Anderson R.M. and Crombie, J.A. (1985) Experimental studies of age-intensity and age-prevalence profiles of infection: *Schistosoma mansoni* in Snails and Mice. In: *Ecology and Genetics of Host-parasite Interactions.* (eds D. Rollinson and R.M. Anderson), 111–145. Academic Press, New York.

Anderson, R.M. and Gordon, D.M. (1982) Processes influencing the distribution of parasite numbers within host populations with special emphasis on parasite induced host mortalities. *Parasitology* **85**, 373–398.

Anderson, R.M. and May, R.M. (1978) Regulation and stability of host –

parasite population interactions: I Regulatory processes. *Journal of Animal Ecology* **47**, 219–249.

Anderson, R.M. and May, R.M. (1979) Population biology of infectious diseases. Part I. *Nature* **280**, 361–367.

Anderson, R.M. and Trewhella, W. (1986) Population dynamics of the badger (*Meles meles*) and the epidemiology and bovine tuberculosis (*Mycobacterium bovis*). *Phil. Trans R. Soc. Land B.* **310**, 327–381.

Andersson, M. (1982) Female choice selects for extreme tail length in a widowbird. *Nature* **299**, 818–820.

Andren, H., Angelstam, P., Lindstrom, E. and Widen, P. (1985) Differences in predation pressure in relation to habitat fragmentation: an experiment. *Oikos* **45**, 273–277.

Angelstam, P. (1979) Black grouse reproductive success and survival rate in peak and crash small-rodent years – a preliminary report. In: *Woodland Grouse Symposium 1978.* (ed T.W.I. Lovel) 101–111. World Pheasant Association, Bures, Suffolk, England.

Angelstam, P. (1983) Population dynamics of tetraonids, especially the black grouse *Tetrao tetrix* L. in boreal forests. Unpubl. doctoral thesis, Uppsala University, Sweden. 254 pp.

Angelstam, P. (1984) Sexual and seasonal differences in mortality of the black grouse *Tetrao tetrix* in boreal Sweden. *Ornis Scandinavica* **15**, 123–124.

Angelstam, P. (1986) Predation on ground-nesting birds' nests in relation to predator densities and habitat edge. *Oikos* **47**, 365–373.

Anglestam, P.K. (1987) Population dynamics in tetranoids: the role of extrinsic factors. *International Ornithological Congress 1986* (in press).

Angelstam, P., Lindstrom, E. and Widen, P. (1982) Cyclic shifting of predation and other interrelationships in a south taiga of small game community. *Transactions International Congress Game Biologists* **14** (1982), 53–60.

Angelstam, P., Lindstrom, E. and Widen, P. (1984) Role of predation in short-term population fluctuations of some birds and mammals in Fennoscandia. *Oecologia* **62**, 199–208.

Angelstam, P., Lindstrom, E. and Widen, P. (1985) Synchronous short-term population fluctuations of some birds and mammals in Fennoscandia – occurrence and distribution. *Holarctic Ecology* **8**, 285–298.

Ankney, C.D. (1980) Egg weight, survival and growth of lesser snow goose goslings. *Journal of Wildlife Management* **44**, 174–182.

Ankney, C.D. and Bisset, A.R. (1976) An explanation of egg weight variation in the lesser snow goose. *Journal of Wildlife Management* **40**, 729–734.

Ankney, C.D. and MacInnes, C.D. (1978). Nutrient reserves and reproductive performance of female lesser snow geese. *Auk* **95**, 459–471.

Atkinson-Willes, G.L. and Frith, J.C. (1964) Trends in the population of British wintering ducks 1961–64. *Wildfowl Trust Annual Report for 1964*, 21–29.

Balfour, E. (1962–63) The hen harrier in Orkney. Part 3. Courtship, display and sociability. *Bird Notes* **300**, 145–53.

Ball, K.E. (1950) Breeding behaviour of the ring-necked pheasant on Pelee Island, Ontario. *Canadian Field Naturalist* **64**, 201–207.

Ballard, W.B. and Robel, R.J. (1974) Reproductive importance of dominant male Greater Prairie Chickens. *Auk* **91**, 75–85.

Balser, D.S. (1964) Management of predator populations with antifertility agents. *Journal of Wildlife Management* **28**(2): 352–358.

Balser, D.S., Dill, H.H. and Nelson H.K. (1968) Effect of predator reduction on waterfowl nesting success. *Journal of Wildlife Management* **32**, 669–682.

Barlow, N. and Dixon, A.F.G. (1980) *Simulation of lime aphid populations.* Simulation Monographs. Pudoc, Wageningen, The Netherlands, 171 pp.

Barnes, R.F.W. (1984) *The decline in Red Grouse bags in Scotland.* Unpublished Game Conservancy Report.

Barry, W.T. (1962) Effect of late seasons on Atlantic Brant reproduction. *Journal of Wildlife Management* **26**, 19–26.

Beattie, K.H. (1981) The influence of game laws and regulations on hunting satisfaction. *Wildlife Society Bulletin* **9**, (3) 229–231.

Beddington, J.R. (1974) Age structure, sex ratio and population density in the harvesting of natural animal populations. *Journal of Applied Ecology* **11**, 915–924.

Beddington, J.R. and Taylor, D.B. (1973) Optimal age specific harvesting of a population. *Biometrics* **29**, 801–809.

Begon, M., Harper, J.L. and Townsend, C.R. (1986) *Ecology: Individuals, Populations and Communities.* Blackwell Scientific Publications, Oxford.

Bergerud, A.T. (1970) Population dynamics of the willow ptarmigan *Lagopus lagopus alleni* L. in Newfoundland 1955–1965. *Oikos* **21**: 299–325.

Bergerud, A.T., Mossop, D.H. and Myrberget, S. (1985) A critique of the mechanics of annual changes in ptarmigan numbers. *Canadian Journal of Zoology* **63**, 2240–2248.

Beverton, R.J.H. and Holt, S.J. (1957) On the dynamics of exploited fish populations. Fishery Investigations, *H.M.S.O. London*, Series 2 **19**, 533 pp.

Blackford, J.L. (1958) Territoriality and breeding behaviour of a population of Blue Grouse in Montana. *Condor* **60**, 145–158.

Blackford, J.L. (1963) Further observations on the breeding behaviour of a Blue Grouse population in Montana. *Condor* **65**, 485–513.

Blank, T.H. (1969) Red-legged partridge. *Eley Game Advisory Station Annual Review* 1968/69, 45–50.

Blank, T.H., Southwood, T.R.E. and Cross, D.J. (1967) The ecology of the partridge. I. Outline of population processes with particular reference to chick mortality and nest density. *Journal of Animal Ecology* **36**, 549–556.

Boatman, N. (1986) The agronomic implications of unsprayed headlands. *Game Conservancy Annual Review* **17**, 61–64.

Bowman, G.B. and Harris, L.D. (1980) Effect of spatial heterogeneity on ground nest predation. *Journal of Wildlife Management* **44**, 806–813.

Box, G.E. and Jenkins, G.H. (1974) *Time-series analysis. Forecasting and control*, Holden-Day, San Francisco.

Braun, C.E. (1975) Mortality, survival and effects of hunting on grouse, partridge, pheasants and quail. *Colorado Division of Wildlife, Division Report No. 3.*

Braun, C.E. and Beck, T.D.I. (1985) Effects of changes in hunting regulations on sage grouse harvest and populations. In: *Game Harvest Management* (eds S.L. Beamson and S.F. Roberson), 335–344. Caesar Kleberg Wildlife Research Institute, Kingsville, Texas.

Breckenridge, W.J. (1929) The booming of the Prairie Chicken. *Auk* **46**, 540–543.

Brittas, R. (1984) Seasonal and annual changes in condition of the Swedish willow grouse, *Lagopus lagopus. Finnish Game Research* **42**: 5–17.

Brooke, M.M. (1945) Effect of dietary change upon avian malaria. *American Journal of Hygiene* **41**, 81–108.

Brower, L.P., Cook, L.M. and Croze, H.J. (1967) Predator responses to artificial batesian mimics released in a neotropical environment. *Evolution* **21**, 11–23.

Brown, D.E., Cochran, C.L. and Wadell, T.E. (1978) Using call counts to predict hunting success for scaled quail. *Journal of Wildlife Management* **42**, 281–287.

Brown, G.M., Hammack, J. and Tillman, M.F. (1976) Mallard population dynamics and management models. *Journal of Wildlife Management* **40**, 542–555.

Brownie, C., Anderson, D.R., Burnham, K.T. and Robson, E.F. (1978) Statistical inference from band recovery data – a handbook. *U.S. Fish & Wildlife Service Resource Publication* **131**. Washington DC. 212 pp.

Bryant, D.M. (1979) Reproductive costs in the House Martin. *Journal of Animal Ecology* **48**, 655–675.

Buechner, H.K. (1960) The bighorn sheep in the United States, its past, present and future. *Wildlife Monographs* **4**, 1–74.

Bulmer, M.G. (1974) A statistical analysis of the 10-year cycle in Canada. *Journal of Animal Ecology* **43**, 119–134.

Burger, G.V. (1966) Observations on aggressive behaviour of male Ring-necked pheasants in Wisconsin. *Journal of Wildlife Management* **30**, 57–64.

Carter, N., Dixon, A.F.G. and Rabbinge, R. (1982) *Cereal Aphid Populations: Biology, Simulation and Prediction.* Simulation Monographs. Pudoc, Wageningen, The Netherlands, 94 pp.

Caswell, H., Koerig, H.E., Resh, J.A. and Ross, Q.E. (1972) An introduction to systems science for ecologists. In: *Systems Analysis and Simulation in Ecology*, (ed B.C. Patten) 3–78, Academic Press, New York, 592 pp.

Caughley, G. (1977) *Analysis of vertebrate populations*. John Wiley and Sons, London. 234 pp.

Caughley, G. (1985) Harvesting of wildlife: past, present and future. In: *Game Harvest Management* (eds S.L. Beamson and S.F. Roberson), 3–14. Ceasar Kleberg Wildlife Research Institute, Kingsville, Texas.

Charnov, E.L. (1976) Optimal foraging: the marginal value theorem. *Theoretical Population Biology* **9**, 129–136.

Charnov, E.L. and Krebs, J.R. (1974) On clutch size and fitness. *Ibis* **116**, 217–219.

Chesness, R.A., Nelson, M.M. and Longley, W.H. (1968) The effect of predator control on pheasant reproductive success. *Journal of Wildlife Management* **32**, 683–697.

Chitty, D. (1967) The natural selection of self-regulatory behaviour in animal populations. *Proceedings of the Ecological Society of Australia* **2**, 51–78.

Christiansen, E. (1979) Skog-og jordbruk, smagnagere og rev. *Tidskrift for skogsbruk* **87**(3), 115–119.

Clark, C.W. (1976) *Mathematical Bioeconomics: the optimal management of renewable resources*. John Wiley and Sons, New York. 352 pp.

Clutton-Brock, T.H. and Harvey, P.H. (1984) Comparative approaches to investigating adaptation. In: *Behavioural Ecology* (eds J.R. Krebs and N.B. Davies) 7–29. Blackwell Scientific Publications, Oxford.

Cobham, R. and Rowe, J. (1986) Evaluating the wildlife of agricultural environments: an aid to conservation. In: *Wildlife conservation evaluation* (ed M.B. Usher) 223–246. Chapman and Hall, London.

Cody, M.L. (1966) A general theory of clutch size. *Evolution* **20**: 174–184.

Cole, L.C. (1951) Population cycles and random oscillations. *Journal of Wildlife Management* **15**, 233–252.

Cole, L.C. (1954) Some features of random population cycles. *Journal of Wildlife Management* **18**, 2–24.

Compton, M.M., Van Krey, H.P. and Siegal, P.B. (1978) The filling and emptying of the uterovaginal sperm-host glands in the domestic hen. *Poultry Science* **57**, 1696–1700.

Cooke, J.G. and Beddington, J.R. (1984) The relationship between catch rates and abundance in fisheries. *IMA Journal of Mathematics Applied in Medicine and Biology* **1**, 391–405.

Cooper, M. McGregor, and Thomas, R.J. (1975) *Profitable Sheep Farming*. Farming Press Ltd., Ipswich.

Coulson, J.C. and Butterfield, J.E.L. (1982) *The geographic characterisation of moorland using invertebrates*. Unpublished report to the Nature Conservancy Council.

Cowardin, L.M. and Johnson, D.H. (1979) Mathematics and mallard management. *Journal of Wildlife Management*, **43**, 18–35.

Cram, E.B. and Cuviellier, E. (1934) Observations on *Trichostrongylus tenuis* in domestic and gamebirds in the United States. *Parasitology* **26**, 340–346.

Cramp, S. and Simmons, K.E.L. (1977) *Handbook of the Birds of Europe, the Middle East and North Africa: the Birds of the Western Palearctic.* Vol. 1: Ostrich – Ducks. Oxford University Press, Oxford.

Cramp, S. and Simmons, K.E.L. (1980) *Handbook of the Birds of Europe, the Middle East and North Africa: the Birds of the Western Palearctic.* Vol. II: Hawks – Bustards. Oxford University Press, Oxford.

Crofton, H.D. (1971) A quantitative approach to parasitism. *Parasitology* **62**, 179–193.

Crook, J.H. (1964) The evolution of social organisation and visual communication in the weaver birds (Ploceinae). *Behaviour, Supplement* **10**, 1–178.

Cross, D.A. (1966) Approaches towards an assessment of the role of insect food in the ecology of gamebirds, especially the partridge (*Perdix perdix*). Unpublished PhD Thesis, University of London.

Cussans, G.W. (1975) Weed control in reduced cultivation and direct drilling systems. *Outlook on Agriculture* **8**, 240–242.

Darwin, C. (1859) *The Origin of Species by means of natural selection.* John Murray, London.

Darwin, C. (1871) *The descent of man and selection in relation to sex.* John Murray, London.

Davies, N.B. (1978) Ecological questions about territorial behaviour. In: *Behavioural Ecology. An Evolutionary Approach* (eds J.R. Krebs and N.B. Davies), 317–350. Blackwell Scientific Publications, Oxford.

Davison, G.W.H. (1981a) Sexual selection and the mating system of *Argusianus argus* (Aves: Phasianidae). *Biological Journal of the Linnaean Society* **15**, 91–104.

Davison, G.W.H. (1981b) Diet and dispersion of the Great Argus Pheasant, *Argusianus argus. Ibis* **123**, 485–494.

Dawkins, R. (1976) *The Selfish Gene.* Oxford University Press, Oxford.

Deevey, E.S. (1947) Life tables for natural populations of animals. *Quarterly Review of Biology* **22**, 283–314.

De Franceschi, P. (1982) Fluttuazioni delle popolazioni di tetraonidi sulli Alpi Carniche. *Estratto da Dendronatura n.* **3**, 19–38.

DeSteven, D. (1980) Clutch size, breeding success and parental survival in the tree swallow (*Iridopiocne bicolor*). *Evolution* **34**, 278–291.

Dobson, A.P. and Hudson, P.J. (1986) Parasites, diseases and the structure of ecological communities. *Trends in Ecology and Evolution,* **1**, 11–15.

Dobson, A.P. and Hudson, P.J. (1987) The population dynamics and control of the parasite nematode *Trichostrongylus tenuis* in red grouse in the north of England. *Applied Population Biology.* (eds S. Jain and L. Botsford.)

Dover, J. (1986) The benefits of unsprayed headlands: butterflies on farmland. *Game Conservancy Annual Review* **17**, 65–68.

Draper, N.R. and Smith, H. (1966) *Applied regression analysis.* John Wiley and Sons, New York.

Duebbert, H.F. and Kantrud, H.A. (1974) Upland duck nesting related to land use and predator reduction. *Journal of Wildlife Management* **38**, 257–265.

Duebbert, H.F. and Lokemoen, J.T. (1980) High duck nesting success in a predator-reduced environment. *Journal of Wildlife Management* **44**, 428–437.

Dumke, R.T. and Pils, C.M. (1973) Mortality of radio-tagged pheasants on the Waterloo Wildlife Area. *Wisconsin Department of Natural Resources Technical Bulletin* **72**. 51 pp.

Eadie, J. (1985) Trends in agricultural land use: the hills and uplands. In: *Agriculture and the Environment.* (ed D. Jenkins). ITE Symposium No. **13**. 13–19.

Edwards, W.R. (1962) Hen pheasant kill by hunting. *Game Research in Ohio* **1**, 26–27.

Edwards, W.R. (1963) Proportionate harvest of Ring-necked pheasant cocks and hens. *Game Research in Ohio* **2**, 11–22.

Einarsen, A.S. (1942) Specific results from ring-necked pheasant studies in the Pacific Northwest. *Transactions of the VIIth North American Wildlife Conference*, 130–138.

Ellison, L.N. and Magnani, Y. (1985) Changes in black grouse densities in the French Alps. *Proceedings of the Third International Grouse Symposium.* International Council for Game and Wildlife Preservation, Paris, 434–460.

Ellison, L.N., Magnani, Y. and Corti, R. (1982) Comparison of a hunted and three protected black grouse populations in the French Alps. In: *Proceedings of the Second International Symposium on Grouse* (ed T.W.I. Lovel). 175–187. World Pheasant Association, Bures, Suffolk, England.

Elton, C., and Nicholson, M. (1942) The ten-year cycle in numbers of the lynx in Canada. *Journal of Animal Ecology* **11**, 215–244.

Emlen, J.M. (1973) *Ecology: an Evolutionary Approach.* Addison-Wesley Publ. Co., Reading, Mass. 493 pp.

Emlen, S.T. and Oring, L.W. (1977) Ecology, sexual selection and the evolution of mating systems. *Science* **197**, 215–223.

Erikstad, K.J., Pedersen, H.C. and Steen, J.B. (1985) Clutch size and egg size variation in willow grouse *Lagopus l. lagopus. Ornis Scandinavica* **16**, 88–94.

Erlinge, S., Frylestam, B., Göransson, G., Högstedt, G., Liberg, O., Loman, J., Nilsson, I.N. Von Schantz, T. and Sylven, M. (1984) Predation on brown hare and ring-neck pheasant populations in southern Sweden. *Holarctic Ecology* **7**, 300–304.

Erlinge, S., Göransson, G., Hansson, L., Högstedt, G., Liberg, O., Nilsson,

I.N., Nilsson, T., Von Schantz, T. and Sylven, M. (1984) Can vertebrate predators regulate their prey? *The American Naturalist* **123**, 125–133.

Errington, P.L. (1934) Vulnerability of Bobwhite populations to predation. *Ecology* **15**, 110–127.

Errington, P.L. (1943) An analysis of mink predation upon muskrats in North Central U.S.A. *Agricultural Experimental Station, Iowa State College of Agriculture. Research Bull* **320**, 798–924.

Errington, P.L. (1945) Some contributions of a fifteen-year local study of the northern bobwhite to a knowledge of population phenomena. *Ecological Monographs* **15**, 1–34.

Errington, P.L. (1946) Predation and vertebrate populations. *Quarterly Review of Biology* **21**, 144–177.

Finerty, J.P. (1980) *The Population Ecology of Cycles in Small Mammals.* Yale University Press, New Haven & London.

Fisher, R.A. (1930) *The Genetical Theory of Natural Selection.* Clarendon Press, Oxford.

Fitter, R. (1986) *Wildlife for man. How and why we should conserve our species.* Collins, London.

Ford, N.L. (1983) Variation in mate fidelity in monogamous birds. In: *Current Ornithology* 1 (ed. R.F. Johnston).

Frank, H. (1970) Die auswirkung von raubwild- und raubzeugminderung auf die strecken von hase, fasan und rebhuhn in einem revier mit intensivster land wirtshaftlicher natzung. In: *Proceedings of the IXth International Congress of Game Biologists*, 1969, 472–479. Moscow, U.S.S.R.

Gardarsson, A. and Moss, R. (1970) Selection of food by Icelandic ptarmigan in relation to its availability and nutritive value. In: *Animal Populations in Relation to their Food Resources* (ed A. Watson), 47–71. 10th Symposium of the British Ecological Society, Blackwell Scientific Publications, Oxford.

George, R.R., Wooley, J.B., Kienzler, J.M., Farris, A.L. and Berner, A.H. (1980) Effects of hunting season length on ring-necked pheasant populations. *Wildlife Society Bulletin* **8**, 279–283.

Gilbert, N., Gutierrez, A.P., Frazer, B.D. and Jones, R.E. (1976) *Ecological Relationships.* W.H. Freeman, Reading, 157 pp.

Goransson, G. (1980) *Dynamics, Reproduction and Social Organisation in Pheasant* Phasianus Colchicus *Populations in South Scandinavia.* Unpublished Ph.D. dissertation, University of Lund.

Graham, A.D. (1973) *The Gardeners of Eden.* Unwin Ltd. London 246 pp.

Grant, P.R. (1986) *Ecology and evolution of Darwin's Finches.* Princeton University Press, Princeton.

Gray, N. (1986) *Woodland Management for Pheasants and Wildlife.* David and Charles, Newton Abbot. 176 pp.

Green, R.E. (1981) Double nesting in red-legged partridges. *Game Conservancy Annual Review* **12**, 35–38.

Green, R.E. (1983) Spring dispersal and agonistic behaviour of the red-legged partridge (*Alectoris rufa*). *Journal of Zoology* **201**, 541–555.

Green, R.E. (1984) The feeding ecology and survival of partridge chicks (*Alectoris rufa* and *Perdix perdix*) on arable farmland in East Anglia, UK. *Journal of Applied Ecology* **21**, 817–830.

Greenwood, P.J. (1980) Mating systems, philopatry and dispersal in birds and mammals. *Animal Behaviour* **28**, 1140–1162.

Gulland, J.A. (1983) *Fish Stock Assessment: a Manual of Basic Methods.* John Wiley and Sons, London. 223 pp.

Haartman, L. von (1969) Nest site and the evolution of polygamy in European passerine birds. *Ornis Fennica* **46**, 1–12.

Hagen, Y. (1952) *Rovfuglene og viltpleien.* Gyldendal Norsk Forlag, Oslo, Norway. 603 pp.

Halliday, T.R. (1983) The study of mate choice. *Mate Choice* (ed P. Bateson). 3–32. Cambridge University Press, Cambridge.

Hamilton, W.D. and Zuk, M. (1983) Heritable true fitness and bright birds: a role for parasites? *Science* **218**, 384–387.

Hannon, S.J. (1983) Spacing and breeding density of willow ptarmigan in response to an experimental alternata of sex ratio. *Journal of Animal Ecology* **52**, 807–820.

Hanssen, I., Ness, J. and Steen, J.B. (1982) Parental nutrition and chick production in captive willow ptarmigan (*Lagopus l. lagopus*). *Acta Vet Scand* **23**, 528–538.

Hanssen, I. and Utne, F. (1985) Spring phenology, egg quality and chick production in willow grouse *Lagopus l. lagopus* in northern Norway. *Fauna Norv Ser. C, Cinclus* **8**, 77–81.

Harper, H.T., Hart, C.M. and Shaffer, D.E. (1951) Effects of hunting pressure and game farm stocking on pheasant populations in the Sacramento valley, California, 1946–1949. *Journal of Wildlife Management* **37**, 141–176.

Harrison, J. (1974) *The Sevenoaks Gravel Pit Reserve.* W.A.G.B.I. Conservation Publication, Marford Mill, Rossett, Clwyd.

Hassell, M.P. (1978) *The Dynamics of Arthropod Predator-Prey Systems* Princeton University Press, Princeton.

Hassell, M.P. (1981) Arthropod Predator-Prey Systems. In: *Theoretical Ecology*, (ed R.M. May). Blackwell Scientific Publications, Oxford.

Hendee, J.A. (1972) A multiple satisfaction approach to game management. *Wildlife Society Bulletin* **2**, 104–113.

Hepp, G.R., Blohm, R.J., Reynolds, R.E., Hines, J.E. and Nichols, J.D. (1986) Physiological condition of autumn banded mallards and its relation to hunting vulnerability. *Journal of Wildlife Management* **50**, 177–183.

Hewson, R. (1976) Grazing by mountain hares *Lepus timidus* L., red deer *Cervus elaphus* L. and red grouse *Lagopus l. scoticus* on heather moorland in north-east Scotland. *Journal of Applied Ecology* **13**, 657–666.

Hewson, R. and Kolb, H.H. (1975) The food of foxes (*Vulpes vulpes*) in Scottish forests. *Journal of Zoology* **176**, 287–292.

Hewson, R. and Kolb, H.H. (1980) A study of fox populations in Scotland from 1971 to 1976. *Journal of Applied Ecology* **17**, 7–19.

Hewson, R. and Leitch, A.F. (1983) The food of foxes in forests and on the hill. *Scottish Forestry* **37**, 39–50.

Hickling, R. (1983) *Enjoying Ornithology*. Poyser, Calton.

Hill, D.A. (1982) *The Comparative Population Ecology of Mallard and Tufted Duck*. Unpublished D. Phil Thesis, University of Oxford.

Hill, D.A. (1984a) Population regulation in the mallard (*Anas platyrhynchos*). *Journal of Animal Ecology* **53**, 191–202.

Hill, D.A. (1984b) Clutch predation in relation to density in Mallard and Tufted Duck. *Wildfowl* **35**, 151–156.

Hill, D.A. (1985) The feeding ecology and survival of pheasant chicks on arable farmland. *Journal of Applied Ecology* **22**, 645–654.

Hill, D.A. (1986) Report of the Woodlands and Pheasants Research Project, *Game Conservancy*, June 1986.

Hill, D.A. (1987) A population model as an aid to pheasant management. Proceedings of a Symposium on Pheasants. *Illinois Natural History Survey*.

Hill, D.A. and Ridley, M.W. (1987) Sexual segregation, spring dispersal and habitat use in the pheasant (*Phasianus colchicus*). *Journal of Zoology*.

Hill, D.A. and Robertson, P.A. (1986) Hand-reared pheasants: How do they compare with wild birds. *Game Conservancy Annual Review* **17**, 76–84.

Hill, D.A. and Robertson, P.A. (1988) *The Pheasant: Ecology, Management and Conservation*. Pub. Collins, London.

Hill, D.A., Wright, R. and Street, M. (1987) Survival of mallard ducklings and competition with fish for invertebrates on a flooded gravel quarry in England. *Ibis* **129**, 159–167.

Hines, J.E. (1986) Social organization, movements and home ranges of blue grouse in fall and winter. *Wilson Bulletin*, **98**, 419–432.

Hochbaum, G.S. and Caswell, F.D. (1978) A forecast of long-term trends in breeding mallard populations in the Canadian Prairies. *Canadian Wildlife Service Progress Notes* No. 90.

Hoffmann, R.S. (1956) Observations on a Sooty Grouse population at Sage Hen Creek, California. *Condor* **58**, 321–337.

Hoffman, R.W. (1985) Effects of changing hunting regulations on blue grouse populations. In: *Game Harvest Management* (eds S.L. Beamson and S.F. Roberson), 327–334. Caesar Kleberg Wildlife Research Institute, Kingsville, Texas.

Höglund, N.H. (1964) *Viltrevy* **2**, 271–328.

Holling, C.S. (1959) Some characteristics of simple types of predation and parasitism. *Canadian Entomologist* **91**, 385–398.

Hornfeldt, B. (1978) Synchronous population fluctuations in voles, small game and tularemia in northern Sweden. Oecologia **32**, 141–152.

Hornfeldt, B., Lofgnen, O. and Carlsson, B.G. (1986) Cycles in voles and small game in relation to variations in plant production indices in Northern Sweden. *Oecologia* (Berl) **68**, 496–502.

Hoskins, W.G. (1970) *The making of the English Landscape.* Pelican, London.

Hudson, P.J. (1985) Harvesting red grouse in the north of England. In: *Game Harvest Management* (eds S.L. Beamson and S.F. Robertson). 319–326. Caesar Kleberg Wildlife Research Institute, Texas, USA.

Hudson, P.J. (1986a) *Red Grouse: The Biology and Management of a Wild Gamebird.* The Game Conservancy Trust, Fordingbridge.

Hudson, P.J. (1986b) The effect of a parasitic nematode on the breeding production of red grouse. *Journal of Animal Ecology* **55**, 85–92.

Hudson, P.J. (1986c) Bracken and ticks on grouse moors in the north of England. In: *Bracken. Ecology and land use and technology* (eds R.T. Smith and J.A. Taylor) 161–170. Parthenon Press, Carnforth, Lancs.

Hudson, P.J. and Dobson, A.P. (1988) The population dynamics of the caecal nematode, *Trichostrongylus tenuis* in red grouse. (In manuscript.)

Hudson, P.J., Dobson, A.P. & Newborn, D. (1985) Cyclic and non-cyclic populations of red grouse: a role for parasitism? In: *Ecology and Genetics of Host-Parasite Interactions,* (eds D. Rollinson, R.M. and Anderson), 79–86. Academic Press.

Hudson, P.J. and Watson, A. (1985) The Red Grouse. *Biologist* **32**, 13–18.

Huffaker, C.B. (1958) Experimental studies on predation: dispersion factors and predator-prey oscillations. *Hilgardia* **27**, 343–383.

Hutchinson, G.E. (1978) *An Introduction to Population Ecology* Yale University Press. New Haven. 260 pp.

Inglis, I.R. (1977) The breeding behaviour of the pink-footed grouse. Behavioural correlates of nesting success. *Animal Behaviour,* **25**, 747–764.

Jarman, P.J. (1974) The social organisation of antelope in relation to their ecology. *Behaviour* **48**, 215–267.

Jeffers, J.N.R. (1978) *An Introduction to Systems Analysis: With Ecological Applications.* Edward Arnold, London, 198 pp.

Jenkins, D. (1957) The breeding of the Red-legged Partridge. *Bird Study* **4**, 97–100.

Jenkins, D. (1961) Social behaviour in the partridge (*Perdix perdix*). *Ibis* **103a**, 155–188.

Jenkins, D., Watson, A. and Miller, G.R. (1963) Population studies on red grouse *Lagopus lagopus scoticus* (Lath.) in north-east Scotland. *Journal of Animal Ecology* **32**, 317–376.

Jenkins, D., Watson, A. and Miller, G.R. (1964) Predation and Red Grouse populations. *Journal of Applied Ecology* **1**, 183–195.

Jenkins, D., Watson, A. and Miller, G.R. (1967) Population fluctuations in the red grouse *Lagopus lagopus scoticus. Journal of Animal Ecology* **36**, 97–122.

Jenkins, D., Watson, A. and Picozzi, N. (1965) Red Grouse chick survival in captivity and in the wild. *Transactions of VI International Congress of Game Biologists*, 63–70.

Jensen, B. (1970) Effect of a fox control programme on the bag of some other game species. *Transactions of the IX International Congress of Game Biologists, Moscow*, 480.

Johnsgard, P.A. (1973) *Grouse and Quails of North America.* University of Nebraska Press, Lincoln, Nebraska.

Jones, A.M. (1984) Nesting habitat of capercaillie in Scottish plantations. In: *Grouse 1984 (3rd International Grouse Symposium)* (eds P.J. Hudson and T.W.I. Lovel), 301–316. World Pheasant Association, Reading.

Jorgensen, S.E. (1986) *Fundamentals of ecological modelling.* Elsevier, Amsterdam. 389 pp.

Keith, L.B. and Rusch, D.H. (1987) Predation's role in the cyclic fluctuations of ruffed grouse. (Unpublished Manuscript).

Keith, L.B., Todd, A.W., Brand, C.J., Adamcik, R.S. and Rusch, D.H. (1977) An analysis of predation during a cyclic fluctuation of snow-shoe hares. *Proceedings of International Congress of Game Biologists*, **13**, 151–175.

Kendall, M. (1973) *Time-series.* Charles Griffen, London.

Kenward, R. (1986) Problems of goshawk predation on pigeons and other game. *International Ornithological Congress XVIII*, 666–677.

Kenward, R.E. and Marcström, V. (1982) Goshawk predation problems and solutions. In: *Understanding the Goshawk.* (eds R.E. Kenward and I.M. Lindsay), The International Association for Falconry and Conservation of Birds of Prey.

Kenward, R.E., Marcström, V and Karlbom, M. (1981) Goshawk winter ecology in Swedish pheasant habitats. *Journal of Wildlife Management* **45**, 397–408.

Keymer, A.E. (1982) Tapeworm Infections. In: *Population dynamics of Infectious disease. Theory and Applications* (ed R.M. Anderson) 109–138. Chapman and Hall, London.

Keymer, A.E. (1985) Experimental epidemiology; *Nematospiroides dubius* and the laboratory mouse. In: *Ecology and Genetics of Host-Parasite Interactions* (eds: D. Rollinson and R.M. Anderson) 55–75. Academic Press, New York.

Kie, J.G., White, M. and Knowlton, F.M. (1979) Effects of coyote predation on population dynamics of white-tailed deer. In: *Proceedings of The First Welder Wildlife Foundation Symposium* (ed D.L. Drawe) 65–82 Sinton, Texas, 275 pp.

Kitchen, D.W. (1974) Social behaviour and ecology of the pronghorn. *Wildlife Monographs* **38**, 1–96.

Krebs, J.R. (1971) Territory and breeding density in the Great Tit *Parus major L., Ecology* **52**, 2–27.

Krebs, J.R. and Davies, N.B. (1984) 2nd Ed. *Behavioural Ecology: An Evolutionary Approach.* Blackwell Scientific Publications, Oxford. 494 pp.

Kruijt, J.P. and Hogan, J.A. (1967) Social behaviour on the lek in Black Grouse, *Lyrurus tetrix tetrix. Ardea* **55**, 203–240.

Kruijt, J.P., Vos, G.J. de and Bossema, I. (1972) The arena system of the Black Grouse. *Proceedings of the XVth International Ornithological Congress, The Hague* 1970, 399–423.

Kruuk, H. and Macdonald, D. (1984) Group territories of carnivores: empires and enclaves. In: *Behavioural Ecology* (eds R.M. Sibly and R.H. Smith). 521–536. Blackwell Scientific Publications, Oxford.

Lachlan, C. and Bray, R.P. (1976) Habitat selection by cock pheasants in spring. *Journal of Applied Ecology* **13**, 691–704.

Lack, D.L. (1946) Blackcock display. *British Birds* **39**, 287–288.

Lack, D. (1948) The significance of clutch size. *Ibis* **89**: 302–352; **90**: 25–45.

Lack, D. (1954) *The Natural Regulation of Animal Numbers.* University Press, Oxford.

Lack, D. (1966) *Population Studies of Birds.* University Press, Oxford.

Lack, D. (1968) *Ecological Adaptations for Breeding in Birds.* Methuen, London.

Lack, P. (1986) *The Atlas of Wintering Birds in Britain and Ireland.* Poyser, Caton.

Lamb, H. (1927) *Ghenghis Khan: Emperor of All Men.* McBride and Coy, New York, 240 pp.

Lance, A.N. (1983) Selection of feeding sites by hen red grouse *Lagopus lagopus scoticus* during breeding. *Ornis Scandinavica* **14**, 78–80.

Langley, P.J.W. and Yalden, D.W. (1977) The decline of the rarer carnivores in Great Britain during the nineteenth century. *Mammal Review* **7**, 95–116.

Lazarus, J.R. and I.R. Inglis (1986) Shared and unshared parental investment, parent-offspring conflict and brood size. *Animal Behaviour* **34**, 1791–1801.

Lefkovitch, L.P. (1965) The study of population growth in organisms grouped by stages. *Biometrics* **21**, 1–18.

Lefkovitch, L.P. (1966) The effects of adult emigration on populations of *Lasioderma serricorne* (F.) (coleoptera: Anobiidae). *Oikos* **15**, 200–210.

Lefkovitch, L.P. (1967) A theoretical evaluation of population growth after removing individuals from some age groups. *Bulletin of Entomological Research* **57**, 437–445.

Leopold, A. (1933) *Game Management.* Scribner's, New York.

Leslie, P.H. (1945) On the use of matrices in certain population mathematics. *Biometrica* **33**, 183–212.

Leslie, P.H. (1948) Some further notes on the use of matrices in population matrices. *Biometrika* **35**, 213–245.

Lessels, C.M. (1986) Brood size in Canada Geese: a manipulation experiment. *Journal of Animal Ecology* **55**, 669–689.

Lessels, C.M. (1987) Parental investment, brood size and time budgets: behaviour of lesser snow geese. *Oecologia* (in press).

Levins, R. (1966) The strategy of model building in population biology. *American Scientist* **54**, 421–431.

Lewis, E.G. (1942) On the generation and growth of a population. *Sankhya* **6**, 93–96.

Lewis, R.A. and Zwickel, F.C. (1982). Differential use of territorial sites by male Blue Grouse. *Condor* **83**, 171–176.

Linden, H. (1981) Estimation of juvenile mortality in the capercaillie, *Tetrao urogallus*, and the black grouse, *Lyrus tetrix* from indirect evidence. *Finnish Game Res.* **39**, 35–51.

Linden, H. and Wikman, M. (1983) Goshawk predation on tetraonids: availability of prey and diet of the predator in the breeding season. *Journal of Animal Ecology* **52**, 953–968.

Lindström, E. (1983) Condition and growth of red foxes (*Vulpes vulpes*) in relation to food supply. *Journal of Zoology* **199**: 117–122.

Lindström, E., Angelstam, P., Widen, P. and Andren, H. (1987). Do predators synchronize vole and grouse fluctuations? – An experiment. *Oikos* **48**: 121–124.

Linhart, S.B. and Enders, R.K. (1964) Some effects of diethylstilbestrol on reproduction in captive red foxes. *Journal of Wildlife Management* **28**, 358–365.

Lomnicki, A. (1982) Individual heterogeneity and population regulation. In: *Current Problems in Sociobiology* (eds King's College Sociobiology Group), 153–167. University Press, Cambridge.

Longrigg, R. (1977) *The English Squire and his Sport.* Michael Joseph, London, 302 pp.

Loomis, R.S., Rabbinge, R. and Ney, E. (1979) Explanatory models in crop physiology. *Annual Review of Plant Physiology* **30**, 339–367.

Lovat, Lord (1911) *The grouse in health and in disease. Vol. I* The final report of the committee of inquiry on grouse disease. Smith, Elder & Co., London.

Lumsden, H.G. (1961) The display of the capercaillie. *British Birds* **54**, 257–272.

MacDonald, D.W. (1980) *Rabies and Wildlife.* Oxford University Press, Oxford.

Mackenzie, J.M.D. (1952) Fluctuations in the numbers of British tetraonids. *Journal of Animal Ecology* **21**, 128–153.

Mannix (1968) *A Sporting Chance. Unusual Methods of Hunting.* Longmans, London.

Marchington, J. (1984) *The Natural History of Game.* Boydell Press, Woodbridge.

Marcström, V., Engren, E. and Kenward, R.E. (1986) An experimental study of fox and marten predation on boreal tetraonids. (Manuscript)

Marcström, V., Engren, E. and Kenward, R.E. (1987) Relationship between predation, voles and boreal tetraonids: An experimental study. (Manuscript.)

Margalef, R. (1968) *Perspectives in Ecological Theory.* University of Chicago Press, Chicago.

Martin, K. and Cooke, F. (1987) Biparental care in willow ptarmigan: a luxury? *Animal Behaviour* **35**, 369–379.

May, R.M. (1981) *Theoretical Ecology, Principles and Applications.* Blackwell Scientific Publications, Oxford.

May, R.M. and Anderson, R.M. (1978) Regulation and stability of host-parasite population interactions. II. *Journal of Animal Ecology* **47**, 249–267.

May, R.M. and Anderson, R.M. (1979) Population biology of infectious diseases Part II. *Nature* **280**, 455–461.

McCall, I. (1986) *How to Manage Your Shoot* David & Charles, Newton Abbot.

McKelvie, C.L. (1985) *A Future for Game?* Allen & Unwin, London.

McKinney, F., Cheng, K.M. and Bruggers, D.J. (1984) Sperm competition in apparently monogamous birds. In: *Sperm competition and the evolution of animal mating systems.* (ed R.L. Smith).

Mercer, W.E. (1969) *Ecology of an island population of Newfoundland willow ptarmigan.* Unpubl. MSc Thesis, University of Wisconsin, Madison, Wisconsin.

Middleton, A.D. (1934) Periodic fluctuations in British game populations. *Journal of Animal Ecology* **3**, 231–249.

Middleton, A.D. (1967) Predatory Mammals and the conservation of game in Great Britain. *Annual Report of the Game Research Association* **5**, 14–25.

Miller, G.R., Jenkins, D. and Watson, A. (1966) Heather performance and red grouse populations. I. Visual estimates of heather performance. *Journal of Applied Ecology* **3**, 313–326.

Miller, G.R., Watson, A. and Jenkins, D. (1970) Responses of red grouse populations to experimental improvement of their food. In: *Animal Populations in Relation to their Food Resources* (ed A. Watson), 323–334. Symposia of the British Ecological Society **10**. Blackwell Scientific Publications, Oxford.

Ministry of Agriculture, Fisheries and Food (1957) *Crop Protection Products Approval Scheme. Approved List 1957.* HMSO.

Ministry of Agriculture, Fisheries and Food (1966) *Agricultural Chemicals*

Approval Scheme. List of Approved Products 1967 For Farmers and Growers. HMSO.

Ministry of Agriculture, Fisheries and Food (1973) *Agricultural Statistics England & Wales 1972. Agricultural Censuses and Production.* London: HMSO.

Ministry of Agriculture, Fisheries and Food (1974) *Agricultural Chemicals Approval Scheme. 1975 List of Approved Products and their Uses for Farmers and Growers.* HMSO.

Ministry of Agriculture, Fisheries and Food (1985) *Agricultural Chemicals Approval Scheme. 1985 List of Approved Products and their Uses for Farmers and Growers.* HMSO.

Ministry of Agriculture, Fisheries and Food (1986) *Agricultural Statistics United Kingdom 1984.* London: HMSO.

Mock, D.W. (1983) On the study of avian mating systems. In: *Perspectives in ornithology* (eds A.H. Brush, and G.A. Clark, Jr.).

Moksnes, A. (1972) Bestandssvingninger hos smaviltarter i Trolheimsom-radet. Naturen **5**, 315–319.

Moore, J. (1984) Parasites that change the behaviour of their hosts. *Scientific American* **250**, 108–113.

Moore, N.W. (1957) The past and present status of the buzzard in the British Isles. *British Birds* **50**, 173–197.

Moore, N.W. (1965) Pesticides and birds – a review of the situation in Great Britain. *Bird Study* **12**, 222–252.

Moran, P.A.P. (1949) The statistical analysis of the sunspot and lynx cycles. *Journal of Animal Ecology* **18**, 115–16.

Moran, P.A.P. (1952) The statistical analysis of game-bird records. *Journal of Animal Ecology* **21**, 154–158.

Moran, P.A.P. (1953) The statistical analysis of the Canadian lynx cycle. I. Structure and prediction. *Australian Journal of Zoology* **1**, 163–173.

Moss, R. (1968) Food selection and nutrition in ptarmigan (*Lagopus mutus*). *Symposium of the Zoological Society of London* **21**, 207–216.

Moss, R. (1969) A comparison of red grouse (*Lagopus l. scoticus*) stocks with the production and nutritive value of heather (*Calluna vulgaris*). *Journal of Animal Ecology* **38**, 103–112.

Moss, R. (1972) Food selection by red grouse (*Lagopus lagopus scoticus* (Lath.)) in relation to chemical composition. *Journal of Animal Ecology* **41**, 411–418.

Moss, R. (1985) Nutrition of wild red grouse (*Lagopus lagopus scoticus*). A reply to Wise. In: *3rd International Grouse Symposium.* (ed P.J. Hudson, P.J. and T.W.I. Lovel), 108–121.

Moss, R. and Watson, A. (1979) Population cycles in the Tetraonidae. *Ornis Fennica*, **56**, 87–109.

Moss, R. and Watson, A. (1984) Adaptive value of spacing behaviour in population cycles of red grouse and other animals. In: *Behavioural*

Ecology, Ecological consequences of adaptive behaviour (eds R.M. Sibly and R.M. Smith) 275–294. Blackwell Scientific Publications, Oxford.

Moss, R. and Watson, A. (1985) Adaptive value of spacing behaviour in population cycles of red grouse and other animals. In: *Behavioural Ecology. Ecological Consequences of Adaptive Behaviour* (eds R.M. Sibly and R.H. Smith), 275–294. Blackwell Scientific Publications, Oxford.

Moss, R., Miller, G.R. and Allen, S.E. (1972) Selection of heather by captive red grouse in relation to the age of the plant. *Journal of Applied Ecology* **9**, 771–781.

Moss, R., Watson, A. and Parr, R. (1975) Maternal nutrition and breeding success in red grouse (*Lagopus lagopus scoticus*). *Journal of Animal Ecology* **44**, 171–190.

Moss, R., Watson, A., Rothery, P. & Glennie, W. (1981) Clutch size, egg size, hatch weight and laying date in relation to early mortality in red grouse *Lagopus lagopus scoticus. Ibis* **123**, 450–462.

Munton, R.J.C. (1974) Agriculture and conservation in lowland Britain. In: *Conservation in Practice* (eds A. Warren and F.B. Goldsmith) 323–336, John Wiley & Son Ltd, Chichester.

Murie, A. (1944) *The wolves of Mount McKinley* U.S. National Park Services Fauna Series No. 5. 238 pp.

Murton, R.K., Westwood, N.J. and Isaacson, A.J. (1974) A study of Wood-pigeon shooting: the exploitation of a natural animal population. *Journal of Animal Ecology* **11**, 61–81.

Myrberget, S. (1972) Fluctuations in a north Norwegian population of willow grouse. *Proceedings of the XVth International Ornithological Congress (The Hague)*, 107–120.

Myrberget, S. (1984) Population cycles of willow grouse *Lagopus lagopus* on an island in northern Norway. *Fauna Norvagica Serie C. Cinclus* **7**, 46–56.

Myrberget, S. (1984) Population dynamics of willow grouse *Lagpous lagopus* on an island in north Norway. *Fauna Norvegica Serie C. Cinclus* **7**, 95–105.

Myrberget, S. (1985) Egg predation in an island population of willow grouse *Lagopus lagopus. Fauna Norvegica Serie C. Cinclus* **8**, 82–87.

Myrberget, S. (1985) A working hypothesis about the causes of the 3–4 year cyclic fluctuations in willow grouse populations in Fennoscandia. *Proceedings of the Third International Grouse Symposium* (eds P.J. Hudson and T.W.I. Lovel). 12–34.

Myrberget, S. (1985) Characteristics of individual willow grouse hens which lose their eggs to predators. *Proceedings of the Third International Grouse Symposium* (eds P.J. Hudson and T.W.I. Lovel) 80–92.

Myrberget, S. (1986) Annual variation in clutch sizes of a population of willow grouse *Lagopus lagopus Fauna Norvegica Serie C. Cinclus* **9**.

Nature Conservancy Council (1986) *Nature Conservation and Afforestation in Britain.* NCC, Peterborough.

Newton, I. (1979) *Population Ecology of Raptors.* T. and A.D. Poyser, Berkhamsted.

Newton, I. (1980) The role of food in limiting bird numbers. *Ardea* **68**, 11–30.

Newton, I. (1986) *The Sparrowhawk.* Poyser, Calton.

Nichols, J.D., Conroy, M.J., Anderson, D.R. and Burnham, K.P. (1984) Compensatory mortality in waterfowl populations: a review of the evidence and implications for research and management. *Transactions of North American Wildlife and Natural Resources Conference* **49**, 535–554.

Nisbet, R.M. and Gurney, W.S.C. (1982) *Modelling fluctuating populations.* John Wiley and Sons, Chichester.

Nur, N. (1984) The consequence of brood size for breeding blue tits. I. Adult survival weight change and the cost of reproduction. *Journal of Animal Ecology* **53**, 479–496.

O'Connor, R.J. and Shrubb, M. (1986) *Farming and Birds.* Cambridge University Press, Cambridge.

Orians, G.H. (1969) On the evolution of mating systems in birds and mammals. *American Naturalist* **103**, 589–603.

Orians, G.H. and Pearson, N.E. (1979) On the theory of central plane foraging. In: *Analysis of Ecological Systems* (eds D.J. Horn, R. Mitchell and G.R. Stair. Ohio State University Press, Columbus.

Oring, L.W. (1982) Avian mating systems. In: *Avian Biology* **6** (eds D. Farner, J. King and K. Parkes), 1–92. Academic Press, New York.

Overton, W.S. (1971) Estimating the numbers of animals in wildlife populations. In: *Wildlife Management Techniques* (ed R.H. Giles), The Wildlife Society, Washington.

Overton, W.S. (1977) A strategy of model construction. In: *Ecosystem Modelling in Theory and Practice: An Introduction with Case Histories,* (eds C.A.S. Hall and J.W. Day), 50–73. Wiley-Interscience, New York, 684 pp.

Owen, M., Atkinson-Willes, G.L. and Salmon, D.G. (1986) *Wildfowl in Great Britain.* Cambridge University Press, Cambridge.

Page, R.E. and Bergerud, A.T. (1984) A genetic explanation for ten year cycles of grouse. *Oecologia* **64**, 54–60.

Parker, H. (1981) Renesting biology of Norwegian willow ptarmigan. *Journal of Wildlife Management* **45**, 858–864.

Parker, H. (1984) Effect of corvid removal on reproduction of willow ptarmigan and black grouse. *Journal of Wildlife Management* **48**, 1197–1205.

Parslow, J.L.F. (1969) Breeding birds of hedges. *Monks Wood Experimental Station Report 1966–68* **21**.

Patterson, I.J. (1980) Territorial behaviour and the limitation of population density. *Ardea* **68**, 53–62.

Pedersen, H.C. and Steen, J.B. (1979) Behavioural thermoregulation in willow ptarmigan *Lagopus lagopus* chicks. *Ornis Scandinavica* **10**, 17–21.

Pedersen, H.C. and Steen, J.B. (1985) Parental care and chick production in a fluctuating population of willow ptarmigan. *Ornis Scandinavica* **16**, 270–276.

Peel, The Earl (1983) Integrated management of upland environment. In: *Management of natural and semi-natural vegetation* (ed J.M. Way), 155–167. Ashford-Wye College.

Perrins, C.M. (1977) The role of predation in the evolution of clutch size. In: *Evolutionary Ecology* (eds B.M. Stonehouse and C.M. Perrins), London, Macmillan, 181–191.

Perrins, C.M. (1979) *British Tits*. Collins, London.

Perrins, C.M. and Birkhead, T.R. (1984) *Avian Ecology*. Blackie, Glasgow.

Petrides, G.A. and C.R. Bryant (1951) An analysis of the 1949–50 Fowl Cholera epizootic in Texan panhandle waterfowl. *Transactions of North American Wildlife Conference*, **16**, 193–216.

Phillips, J., Raen, S.G. and Aelerud, F. (1984) Response of willow grouse to serial burning of mountain vegetation in Numedal, S. Norway. In: *Grouse 1984, (3rd International Grouse Symposium)* (eds P.J. Hudson and T.W.I. Lovel), 55–68. World Pheasant Association, Reading.

Picozzi, N. (1968) Grouse bags in relation to the management and geology of heather moors. *Journal of Applied Ecology* **5**, 483–488.

Pils, C.M. and Martin, M.A. (1978) Population dynamics, predator-prey relationships and management of the red fox in Wisconsin. *Department of Natural Resources, Madison, Wisconsin*, Technical Bulletin No. **105**, 56 pp.

Pitcher, T.J. and Hart, P.J.B. (1982) *Fisheries Ecology*. Croom Helm, London. 414 pp.

Podoler, H. and Rogers, D. (1975) A new method for the identification of key factors from life-table data. *Journal of Animal Ecology* **44**, 85–114.

Potts, G.R. (1970) Studies on the changing role of weeds of the genus *Polygonum* in the diet of Partridges. *Journal of Applied Ecology* **7**, 567–576.

Potts, G.R. (1973) Factors governing the chicks survival rate of the grey partridge. In: *Proceedings of the Xth International Congress of Game Biologists* **1971**, 85–86, Paris, France.

Potts, G.R. (1974) The grey partridge: problems of quantifying the ecological effects of pesticides. In: *Proceedings of the XIth International Congress of Game Biologists* 1973, 405–413. Stockholm, Sweden.

Potts, G.R. (1980) The effects of modern agriculture, nest predation and game management on the population ecology of partridges (*Perdix perdix* and *Alectoris rufa*). *Advances in Ecological Research* **11**, 2–79.

Potts, G.R. (1985) The partridge situation in Italy: a view from Britain. In:

Seminario tenuto all'Università della Calabria. *Biologia dei Galliformi, Problemi di Gestione Venatoria e Conservazione* (eds F. Dessi Fulgheri and T. Mingozzi), 9–13. Dipartimento di Ecologia dell'Università della Calabria, Arcavacata, Italy.

Potts, G.R. (1986) *The Partridge. Pesticides, Predation and Conservation.* Collins, London. 274 pp.

Potts, G.R. and Vickerman, G.P. (1974) Studies on the cereal ecosystem. *Advances in Ecological Research* **8**, 107–197.

Potts, G.R., Coulson, J.C. and Deans, I.R. (1980) Population dynamics and breeding success of the shag *Phalacrocorax aristotelis* on the Farne Islands, Northumberland. *Journal of Animal Ecology* **49**, 465–484.

Potts, G.R., Tapper, S.C. and Hudson, P.J. (1984) Population fluctuations in Red Grouse: analysis of bag records and a simulation model. *Journal of Animal Ecology* **53**, 21–36.

Price, P.W. (1980) *Evolutionary Biology of Parasites.* Princeton University Press, New Jersey.

Rands, M.R.W. (1982) *The influence of habitat on the population ecology of partridges.* Unpublished D.Phil Thesis, University of Oxford.

Rands, M.R.W. (1985) Pesticide use on cereals and the survival of grey partridge chicks: a field experiment. *Journal of Applied Ecology* **22**, 49–54.

Rands, M.R.W. (1986a) The survival of gamebird (Galliformes) chicks in relation to pesticide use on cereals. *Ibis* **128**, 57–64.

Rands, M.R.W. (1986b) The effect of hedgerow characteristics on partridge breeding densities. *Journal of Applied Ecology* **23**, 479–487.

Rands, M.R.W. (1987a) Hedgerow management for the conservation of partridges (*Perdix perdix* and *Alectoris rufa*). *Biological Conservation*, **40**, 125–139.

Rands, M.R.W. (1987b) Recruitment of grey and red-legged partridges (*Perdix perdix* and *Alectoris rufa*) in relation to population density and habitat. *Journal of Zoology.* **212**, 407–418.

Rands, M.R.W. (1988) The effect of nest site selection on nest predation in Grey Partridges (*Perdix perdix*) and Red-legged Partridges (*Alectoris rufa*). *Ornis Scandinavica* **19**, 35–40.

Rands, M.R.W., Ridley, M.W. and Lelliott, A.D. (1984) The social organization of feral peafowl. *Animal Behaviour* **32**, 830–835.

Rands, M.R.W., Sotherton, N.W. and Moreby, S.J. (1985) Some effects of cereal pesticides on gamebirds and other farmland fauna. In: *Recent Developments in Cereal Production* (ed C. Green), 98–113. Proceedings of a Symposium at the University of Nottingham.

Rands, M.R.W. and Sotherton, N.W. (1986) Pesticide use on cereal crops and changes in the abundance of butterflies on arable farmland in England. *Biological Conservation* **36**, 71–82.

Rands, M.R.W. and Sotherton, N.W. (1987) The management of field margins for the conservation of gamebirds. In: *1987 British Crop Protection Conference Monograph Number 35 – Field Margins*. (eds J.M. Way and P.W. Greig-Smith). 95–104.

Redmond, G.W., Keppie, D.M. and Herzog, P.W. (1982) Vegetative structure, concealment and success at nests of two races of spruce grouse. *Canadian Journal of Zoology* **60**, 670–675.

Reed, T. (1985) Grouse moors and wading birds. *Game Conservancy Annual Review* **17**, 57–60.

Ricker, W.E. (1975) *Computation and Interpretation of Biological Statistics of Fish Populations*. Bulletin 191, Fisheries Research Board of Canada, 382 pp.

Ridley, N.W. (1983) *Mating System of the Pheasant* (Phasianus colchicus). D.Phil Thesis, University of Oxford.

Ridley, M.W., Lelliott, A.D. and Rands, M.R.W. (1985) The courtship display of feral Peafowl. *World Pheasant Association Journal* **9**, 57–68.

Ridley, M.W. and Hill, D.A. (1987) Social organisation in the pheasant: harem formation, mate selection and the role of mate guarding. *Journal of Zoology* (in press).

Robbins, C.S. (1985) Summary of bird censusing and atlasing in North America. In: *Bird Census and Atlas Studies* (eds K. Taylor, R.J. Fuller and P.C. Lack) British Trust for Ornithology, Tring.

Robel, R. (1969) Nesting activities and brood movements of Black Grouse in Scotland. *Ibis* **111**, 395–399.

Robel, R.J. and Ballard, W.B. (1974) Lek social organisation and reproductive success in the Greater Prairie Chicken. *American Zoologist* **14**, 121–128.

Robertson, P.A. (1986) *The Ecology and Management of Hand-reared and Wild Pheasants in Ireland*. Unpublished Ph.D. Thesis, National University of Ireland.

Robertson, P.A. and Hill, D.A. (1987) Nesting dynamics and intraspecific nest parasitism in the pheasant. (Unpublished manuscript.)

Robertson, P.A. and Hill, D.A. (in prep) Intraspecific nest parasitism and clutch predation in the pheasant (*Phasianus colchicus*).

Roe, R.G. (1951) *The North American Buffalo*. Toronto Press, Toronto, Canada. 957 pp.

Rogers, J.P., Nichols, J.D., Martin, R.W., Kimball, C.F. and Pospahala, R.S. (1979). *Transactions of the 44th North American Wildlife and Natural Resources Conference*, 1979, 114–126.

Roseberry, J.L. (1979) Bobwhite population responses to exploitation: real and simulated. *Journal of Wildlife Management* **43**, 285–305.

Royal Commission on Environmental Pollution (1979) *Agriculture and Pollution*. (Cmnd. 7644.) London: HMSO.

Ruesink, W.G. (1976) Status of the systems approach to pest management. *Annual Review of Entomology* **21**, 27–46.

Ruwet, J.-C. (1982) Statut et évolution, dans le contexte européen, des populations de tetras lyre (*Tetrao tetrix*) dans les Ardennes Belges. Cahiers d'Éthologie appliquée **2**, 81–104.

Safriel, U.N. (1975) On the significance of clutch size in nidifugeous birds. *Ecology* **56**, 703–708.

Sargeant, A.B., Allen, S.H. and Eberhardt, R.T. (1984) Red fox predation on breeding ducks in midcontinent North America. *Wildlife Monographs* **89**, 1–41.

Savory, C.J. (1977) The food of red grouse chicks (*Lagopus lagopus scoticus*). *Ibis* **119**, 1–9.

Savory, C.J. (1978) Food consumption of red grouse in relation to the age and productivity of heather. *Journal of Animal Ecology* **47**, 269–282.

Savory, C.J. (1983) Selection of heather age and chemical composition by red grouse in relation to physiological state, season and time of day. *Ornis Scandinavica* **14**, 135–143.

Schumacher, W. (1980) Schutz und Erhaltung gefahrdeter Ackerwildkrauter durch Integration von landswirtschaftlicher Nutzung und Naturschutz. *Natur und Landschaft* **55**, 447–453.

Schumacher, W. (1981) Artenschutz fur Kalkackerunkrauter. *Zeitschrift Pflanzenkrankheiten Pflanzenschutz, Sonderheft* **9**, 95–100.

Schwartz, C.W. (1945) The ecology of the Prairie Chicken in Missouri. *University of Missouri Studies* **20**, 1–99.

Scott, J.W. (1942) Mating behaviour of the Sage Grouse. *Auk* **59**, 477–498.

Selous, E. (1909–10) An observational diary on the nuptual habits of the blackcock (*Tetrao tetrix*) in Scandinavia and England. *Zoologist* **13**, 401–413; **14**, 23–29, 51–56, 176–182, 248–265.

Sharrock, J.T.R. (1976) *The Atlas of Breeding Birds in Britain and Ireland.* Poyser, Calton.

Shepherd, J.G. (1982) A versatile new stock recruitment relationship for fisheries and the construction of sustainable yield curves. *Journal de Conservation Internationale d'Exploration de la Mer.* **40**, 67–75.

Sih, A., Crowley, P., McPeek, M., Petranka, J. and Strohmeier, K. (1986) Predation, competition and prey communities. A review of field experiments. *Annual Review of Ecology and Systematics* **16**, 269–311.

Siivonen, L. (1948) Structure of short-cycle fluctuations in numbers of mammals and birds in the northern parts of the northern hemisphere. *Papers on Game Research* **1**.

Siivonen, L. (1952) On the reflection of short-term fluctuations in numbers in the reproduction of tetraonids. *Papers on Game Research* **9**, 1–43.

Siivonen, L. (1954) On the short-term fluctuations in numbers of tetraonids. *Papers on Game Research* **13**

Siivonen, L. (1954) Some essential features of short-term population fluctuations. *Journal of Wildlife Management* **18**, 38–45.

Siivonen, L. (1957) The problem of short-term fluctuations in number of tetraonids in Europe. *Papers on Game Research* **19**.

Siivonen, L. (1957) The correlation between the fluctuations of partridge and European hare populations and the climatic conditions of winters in South West Finland during the last thirty years. *Finnish Game Foundation Papers on Game Research*, Helsinki. **17**, 1–30.

Simon, J.R. (1940) Mating performance of the Sage Grouse. *Auk* **57**, 467–471.

Sinclair, A.R.E. (1979) The eruption of the ruminants. In: *Serengeti, Dynamics of an Ecosystem* (eds A.R.E. Sinclair and M. Norton-Griffiths) 82–103. University of Chicago Press, Chicago.

Sinclair, G.A. (1983) *The Upland Landscape Study*. London. Countryside Commission.

Sissenwine, M.P. (1978) Is MSY an adequate foundation for optimum yield? *Fisheries* **3** (6).

Slagsvold, T. (1978) Production of young by the willow grouse in Norway in relation to temperature. *Norwegian Journal of Zoology* **23**, 269–275.

Sly, J.M.A. (1977) *Review of Usage of Pesticides in Agriculture and Horticulture in England and Wales, 1965–1975.* (Pesticide Usage Survey report no. 8.) Pinner: Ministry of Agriculture, Fisheries and Food.

Sly, J.M.A. (1981) *Review of Usage of Pesticides in Agriculture and Forestry in England and Wales, 1965–1979.* (ADAS Survey report no. 23.) Pinner: Ministry of Agriculture, Fisheries and Food.

Sly, J.M.A. (1984) *Pesticide Usage England and Wales: Preliminary Report no. 35: Arable Farm Crops and Grass 1982.* Pinner: Ministry of Agriculture, Fisheries and Food.

Sly, J.M.A. (1986) *Review of Usage of Pesticides in Agriculture, Horticulture and Animal Husbandry in England and Wales, 1980–1983.* (Pesticide Usage Survey report no. 41.) Pinner: Ministry of Agriculture, Fisheries and Food.

Smith, C.C. and Fretwell, S.D. (1974) The optimal balance between size and numbers of offspring. *American Naturalist* **108**, 499–506.

Smyth, K.E. and Boag, D.A. (1984) Production in spruce grouse and its relationship to environmental factors and population parameters. *Canadian Journal of Zoology*, **62**, 2250–2257.

Sotherton, N.W. (1980) *The Ecology of Gastrophysa Polygoni (L.) Coleoptera: Chrysomelidae) in Cereals.* Unpublished Ph.D. Thesis, University of Southampton.

Sotherton, N.W. (1982) Observations on the biology and ecology of the chrysomelid beetles *Gastrophysa polygoni* in cereal fields. *Ecological Entomology* **7**, 197–206.

Sotherton, N.W. (1982) Effects of herbicides on the chrysomelid beetle *Gastrophysa polygoni* (L.) in laboratory and field. *Zeischrift fur Angewandte Entomologie* **94**, 446–451.

Sotherton, N.W., Rands, M.R.W. and Moreby, S.J. (1985) Comparison of herbicide treated and untreated headlands for the survival of game and wildlife. *1985 British Crop Protection Conference – Weeds* **3**, 991–998.

Southwood, T.R.E. (1967) The ecology of the partridge. II. The role of pre-hatching influences. *Journal of Animal Ecology* **36**, 557–562.

Southwood, T.R.E. (1978) *Ecological Methods with Particular Reference to the Study of Insect Populations.* Chapman and Hall, London.

Steed, J.M., Sly, J.M.A., Tucker, C.G. and Gutter, J.R. (1979) *Arable Farm Crops 1977* (Pesticide Usage Survey Report No. 18). MAFF, Pinner.

Stoddard, H.L. (1951) *The Bobwhite Quail – its Habits, Preservation and Increase.* Charles Scribner's Sons, New York, 559 pp.

Stone, M. (1974) Cross-validatory choice and assessment of statistical predictions. *Journal of the Royal Statistical Society, B* **36**, 111–147.

Storaas, T. and Wegge, P. (1985) High nest losses in Capercaillie and Black Grouse in Norway. In: *3rd International Grouse Symposium.* (eds P.J. Hudson and T.W.I. Lovel). 481–498.

Storaas, T., Wegge, P., and Sonerud, G. (1982) Destruction des nids de grand tetras et cycle des petits rongeurs dans l'ést de la Norwège. In: *Actes du Colloque International Sur le Grand Tetras.* Union nationale des associations ornithologique. Duo-print, Schweighouse, France. 166–178.

Strandgaard, H. (1964) The Danish bag record I. Studies in game geography based on the Danish bag record for the years 1956–57 and 1957–58. *Danish Review of Game Biology* **4** (2), 116 pp.

Strandgaard, H. and Asferg, T. (1980) The Danish bag record II. Fluctuations and trends in the Game Bag Record in the years 1941–1976 and the geographical distribution of the bag in 1976. *Danish Review of Game Biology* **11** (5), 1–112.

Sturkie, P.E. (1976) *Avian Physiology*, 3rd Edition. Springer-Verlag: New York.

Sulkava, S. (1964) Zur nahrungsbiologie des habichts, *Accipiter g. gentilis* (L.) BWP. *Aquilo. Ser. Zool* **3**, 1–103.

Taber, R.D. (1949) Observations on the breeding behaviour of the Ring-necked Pheasant. *Condor* **51**, 153–175.

Tapper, S.C. (1979) The effect of fluctuating vole numbers (*Microtus agrestis*) on a population of weasels (*Mustela nivalis*) on farmland. *Journal of Animal Ecology* **48**, 603–617.

Tapper, S.C. and Hirons, G. (1983) Recent Trends in Woodcock Bags in Britain. *Proceedings of the Second European Woodcock and Snipe Workshop*, (ed H. Kalchreuter). International Wildfowl Research Bureau, Slimbridge, England.

Tapper, S.C., Green, R.E. and Rands, M.R.W. (1982) Effects of mammalian predators on partridge populations. *Mammal Review* **12**, 159–168.

Taylor, L.R. and Taylor, R.A.J. (1977) Aggregation, migration and population mechanics. *Nature* **265**, 415–421.

Teng, P.S., Blackie, M.J. and Close, R.C. (1980) Simulation of the barley leaf rust epidemic: Structure and validation of BARSIM-I. *Agricultural Systems* **5**, 85–103.

Tipton, A.R. and Kendall, R.J. (1980) A model of the impact of methyl parathion spraying on a quail population. *Bulletin of Environmental Contamination and Toxicology* **25**, 586–593.

Tittensor, R. (1981) A sideways look at nature conservation in Britain. *Discussion Papers in Conservation* **29**, University College, London.

Trautman, C.G., Fredrickson, L.F. and Carter, A.V. (1973) Relationship of red foxes and other predators to populations of ring-necked pheasants and other prey, South Dakota. *Proceedings of the Thirty-Ninth North American Wildlife Conference*, 241–253.

Turner, T.W. (1955) *Memoirs of a Gamekeeper*. Geoffrey Bles, London.

Twining, H., Hjersman, H.A. and Wallace, M. (1948) Fertility of eggs of the ring-necked pheasant. *California Fish and Game* **34**, 209–216.

Usher, M.B. (1972) Developments in the Leslie Matrix Model. In: *The 12th Symposium of the British Ecological Society – Mathematical Models in Ecology*, (ed J.N.R. Jeffers), 29–60.

Usher, M.B. (1983) Species diversity: a comment on a paper by W.B. Yapp. *Field Studies* **5**, 825–832.

Van Riper, C. III, Van Riper, S.G., Goff, M.L. and Land, M. (1986) The epizootiology of avian malaria in Hawian avifauna. *Ecological Monographs* **56**, 327–344.

Vandervell, C.A. and Coles, C.L. (1983) *Game and the English Landscape*. Debrett's Peerage Ltd., London.

Varley, G.C. and Gradwell, G.R. (1968) Population models for the winter moth. In: *Insect Abundance*, (ed T.R.E. Southwood), Symposium of the Royal Entomological Society, London. **4**, 132–142.

Vaught, R.W., McDougle, H.C. and H.H. Burgess (1967) Fowl cholera in waterfowl at Syvaw Creek National Wildlife Refuge, Missouri. *Journal of Wildlife Management* **31**, 248–253.

Verner, J. and Willson, M.F. (1966) The influence of habitats on mating systems of North American passerine birds. *Ecology* **47**, 143–147.

Vesey Fitzgerald, B. (1946) *British Game*. Collins, London.

Vickerman, G.P. (1974) Some effects of grass weed control on the arthropod fauna of cereals. *Proceedings of the 12th British Weed Control Conference* 1974, 929–939.

Vickerman, G.P. (1974) The effects of straw burning on invertebrates. In: *Straw Burning and Its Effects on Wildlife*, 7–11. Fordingbridge: U.K.

Vickerman, G.P. (1978) The arthropod fauna of undersown grass and cereal fields. *Scientific Proceedings of the Royal Dublin Society* **6**, 156–165.

Vos, G.J. de (1979) Adaptedness of arena behaviour in Black Grouse (*Tetrao tetrix*) and other grouse species (Tetraoninae). *Behaviour* **68**, 277–314.

Vos, G.J. de (1983) Social behaviour of Black Grouse: an observational and experimental field study. *Ardea* **71**, 1–103.

Wagner, B.H., Besadny, C.D. and Kabat, C. (1965) Population ecology and management of Wisconsin Pheasants. *Technical Bulletin No. 34. Wisconsin Conservation Department*, Madison, Wisconsin.

Walsingham, Lord and Payne Gallway, R. (1895) The Badminton Library: *Shooting, Field and Covert.* Longmans, Green, and Co., London.

Walters, C.J., Hilborn, E.O., Peterson, R.M. and Stander, J.M. (1974) Development of a simulation model of mallard duck populations. *Canadian Wildlife Service Occasional Paper, No. 20.*

Watson, A. (1965) A population study of ptarmigan (*Lagopus mutus*) in Scotland. *Journal of Animal Ecology,* **34**, 135–172.

Watson, A. (1967) Social status and population regulation in the red grouse (*Lagopus lagopus scoticus*). *Abstract of the Proceedings of the Royal Society Population Study Group* No. **2**, 22–30.

Watson, A. (1985) Social class, socially induced loss, recruitment and breeding of red grouse. *Oecologia* **67**, 493–498.

Watson, A. and Jenkins, D. (1968) Experiments on population control by territorial behaviour in red grouse. *Journal of Animal Ecology* **37**, 595–614.

Watson, A. and Miller, G.R. (1976) *Grouse Management.* The Game Conservancy, Fordingbridge.

Watson, A. and Moss, R. (1970) Dominance, spacing behaviour and aggression in relation to population limitation in vertebrates. *Animal Populations in Relation to their Food Resources* (ed A. Watson). 167–218. Symposia of the British Ecological Society, **10**. Blackwell Scientific Publications, Oxford.

Watson, A. and Moss, R. (1972) A current model of population dynamics in red grouse. *Proceedings of the International Ornithological Congress* **15**, 134–149.

Watson, A. and Moss, R. (1979) Population cycles in the tetraonidae. *Ornis Fennica* **56**: 87–109.

Watson, A. and R. Moss (1987) The mechanics of annual changes in ptarmigan numbers: a reply to Bergerud, Mossop and Myberget. *Canadian Journal of Zoology,* **66**.

Watson, A., Moss, R., Phillips, J. and Parr, R. (1977) The effect of fertilizers on red grouse stocks on Scottish moors grazing by sheep, cattle and deer. In: *Ecologie du Petit Gibier et Amenagement des Chasses,* (eds P. Pesson and M.G. Birkan), 193–212. Gauthier-Villars, Paris.

Watson, A. and O'Hare, P.J. (1979) Red grouse populations on experimentally treated and untreated Irish bog. *Journal of Applied Ecology* **16**, 433–452.

Watson, A., Moss, R. and Parr, R. (1984) Effects of food enrichment on numbers and spacing behaviour of red grouse. *Journal of Animal Ecology* **53**, 663–678.

Watson, A., Moss, R., Rothery, P. and Parr, R. (1984) Demographic causes and predictive models of population fluctuations in red grouse. *Journal of Animal Ecology*, **53**, 639–662.

Watt, A.D., Vickerman, G.P. and Wratten, S.D. (1984) The effect of the grain aphid, *Sitobion avenae* (F.), on winter wheat in England: an analysis of the economics of control practice and forecasting systems. *Crop Protection* **3**, 209–222.

Watts, C.R. and Stokes, A.W. (1974) The social order of turkeys. *Scientific American* **224**, 112–118.

Weaver, J.K. and Moseby, H.S. (1978) Influence of hunting regulation on the Virginia wild turkey population. *Journal of Wildlife Management* **43**, 128–135.

Weeden, R.B. (1964) Spatial separation of sexes in rock and willow ptarmigan in winter. *Auk* **81**, 534–541.

Whiteside, R.W. and Guthrie, F.F. (1983) Effect of hunting on ring-necked pheasants in North West Texas. *Wildlife Society Bulletin* **11**, 250–252.

Whitfield, P.J. (1979) *The Biology of Parasitism: an Introduction To The Study of Associating Organisms.* Edward Arnold, London.

Wiley, R.H. (1973) Territoriality and non-random mating in the sage grouse *Centrocercus urophasianus. Animal Behaviour Monographs* **6**, 87–169.

Wiley, R.H. (1974) Evolution of social organisation and life history patterns among grouse (Aves: Tetraonidae). *Quarterly Review of Biology* **49**, 201–227.

Williams, G.C. (1966) Natural selection, the costs of reproduction and a refinement of Lack's principle. *American Naturalist* **100**, 687–690.

Williams, G.R. (1954) Population fluctuations in some northern hemisphere game birds (Tetraonidae). *Journal of Animal Ecology* **23**, 1–37.

Williams, J. (1985) The statistical analysis of fluctuations in red grouse bag data. *Oecologia* **65**, 269–272.

Wilson, G.R. (1979) *Effects of caecal threadworm* Trichostrongylus tenuis *on red grouse.* Unpublished Ph.D Thesis, University of Aberdeen.

Wilson, R.A., Smith, G. and M.R. Thomas (1982) Fascioliasis. In: *Population Dynamics of Infectious Diseases. Theory and Application.* (ed R.M. Anderson). 262–319. Chapman and Hall, London.

Winkler, D.W. and Walters, J.R. (1983) The determination of clutch size in precocial birds. In: *Current Ornithology* Vol 1. (ed R. Johnston) Plenum Press, New York. 33–67.

Wise, D.R. (1982) Nutrition of wild red grouse (*Lagopus lagopus scoticus*). *The World Pheasant Association Journal VII*, 1981–1982, 36–41.

Wise, D.R. (1985) Nutrition of wild red grouse (*Lagopus lagopus scoticus*). Comments on Moss's reply to Wise. In: *Third International Grouse Symposium.* (eds P.J. Hudson and T.W.I. Lovel), 122–130.

Wittenberger, J.F. (1978) The evolution of mating systems in grouse. *Condor* **80**, 126–137.

Wonnacott, R.J. and Wonnacott, T.H. (1979) *Econometrics*; second edition. J. Wiley & Son Ltd, New York.

Wood, J.B. (1983) The conservation and management of animal populations. In: *Conservation on Perspective*, (eds A. Warren and F.B. Goldsmith), 119–139. John Wiley & Son Ltd, Chichester.

Zammuto, R.M. (1987) Life histories of birds: clutch size, longevity and body mass among North American game birds. *Canadian Journal of Zoology* **64**, 2739–2749.

Zwickel, F.C. (1975) Nesting parameters of blue grouse and their relevance to populations. *Condor* **77**, 423–430.

Index